The Science of Goodness

Is It Worth Being Good According to Science?

By

Milan Toma, PhD, SMIEEE

2025

Published by: Dawning Research Press
Contact: admin@dawningresearch.org
Website: www.dawningresearch.org

ISBN Number

Paperback: 979-8-9998324-5-0

All information has been carefully verified, and sources are cited throughout the text. The content reflects the author's commitment to evidence-based research and is intended for educational and informational purposes. The views expressed are those of the author and do not necessarily reflect those of any affiliated institutions. While every effort has been made to ensure the accuracy of the information presented, errors or omissions may still occur. If you spot a serious inaccuracy, we encourage you to contact us so that we can make corrections in the next edition. The author and publisher assume no responsibility for errors or omissions, or for damages resulting from the use of the information contained herein.

First Edition

Contents

Chapter 1

Goodness in Leadership

It is a curious thing how we strive to understand the human heart by measuring it. In the vast and dusty library of the science of goodness, no other subject has been taken down from the shelf and examined with such weary persistence as the idea of goodness in leadership. It is the most handled book in the room. We wish to know what makes a leader good. We look at their habits. We look at the rules they live by. We look at the soil of the culture that grew them. By staring at these things, and by reading the old theories alongside the stories of real lives, this chapter attempts to paint a picture of the "good-hearted" leader. It asks why such a person is necessary for the factory, the office, or the state to survive the long winter.

> **Key Point:** We study the science of leadership character to understand why organizations require leaders with good qualities to survive and succeed in difficult times.

1.1 The Role of Personality in Leadership

There is a great pile of research that tries to draw a line between who a person is and how well they lead. Scholars have spent years gathering these facts. They are particularly fond of a map of the human soul known as the Big Five model. This model suggests that the complex storm of human character can be sorted into five distinct baskets. There is Openness, which is the hunger for new things. There is Conscientiousness, which is the love of order and duty. There is Extraversion, the need to be among people and noise. There is Agreeableness, the simple wish to please others. And finally there is Neuroticism, which is the shadow of anxiety and sadness that follows one about.

Judge et al. took on the heavy task of a meta-analysis. This is a method where one does not look at a single life but gathers the fragments of many studies to find a single truth. They collected data from 73 independent samples. They looked at the five baskets of character to see which ones predicted who would become a leader and who would fail. They synthesized 222 correlations and tried to wipe away the errors of measurement to see the thing clearly [1].

To understand their work, one must understand the tool they use. It is called the correlation coefficient, or simply r. It is a cold little number that attempts to weigh the invisible connection between a trait and a result. Imagine a scale that tips from negative one to positive one. If the number is positive, it means that having more of a trait lifts the leader up. If the number is negative, it means the trait drags the leader down like a stone in a pocket. If the number sits near zero, it means there is no connection at all, which is often the way of things in life. For instance, an r of 0.31 for extraversion is a moderate positive bond. An r of -0.24 for neuroticism is a moderate negative bond.

The numbers told a story that was both expected and somewhat sad. Extraversion, with an r of 0.31, and Conscientiousness, with an r of 0.28, stood tall. Openness to experience followed with an r of 0.24. Low neuroticism, meaning a calm spirit, was also important, sitting at -0.24. But Agreeableness, that gentle quality of kindness we value so much in a friend, showed a weak relationship, a mere r of 0.08. As illustrated in Figure 1.1, it is the loud and the organized who rise. Extraversion was the most consistent sign of a leader. These findings support the idea that our traits shape our fate, and they

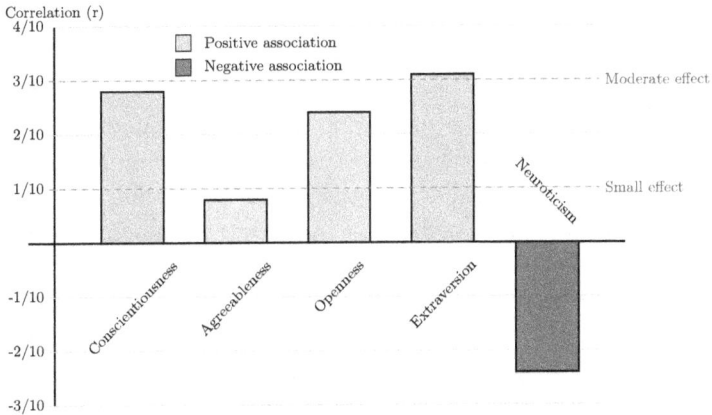

Figure 1.1: Correlation coefficients between Big Five personality traits and leadership based on meta-analysis of 222 correlations from 73 samples [1]. Extraversion shows the strongest positive association (r = 0.31), followed by Conscientiousness (r = 0.28) and Openness to Experience (r = 0.24). Agreeableness shows a weak positive correlation (r = 0.08), while Neuroticism shows a negative association (r = -0.24) with leadership effectiveness and emergence.

remind us that we must look at the whole person, not just one part, to understand the mystery of influence [1].

Building on this foundation, DeRue and colleagues attempted to weave together two threads that usually hang loose. They integrated the theories of what a leader is (i.e., their traits, such as the Big Five, intelligence, and gender) with the theories of what a leader does. They performed a meta-analysis, which, again, is a method of gathering the fragments of many small studies to build a single, larger truth. They tested a model where the actions of a leader serve as the bridge between their character and their success. The study found that when one looks at both the person and the deed, one can explain a minimum of 31% of the variance in effectiveness. Variance is a scholar's cold word for the difference between one fate and another, the gap between success and ruin. Once again, the loud energy of extraversion and the steady hand of conscientiousness were the most reliable signs. It seems that while our nature is the seed, our specific behaviors are the fruit that others taste [2].

Recent studies have cast a net across the oceans to see if these truths hold in every climate. Javalagi, Newman, and Li looked at the world with a wide lens, gathering data from over one hundred samples to study the Big Five. They used meta-analytic techniques to measure the strength of these human connections across different lands. They found that while the Big Five traits are always useful, their value changes with the soil. In collectivist societies (i.e., those places where the village is loved more than the self and the group stands above the individual) agreeableness and extraversion are mighty forces. The study also spoke of the HEXACO model. This is a newer map of the human soul that adds a sixth dimension called Honesty-Humility, measuring fairness and the absence of greed. It appears that this quiet virtue predicts success even better than the old models, reminding us that decency has a value that crosses borders [3].

Silverthorne took a lamp to the United States, Taiwan, and Thailand to compare the souls of effective leaders against those who stumble. He used the NEO PI-R, a long list of questions designed to reveal the heart. In America, the effective leaders stood tall on all five traits. But in the East, the pattern shifted like smoke. In China, conscientiousness was the most precious gold, while surgency was less needed. Surgency is a fancy word for the drive to dominate, the need to be the rooster in the yard; it seems this quality is not always the path to respect. These findings tell us that while the Big Five is a useful tool, one must always look at the setting in which the work is done [4].

Scholars have also reminded us that a person is not a stone, unchanging and hard. Judge and DeRue noted that the situation holds a heavy hand over us. There is a concept known as trait activation theory. It suggests that our true nature lies sleeping until the world wakes it up with a specific demand, just as a match only burns when struck against the box. A quiet person may become a lion if the house is on fire. The effectiveness of a trait like extraversion depends entirely on whether the moment calls for a speech or for silence [1, 2].

In the most recent years, from 2020 to 2025, researchers have looked at the dusty corridors of schools and offices with fresh eyes. Suwardi and colleagues reviewed the lives of educational leaders. They found that conscientiousness and emotional stability (i.e., the ability to remain calm when the bell rings and the day is chaotic) were vital for teaching and leading. Grover and Amit looked at the different ways a person might lead. They concluded that those who understand their own nature and adapt to the needs of the hour are the ones who thrive. They found that prosocial qualities, such as empathy, kindness, and patience, are not merely soft virtues for the weak but are the very things that build a strong organization. It is a comfort to know that a good heart is still worth something in the ledger of success [5, 6].

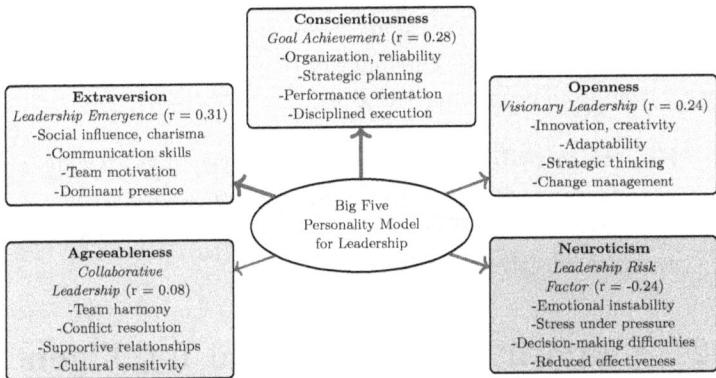

Figure 1.2: The Big Five Personality Model applied to leadership effectiveness. Meta-analytic research demonstrates that extraversion (r = 0.31) and conscientiousness (r = 0.28) are the strongest predictors of leadership emergence and effectiveness, followed by openness to experience (r = 0.24). Agreeableness shows a weak positive relationship (r = 0.08), while neuroticism represents a consistent risk factor (r = -0.24) for leadership effectiveness.

And so, after all the counting and measuring, we arrive at a conclusion that feels almost inevitable. The empirical literature, that vast collection of human observation, demonstrates that the Big Five personality traits are reliably linked to the success or failure of a leader. It is the energetic ones and the careful ones (i.e., those marked by extraversion and conscientiousness) who seem to find the way forward (see Figure 1.2). These traits are not merely decorations of the soul. They shape the way a leader walks through the day and the heavy choices they make. It happens because our nature forces us to adopt specific behaviors, just as a willow bends because it is a willow.

The evidence whispers another truth, one that is perhaps more hopeful. It suggests that prosocial qualities are essential. Prosocial is a dry term for a warm thing; it refers to actions intended to help other people rather than oneself. Qualities like honesty and humility are not just polite ornaments. They are instrumental for effective leadership, particularly in those collectivist cultures where the group breathes as a single body and in our tangled, globalized world. The idea of bringing personality assessment (i.e., the measuring of the spirit) into the training of leaders is supported by a mountain of research. It reinforces the broad and gentle argument that traits oriented toward goodness are not only desirable but are the very things that keep the organization from crumbling into dust.

> **Key Point:** Research consistently shows that specific personality traits, especially extraversion and conscientiousness, are reliable predictors of who becomes a leader and how effective they are.

1.2   Empathy and Emotional Intelligence

In the modern organization, where the air is often stale and the lights hum with a weary persistence, two qualities have come to matter more than the rest. These are empathy and emotional intelligence, or EI as the scholars abbreviate it. They have emerged as the central pillars of leadership that is both effective and ethical. While the personality traits we discussed earlier, such as the energy of extraversion or the diligence of conscientiousness, provide a foundation for a leader, they are merely the floorboards. It is often the leader's capacity for empathy and emotional intelligence that determines whether they can inspire a tired team, motivate the disheartened, and keep the work going through the long winter.

The books on the shelves robustly support the view that empathy and EI are indispensable. These are not luxuries. These competencies enable leaders to understand the silent needs of their followers and to foster trust in a cynical world. They allow a leader to manage the inevitable conflicts that arise when people are tired and to drive the organization toward a better outcome. The importance of this is recognized across all cultures and is grounded in the cold facts of psychological and neurological science. As such, the cultivation of empathy and EI should be the main task of leadership development in any organization that wishes to preserve goodness in its halls.

> **Key Point:** Beyond basic personality traits, a leader's ability to understand and manage emotions is vital for inspiring teams and maintaining ethical, effective leadership.

1.2.1   Conceptual Foundations

To understand this, we must look at what the words mean. Emotional intelligence encompasses the capacity to recognize, interpret, and effectively manage emotions in oneself and in interactions with others [7,8]. It is the ability to read the weather of the human heart. Over the last thirty years, researchers have proposed several frameworks to explain this mystery. The most notable among them are the ability model, the trait model, and the mixed models. Each of these has shaped our theoretical understanding and the practical ways we try to measure the soul.

The ability model was introduced by Mayer and Salovey. They treat EI as a set of cognitive skills. By cognitive, they mean it is a labor of the intellect, a mental process that facilitates the handling of emotional information and guides how one behaves in the company of others. This model identifies four distinct but related abilities. First, there is the accurate perceiving of emotions, which is the ability to see the sadness behind a smile. Second, there is the using of emotions to facilitate thinking, which means allowing a mood to help solve a problem. Third, there is the understanding of emotional meanings, knowing that grief comes from loss. And finally, there is managing emotions reflectively, which is the hard discipline of calming a storm within oneself or another [9–11]. Because this approach views EI as a function of the mind, it typically employs performance-based tasks to evaluate it, asking the person to solve emotional puzzles rather than simply asking them how they feel.

Alternatively, there is the trait model developed by Petrides and Furnham. They view EI differently. To them, it is a collection of self-perceived emotional strengths and behavioral tendencies. It is not necessarily what one can do, but what one believes one is like. These traits are relatively stable and closely linked to personality. This perspective organizes trait EI into fifteen facets, which are further grouped into four domains. There is well-being, which is the general sense that life is bearable. There is self-control, the leash one puts on one's impulses. There is emotionality, the depth of one's feelings. And there is sociability, the knack for being among people without fatigue [12, 13]. Assessment in this model relies on self-report instruments, which are questionnaires that capture an individual's habitual emotional responses.

The mixed models of EI, such as those proposed by Bar-On and Goleman, blend the soup of ability and trait perspectives together. Bar-On offered a framework that emphasizes a range of non-cognitive competencies. These include intrapersonal skills, which is the knowledge of oneself, and interpersonal skills, which is the knowledge of the neighbor. It also includes adaptability, stress management, and general mood, all of which contribute to effective coping with the heavy demands of life [14]. Goleman proposed a model that became very influential in the world of work. He highlights competencies like self-awareness, self-regulation, motivation, empathy, and social skills as essential for effective leadership [15, 16]. Self-regulation here refers to the vital pause before one reacts in anger. These models have been widely adopted in research, reinforcing the view that EI is a vital factor in the success of a leader [17, 18].

A recurring theme across all these models is the centrality of empathy. Empathy involves both sharing the feelings of another and understanding their perspective. In the difficult task of leadership, empathy enables authentic connections. It allows the leader to anticipate what the team needs before they ask and to foster appropriate responses to the shifting emotional dynamics of the room. It is the thread that holds the fabric together.

Key Point: Various theoretical models define emotional intelligence as either a cognitive ability, a personality trait, or a mix of competencies, but all agree that empathy is a core component.

1.2.2 Empirical Evidence: EI, Empathy, and Leadership Effectiveness

There is a heavy and serious collection of books and papers that proves what we perhaps already knew in our hearts. A substantial and methodologically rigorous body of empirical research, including the most recent gatherings of data known as meta-analyses, provides robust evidence for a strong positive relationship between emotional intelligence, empathy, and the ability to lead effectively [19–21]. Mills took on the task of a meta-analysis. This is a method where one does not trust a single story but gathers the numbers from many quantitative studies to find the truth hidden in the noise. By looking only at studies that measured these things with cold, hard numbers, Mills found a moderately strong positive relationship between EI and effective leadership. It suggests that this quality of the soul is not a trifle but a significant factor that must be taught in the training halls [19]. Similarly, Pa and Mathew performed a review of the archives, sourcing empirical studies from the major databases. Their analysis revealed a strong, statistically significant correlation, typically in the range of $\approx r = 0.3$ to 0.5 or higher. In the quiet language of statistics, this is a powerful bond, reinforcing the view that EI is a vital competency and that developing it can change the fate of a leader [21].

Gómez-Leal and colleagues looked specifically at the schoolhouse. They conducted a systematic review of 35 rigorously selected articles to examine EI in school leadership. They found that self-awareness, self-management, empathy, and relationship management were the most vital skills for those who watch over teachers and children. These skills are the foundation for building trust and managing the inevitable conflicts of the day. The review demonstrated that when a leader has intelligence of the emotions, the teachers are more satisfied, the school climate is warmer, and the students learn better. It is a reminder that the headmaster must also have a heart [20].

The studies consistently show that leaders with high EI are seen as better by everyone around them. Edelman and van Knippenberg examined the machinery of this success. They focused on the leader's ability to manage the emotions of their subordinates. Their findings indicate that emotionally intelligent leaders are better equipped to perceive and regulate the feelings of others. This facilitates a positive work climate and reduces the stress that hangs over the workplace like a fog. The study used survey-based assessments, asking both the leaders and the workers what they felt, and found that this ability to manage emotions was linked to higher satisfaction [22].

Rosete and Ciarrochi provided a study of great rigor. They employed the Mayer-Salovey-Caruso Emotional Intelligence Test, or MS-CEIT. This is not a questionnaire where one simply boasts of one's kindness but an ability-based measure that tests skill, much like a mathematics exam for the feelings. They studied 41 senior executives in the Australian Public Service. They assessed leadership effectiveness through 360-degree feedback, a method where a person is judged from all sides by 149 subordinates and managers. The results demonstrated that EI was significantly associated with higher effectiveness ratings ($r = 0.384$, $p < 0.05$), even after accounting for personality and raw intelligence. The ability to perceive emotions emerged as a particularly strong sign of a good leader [23].

A notable study by Kerr and colleagues examined senior managers using the Emotional Quotient Inventory, or EQ-i [24]. They found a significant positive relationship between EI and effectiveness, particularly in the domains of interpersonal skills and stress management. It seems that the ability to remain calm and kind is a predictor of success.

Beyond merely doing the job well, research has established that EI plays a role in who rises to the top in the first place. Côté and colleagues conducted two studies with undergraduate students working in small groups. They used both the hard tests of ability and the softer self-reports. They found that individuals with higher ability-based EI were more likely to be seen as leaders by their peers. The ability to understand emotions was the key. Even when the groups were mixed randomly, the one who understood the human heart was the one who emerged as the leader [25].

Empathy, which is a distinct cousin of EI, has also been shown to be vital. Westover identified empathy, alongside integrity and resilience, as foundational traits for the modern workplace. His work suggests that empathetic leaders are better able to navigate change and create a safe environment where people are not afraid to speak. This is grounded in practical strategies like active listening, which is the art of hearing what is not said [26, 27]. Qualitative analyses by Vivek Mehra and Srivastava, and case studies by Vatsalya Sharma, further corroborate that empathy makes the workers happier and the organization stronger [28, 29].

However, there is a nuance to this, a shadow in the light. Simon and colleagues provided a study on the cost of caring. Using experience sampling methods, which catch life as it happens, they found that leaders with high trait empathy experienced more distress when they had to give negative feedback. They felt the pain of the other person, and this made them less attentive and less effective for the rest of the day. While empathy is generally good, excessive feeling can be a burden in harsh moments [30]. In contrast, Sadri and colleagues looked at evidence across 38 countries and concluded that empathy is generally a foundational skill that enhances effectiveness, particularly in managing relationships [31].

Moreover, the combination of high empathy and EI appears to have a synergistic effect. Côté and colleagues demonstrated that EI predicts leadership emergence above other differences, while Gómez-Leal highlighted the centrality of both. It suggests that the integration of these qualities leads to a superior outcome, reinforcing the importance of developing both competencies [20, 25].

Key Point: Extensive data and meta-analyses confirm that emotional intelligence and empathy are strongly linked

to better leadership performance and the likelihood of
emerging as a leader.

1.2.3 Impact on Team Dynamics, Collaboration, and Conflict Resolution

There is a substantial body of research that underscores the role of
empathy and EI in the delicate life of a team. Hwang conducted
a survey on diverse professional teams and revealed that higher EI
scores correlated with improved communication and trust. When
the members understood each other, they felt a stronger sense of
collective efficacy, which is the belief that they can succeed together
[32]. Similarly, Wu and colleagues used mixed methods, combining
numbers with interviews. They found that teams led by emotionally
intelligent leaders displayed more adaptive conflict management styles.
They did not fight as bitterly, and they were happier [33]. Rapisarda
analyzed work teams and demonstrated that EI is a key predictor of
cohesiveness. The teams that had high EI outperformed the others,
both in their tasks and in their relationships [34]. Bannikov and
colleagues reported that EI fosters efficient communication and enables
teams to adapt to the complex and changing world [35].

Further, emotionally intelligent leadership contributes to constructive communication and reduces the noise of conflict. Ugoani presented
case studies showing that leaders with high EI employ effective strategies to manage disputes and inspire their subordinates [36]. Reilly
conducted a review and concluded that developing EI in teams positively impacts performance and keeps people from leaving the job [37].
Quinn and Wilemon examined project leaders in engineering and
found that EI enhances effectiveness by facilitating open dialogue
and mutual respect [38]. Coronado-Maldonado and Benítez-Márquez
synthesized 104 articles and noted that in certain roles, EI accounts
for up to 58% of job performance. It is a staggering number [39].

Empathy is particularly vital when people disagree. Westover
and Mehra provide evidence that empathetic leaders are adept at
perceiving the emotional undercurrents of a room. They understand

diverse viewpoints and respond with sensitivity [26, 28]. Arghode and
colleagues proposed that empathy enables leaders to bridge the gaps
between people and nurture a climate of safety [40]. Klimecki reviewed
studies of the brain and found that empathy activates neural circuits
linked to prosocial behaviors. These are the physical pathways in the
mind that allow for peace [41]. Shivani and Karuna illustrated that
leaders with high EI are consistently better at de-escalating tensions
and finding solutions that benefit everyone [42].

The practical strategies for this include active listening and the validation of emotions. Vandana and colleagues highlighted the efficacy of
validating emotions, which means acknowledging that a person's feelings are real, to reduce defensiveness [43]. Gerasimova and Khasanova
identified self-regulation skills as central. This is the ability to hold
one's tongue and maintain composure [44]. Costa and colleagues
used an experiment with voice self-perception to demonstrate how
self-regulation can mitigate the negative effects of conflict [45]. Xu
provided a perspective that emotional validity facilitates constructive
management. When individuals feel understood, the storm passes
more quickly [46].

The benefits of this emotional wisdom are sketched out in Figure
1.3. It is a map that shows how a simple understanding of the human
heart contributes to the excellence of leadership and the settling of
the inevitable quarrels that arise when people work together. The
empirical evidence, which is to say the collection of observed facts,
substantiates the value of these high EI teams. Bannikov and colleagues, along with Mekhala and Sandhya, went into the field to
watch how people labor. They demonstrated that teams where the
members possess high EI experience a 25% increase in productivity.
Productivity is a dry word for the amount of work a person can finish
before the sun sets; it seems that when communication is smooth and
the navigation of complex interactions is handled with care, the work
flows like water [35, 47].

On a broader scale, the organizations that decide to teach these
things report a marked change. According to the surveys and interventions by Hwang, Ullah, Rapisarda, and Moore and Mamiseishvili,

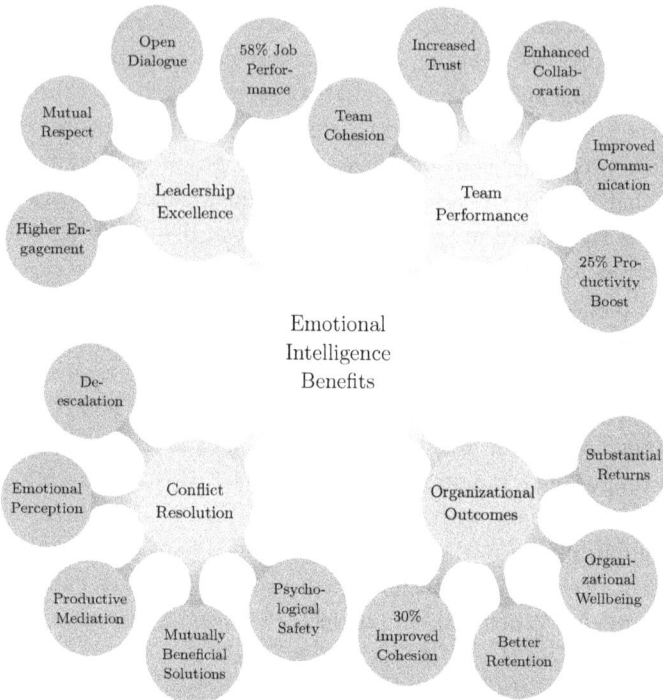

Figure 1.3: Framework illustrating the multifaceted benefits of Emotional Intelligence in organizational contexts. The central concept branches into four key outcome domains: Team Performance demonstrates quantifiable improvements including 25% productivity increases through enhanced communication, collaboration, trust, and cohesion [35,47]; Leadership Excellence shows substantial impact with up to 58% contribution to job performance through facilitating open dialogue, mutual respect, and higher employee engagement [39]; Conflict Resolution encompasses critical capabilities for de-escalation, emotional perception, productive mediation, and creating psychologically safe environments; and Organizational Outcomes represent the broader business value with 30% improvements in team cohesion, better retention rates, enhanced organizational wellbeing, and substantial returns on EI investments [32,34,48,49].

there is an improvement of up to 30% in team cohesion. Cohesion is the invisible glue that keeps a group from scattering; it is the shared belief that they belong to one another and to the task [32,34,48,49]. Collectively, these studies illustrate a simple truth. Investing in empathy and the education of the emotions is not merely a kindness for the individual. It yields substantial organizational returns, which is the scholar's way of saying that goodness, in the end, is also profitable.

Key Point: Teams led by emotionally intelligent managers experience better communication, easier conflict resolution, and significantly higher productivity and cohesion.

1.2.4 Impact on Employee Engagement

Trust is widely recognized as the invisible mortar that holds the bricks of an organization together. Without it, the walls crumble. Both empathy and emotional intelligence, or EI, serve as the critical hands that mix this mortar and maintain it against the weather of the workplace [50]. Yulianti and colleagues sat down and spoke at length with leaders and the people they lead, conducting what scholars call qualitative research. They found that leaders who possessed high EI, particularly those who could see the shadow of an emotion passing over a face and manage it, were more successful. They fostered trust. They created a space for open communication. They built what is known as psychological safety. This is a term for the comfort of knowing that one will not be punished or humiliated for speaking the truth. These findings align with the heavy books of the library, which consistently identify trust as the thing a worker needs to feel satisfied and to stay.

The importance of empathy and this feeling of safety in the building of trust is further substantiated by a series of empirical studies. Zhou conducted a quantitative analysis, gathering survey data from many different lives in diverse organizations. The study looked at inclusive leadership and loyalty, using psychological safety as a mediating variable. A mediating variable is like a bridge; it is the path that connects the cause to the effect. The results indicated that leaders who build this bridge, by encouraging open dialogue and valuing the different ways people see the world, significantly enhance the loyalty and trust of their staff [51]. Similarly, Vaishal utilized an empirical approach to analyze how safety changes the way decisions are made. It was found that in environments where people are not afraid, the decisions are more effective and ethical [52]. Clarke and colleagues extended these findings through a mixed-methods study, which uses both numbers and stories. They demonstrated that leaders who actively promote this safety contribute to the wellbeing of the employee. They make the worker willing to speak up about worries or new ideas [53]. Collectively, these studies underscore a simple truth. Leaders who show a genuine concern for the lives of their team members foster a sense of safety and loyalty, which are the very roots of trust.

A robust body of research confirms that the vast majority of employees perceive empathy as vital. It is the oxygen they need to trust the air in the room. Muss and colleagues conducted a systematic literature review, which is a careful sifting of findings from a wide range of contexts. They concluded that empathetic leadership is consistently associated with higher levels of trust, engagement, and the performance of the organization [54]. Longmire and Harrison employed experiments and surveys to distinguish between two things that often look alike. There is perspective-taking, which is the cognitive act of understanding how another thinks, and there is empathy, which is the emotional act of feeling what another feels. They revealed that while both contribute to trust, it is empathy that has the stronger effect on cooperation [55]. Bahadur and colleagues used structural equation modeling. This is a complex statistical method that tests a theory by looking at the relationships between many variables at once, like a map of the stars. They investigated the effect of employee empathy on the loyalty of those they serve. They identified trust as the key. Their results showed that when interactions are empathetic, trust grows, and loyalty follows [56]. These convergent findings highlight that empathy is central to the process of building trust.

The relationship between EI and trust is further elucidated by studies employing both quantitative and mixed-methods designs. Ruestow conducted an exploratory study in the weary halls of public human services. It was found that the EI of the leaders was positively correlated with the job satisfaction of the followers and their commitment to the organization. Both of these are closely linked to trust [57]. Karim examined the relationship between EI and something called leader-member exchange. This is a scholar's term for the unique quality of the relationship between a boss and a specific worker. The study demonstrated that high EI in leaders facilitates stronger, trust-based relationships [58]. Sanders provided empirical evidence connecting the EI of the followers to their style of following. It indicates that emotionally intelligent followers are more likely to trust and engage with their leaders [59]. Rajesh and colleagues identified follower EI as a mediator between a transforming style of leadership and positive outcomes, including trust [60]. Jordan and Troth found that EI and high-quality relationships are associated with reduced turnover intentions. Turnover intention is the quiet plan a worker makes to leave their job. When trust is present, this desire fades [61]. These studies collectively demonstrate that emotionally intelligent leaders are more likely to inspire trust and commitment.

The positive influence of EI on psychological empowerment and employee engagement has been confirmed through the cold logic of advanced statistical analyses. Hameli and colleagues utilized multiple regression analyses to show that the attributes of a leader, particularly their belief in their own ability and their power to empower others, significantly predict how engaged the employees will be [62]. Psychological empowerment is the feeling that one has control over one's work and that the work has meaning. Alotaibi and colleagues, along with Udod and colleagues, employed survey-based methodologies to examine this. They found that employees feel more empowered and engaged when their leaders demonstrate high EI, especially in recognizing and responding to the quiet cues of emotion [63,64]. These findings reinforce the argument that EI is not only beneficial for leaders but for the climate of the entire organization. It enhances the employee's sense of agency, making them feel less like a cog in a machine and more like a human being.

Empathetic leadership is associated with a wide range of constructive outcomes. Vatsalya Sharma and colleagues presented a qualitative case study of compassionate leadership. It illustrated how management practices driven by empathy lead to increased engagement, reduced stress, improved well-being, and higher retention rates [29]. Retention rate is simply the measure of how many people choose to stay rather than walk out the door. The study highlighted practical strategies, such as active listening and individualized support, which contribute to a culture that is bearable and even positive.

The broader organizational benefits of empathy and EI are further supported by hybrid and systematic literature reviews. Muss and colleagues, and Coronado-Maldonado and Benítez-Márquez, synthesized findings from over a hundred peer-reviewed articles. They concluded that the empathy and EI of a leader are linked to enhanced collaboration, trust, and overall performance. They also found a link to innovation and adaptability in uncertain environments [39,54]. Ma and colleagues conducted a quantitative study examining the relationship between empathetic leadership and the innovative behavior of employees. They found that empathy not only fosters trust but also encourages adaptability and creative problem-solving, particularly when the future is unclear [65]. Abd Nasir and Mahadi explored the integration of moods and emotions into the strategies of development. They demonstrated that emotionally intelligent organizations are better equipped to navigate change [66]. Ridho and Kumar provided additional empirical support, showing that EI is a key determinant of exceptional leadership and transformational change, both of which are grounded in the soil of trust and empathy [67,68].

The empirical literature robustly demonstrates that the building of trust and the satisfaction of the employee are deeply intertwined with the leader's empathy and emotional intelligence. Methodologically diverse studies converge on the conclusion that leaders who embody these qualities foster psychological safety, loyalty, and engagement. They also enhance the performance of the organization. The multifaceted relationship between empathy, emotional intelligence, and these outcomes is illustrated in Figure 1.4. It demonstrates how these competencies create a foundation for trust that cascades through the lives of the employees to the broader benefits of the group. These findings affirm that goodness, as manifested through empathy and EI, is not only morally desirable but is also practically worthwhile in the struggle for success.

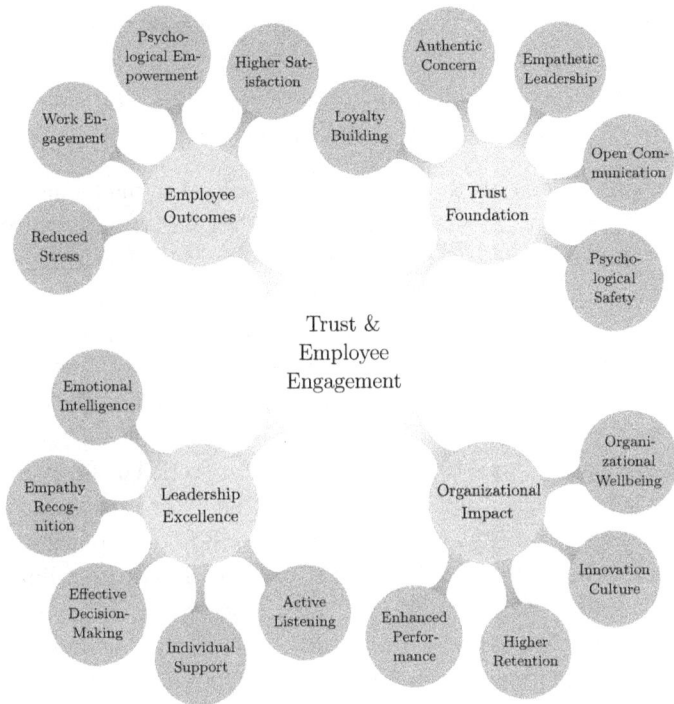

Figure 1.4: Framework illustrating the impact of empathy and emotional intelligence on trust-building and employee engagement. The central concept branches into four key domains: Trust Foundation encompasses the fundamental elements of psychological safety, open communication, empathetic leadership, authentic concern for employee wellbeing, and loyalty building that create the groundwork for organizational success [50, 51, 53]; Employee Outcomes demonstrate the direct benefits including higher satisfaction, psychological empowerment, enhanced work engagement, and reduced stress levels that result from emotionally intelligent leadership [62–64]; Leadership Excellence represents the core competencies of emotional intelligence, empathy recognition, effective decision-making, individualized support, and active listening that enable leaders to build trust and inspire engagement [29, 54]; and Organizational Impact captures the broader business results including enhanced performance, higher retention rates, innovation culture development, and overall organizational wellbeing that emerge from trust-based leadership approaches [65–68].

Key Point: Leaders who demonstrate empathy create an environment of trust and psychological safety, which

directly increases employee loyalty, engagement, and job
satisfaction.

1.2.5   Cross-Cultural Perspectives

A substantial body of research has established that the human heart
is much the same across the globe, and yet the expression of its
goodness changes with the soil on which it stands. The significance
of empathy and emotional intelligence in leadership is global, but
their impact is deeply influenced by the customs of the place. Raghav
and Padmavathi, along with Sadri, Pedersen, and Alon, provide the
empirical and conceptual foundations for understanding these subtle
dynamics [69–71].

Raghav and Padmavathi employed a cross-sectional survey design
across multiple organizations. This is a method that takes a snapshot
of many lives at a single moment in time to see how they connect. They
examined the relationship between a leader's EI and the willingness
of the employee to stay and work hard. Their quantitative analysis
revealed that leaders with higher EI consistently fostered greater
engagement and lower turnover, which is the rate at which people
leave their jobs in despair. However, the magnitude of these effects
varied according to cultural norms. It underscores the universal
value of EI, while highlighting the necessity for cultural adaptation to
maximize its benefits [69].

Sadri and colleagues conducted a large and heavy study involving
over 37,000 leaders across 38 countries. They utilized hierarchical
linear modeling. This is a complex way of calculating that respects
the different layers of the world, distinguishing the individual from
the country they live in. They assessed the relationship between how
subordinates rated a leader's empathy and how supervisors rated
that leader's performance. The results indicated a significant positive
association. However, the strength of this relationship was moderated
by cultural dimensions such as power distance. Power distance is a
scholar's term for the steepness of the stairs between the master and
the servant, or how much a culture accepts that authority is unequal.

In cultures where this distance is high and the boss is a distant figure, the positive impact of empathic emotion was particularly pronounced. It suggests that the "goodness" of empathy is both broadly effective and sensitive to the context. Pedersen and Pope advanced the discourse by critiquing the models of empathy that come only from the West. They proposed the construct of "inclusive cultural empathy." This emphasizes a relational approach that respects the local way of being. Their conceptual analysis argued that effective global leadership requires an expanded understanding of empathy to foster trust in a room filled with strangers.

Alon and Higgins synthesized the literature to propose that success depends on the integration of three things. There is emotional intelligence (EQ), analytical intelligence (IQ), and cultural intelligence (CQ). Their model posits that CQ, which is the wisdom of the traveler who knows the customs of others, moderates the effectiveness of the other two. It enables leaders to adapt to diverse environments and thereby maximize the "goodness" of their leadership. Collectively, these studies demonstrate that while attributes like empathy are universally beneficial, their optimal expression is shaped by the culture, reinforcing the importance of learning the ways of the people one leads [31, 70, 71].

Further empirical support for the value of EI across the oceans is provided by Miao, Humphrey, and Qian [72]. They conducted a comprehensive meta-analysis, synthesizing data from multiple studies across various national cultures. Employing meta-analytic techniques, the authors quantified the relationship between leader EI and two critical outcomes. The first is task performance, which is simply doing the job well. The second is organizational citizenship behavior, or OCB. This creates a dry acronym for a warm concept. OCB refers to the small, unwritten acts of kindness and help that a worker performs not because they must, but because they wish to help the group. The analysis revealed that leader EI is significantly and positively associated with both. However, the strength of these relationships is moderated by cultural dimensions such as individualism-collectivism. This dimension measures whether a person sees themselves as a solitary tree or as part of a forest. This robust evidence affirms that goodness, operationalized as EI, yields tangible benefits, but it also cautions that its impact depends on alignment with local expectations [72].

The expression of empathy is further nuanced by the way power is held. Mullamaa utilized an ethnographic, qualitative case study approach [73]. Ethnography is the patient work of sitting with people, watching their days, and living among them to understand their truth. The study investigated empathetic leadership within international project teams in six Nordic and Baltic countries. Through participant observation and interviews, the study found that empathetic leadership was particularly effective in low power distance cultures. These are places where the leader and the worker stand almost as equals. Here, empathy fostered inclusion and enthusiasm.

Conversely, Islam and colleagues employed quantitative survey methods to examine paternalistic leadership in high power distance cultures [74]. Paternalism is a style where the leader acts like a stern but protective father. They found that while empathy remains important, it must be balanced with clear authority and structure. Their results indicate that benevolent and moral leadership is good, but excessive authoritarianism can ruin it. These findings illustrate that the worth of goodness is context-dependent. In egalitarian cultures, participative styles work best, whereas in hierarchical cultures, goodness is best expressed through a combination of benevolence and firm guidance [73, 74].

The capacity to interpret the signals of a diverse world is further enhanced by cultural intelligence, or CQ, as explored by Judy van Zyl and Sigamoney [75]. Through a review of the concepts and the evidence, they demonstrated that leaders with high CQ are more adept at adapting their communication. They improve trust and collaboration. This research reinforces the argument that cultivating goodness, in the form of cultural sensitivity, is both a moral duty and a practical necessity for the global leader [75].

Finally, the practical development of these qualities is addressed by Ng, Van Dyne, and Ang [76]. They integrated experiential learning theory with research on cultural intelligence. Experiential learning is the idea that one learns best not from books, but from the bruises and triumphs of actual experience. They proposed a model for development that identified self-awareness, cultural immersion, and active listening as key practices. The model emphasizes that the cultivation of goodness through intentional learning is essential for effective leadership in diverse environments. It suggests that such growth is possible for those willing to do the work [76].

The collective evidence from these studies affirms that goodness, as manifested in empathy and emotional intelligence, is a critical asset. However, its expression is deeply influenced by the cultural context. It necessitates an adaptive approach, reminding us that to lead well, one must first understand the people.

> **Key Point:** While empathy and emotional intelligence are valuable worldwide, leaders must adapt how they express these qualities to fit local cultural norms and expectations.

1.2.6   Leadership Intelligence

Modern leadership effectiveness is best understood as the synergistic integration of three distinct gifts, a combination often referred to as leadership intelligence, or LQ. It is a triad of the mind and heart. There is cognitive intelligence (IQ), emotional intelligence (EQ), and cultural intelligence (CQ). As illustrated in Figure 1.5, each of these intelligences contributes distinct but complementary capabilities to the difficult task of guiding others. IQ provides the analytical and strategic foundation; it is the cold, sharp logic needed for decision-making. EQ is the warmth that enables leaders to build trust, manage the fragile web of relationships, and foster engagement. And CQ is the traveler's wisdom, equipping leaders to adapt their behaviors and communication styles to the strange and diverse cultural contexts they encounter.

Crucially, CQ serves as the adaptive mechanism. This is a scholar's term for the hinge upon which the door turns. It allows the raw power of IQ and the empathy of EQ to be expressed appropriately across different environments. This means that even leaders with strong

analytical and emotional skills will stumble if they lack the cultural
awareness to know how their words land in a foreign ear. Research
has shown that CQ moderates the impact of both IQ and EQ. To
moderate, in the statistical sense, means to act like a valve that
regulates the flow; it enhances leadership effectiveness by enabling a
context-sensitive application of these skills [70, 71, 75].

The empirical studies, those ledgers of human behavior, further
support this integrative model. They show that leaders who combine
high EQ with strong CQ are more successful at fostering engagement
and reducing turnover, which is the sad rhythm of people leaving
their work. This is especially true in culturally diverse teams where
misunderstanding is easy [69, 72]. The framework in Figure 1.5 thus
encapsulates the consensus that effective global leadership is not the
product of a single lonely intelligence. Rather, it is the dynamic
interplay of IQ, EQ, and CQ, with cultural intelligence acting as the
key moderator for success in an interconnected world [71, 76].

The necessity of LQ, which is the integrated mastery of these three,
is most pronounced in environments where individuals from diverse
cultural, disciplinary, or social backgrounds must labor together toward
a shared hope. In academia, where faculty and students drift in from
across the continents, leaders must navigate intellectual complexity
and the friction of interpersonal dynamics to foster innovation. In
healthcare, effective leadership is vital for coordinating teams and
delivering compassionate care to patients from varied backgrounds,
often under the high pressure of life and death. The same is true
in international business, global nonprofits, and the offices of public
administration. Success in these places depends on the ability to
harmonize diverse perspectives and to inspire a collective purpose.

But nowhere is the importance of LQ more visible, or perhaps
more consequential, than in the realm of politics and public leadership.
The leaders we elect are tasked with the heavy burden of uniting
increasingly diverse populations. They must mediate between competing interests and make decisions that shape the very fabric of society.
In such high-stakes environments, the ability to combine cognitive
acuity, emotional understanding, and cultural sensitivity is essential.

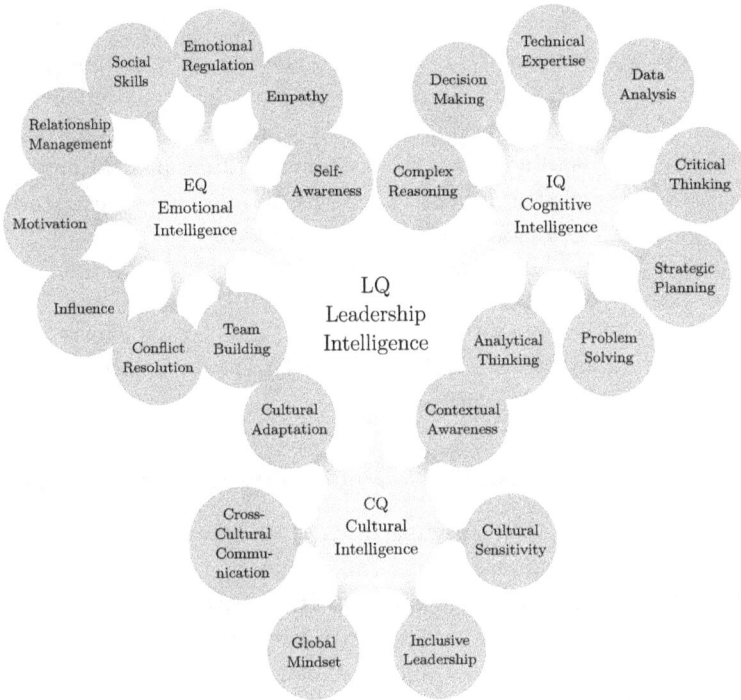

Figure 1.5: Framework illustrating the integration of three critical intelligence types in leadership effectiveness (i.e., LQ). The central concept branches into IQ (cognitive capabilities for analytical thinking and problem-solving), EQ (emotional competencies for relationship management and influence), and CQ (cultural adaptability for global leadership success). Research demonstrates that modern leadership requires the synergistic application of all three intelligences, with CQ serving as a moderator that enhances the contextual effectiveness of IQ and EQ across diverse cultural environments.

It is needed for building trust, fostering social cohesion, and guiding communities through the fog of complexity and change. Political leaders with high LQ are better equipped to bridge the divides, to respond empathetically to their constituents, and to create inclusive policies that reflect the needs of all citizens.

In all of these contexts, the selection and development of leaders who embody all three pillars of LQ is not just beneficial. It is vital

for the survival and resilience of the institution. Leaders with strong
cognitive, emotional, and cultural intelligence are uniquely positioned
to unlock the full potential of their organizations. They foster environments of trust and adaptability. As the world becomes increasingly
interconnected and crowded, the future of thriving institutions will
depend on their commitment to identifying and empowering those
rare souls who excel across the spectrum of LQ.

> **Key Point:** Modern leadership requires a combination
> of cognitive, emotional, and cultural intelligence, where
> cultural intelligence helps apply analytical and emotional
> skills in diverse settings.

1.2.7   Neurological and Psychological Foundations

The neurological basis of empathy is a complex conversation between the ancient, animal parts of our nature and the newer, quieter
rooms of the mind where reason sits. It is characterized by the interplay of lower-order processes, which are automatic and affective,
and higher-order processes, which are cognitive and regulatory. Convergent neuroscientific research, employing a range of methodologies
such as neuroimaging meta-analyses, structural MRI, and behavioral
paradigms, has allowed us to peer into the skull to see this machinery
at work [77–86].

For example, Kim synthesizes the evidence to show that empathy
involves specific territories of the brain: the anterior insula, the anterior cingulate cortex, and the prefrontal regions. It integrates the
sudden, automatic affective responses with the deliberate regulatory
mechanisms that allow us to control them [77]. Kanch and colleagues
review the studies supporting the involvement of the mirror neuron
system. This is the part of the mind that acts as a looking glass,
allowing us to see ourselves in the actions of another. They highlight
the roles of the inferior frontal gyrus and the superior temporal sulcus
in enabling both affective resonance, which is the vibration of shared
feeling, and cognitive perspective-taking, which is the intellectual
understanding of another's view [78].

Kogler and colleagues conducted meta-analyses, gathering many pictures of the brain to distinguish between affective empathy and cognitive empathy. They found they live in different places. Affective empathy is linked to the anterior insula, while cognitive empathy engages the medial prefrontal cortex, supporting the idea that empathy is not one thing but a house with many doors [79]. Further, Uribe and colleagues employed structural and functional MRI. They found that these two types of empathy are associated with distinct neuroanatomical substrates. Substrate is a dry word for the physical foundation, the very soil of the brain. They found increased cortical thickness in the frontal regions for those with high cognitive empathy, and greater volumes in the thalamus for those who feel deeply [80].

Eres, Moore, and Robert used voxel-based morphometry. This is a technique that measures the volume of the brain's matter, much as a grocer weighs grain. They show that both affective and cognitive empathy are associated with structural variations in the insula and prefrontal cortices, reinforcing the idea that our capacity for goodness is written into the bone and tissue [81–83].

Walter and Shamay-Tsoory provide frameworks that combine genetics and neuroimaging, emphasizing that these neural regions are vital for social cognition [84, 86]. Cox and colleagues demonstrated through resting-state fMRI that even when the mind is quiet, individual differences in empathy are reflected in the intrinsic connectivity patterns of the brain. It suggests that empathy is an intrinsic feature of how we are made [85].

Key neural networks implicated in this mystery include the sensorimotor regions and the mirror neuron system. Baird, Rajmohan, and Pfeifer collectively provide evidence for this [87–89]. Pfeifer used neuroimaging in children to link this neural mirroring with interpersonal competence. These studies support the view that the mirror neuron system is central to the vicarious experience of emotion. Vicarious means to feel something through another, a capacity that is fundamental if one wishes to lead effectively.

Then there is the phenomenon of emotional contagion. This is the process by which emotions are transmitted between individuals like a fever. It is supported by these same neural systems and has been extensively studied. Elfenbein and colleagues synthesize the mechanisms of how this contagion influences the mood and motivation of a group [90]. Kudryashov and Simonyan review the psychophysiological aspects, emphasizing that this is a form of communication that requires no words [91].

Rhee and colleagues use network analysis to map how these feelings travel through a team, demonstrating that both explicit and implicit mechanisms shape the spread of emotion [92]. Hirsch employed two-person multimodal imaging to provide direct evidence. They found that when two people share a feeling, their neural activity becomes synchronized, beating in time together [93].

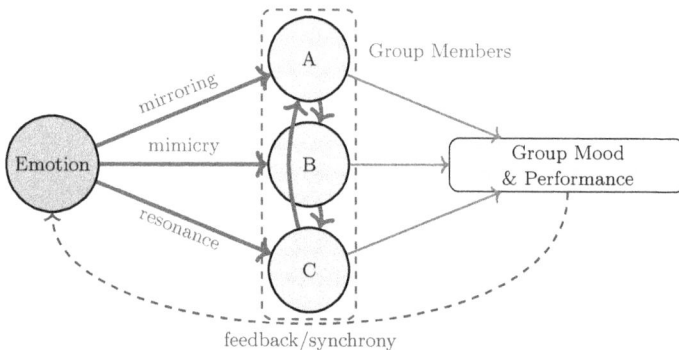

Figure 1.6: Emotional contagion describes the process by which an individual's emotional state (e.g., joy, stress, or anger) is transmitted to others through mechanisms such as facial and vocal mimicry, mirroring, and affective resonance. In this diagram, the initiator's emotion spreads to multiple group members, who in turn influence each other, resulting in a group-wide mood or collective affect. The group's collective emotional climate then feeds back to the original initiator, creating a dynamic loop that can amplify or dampen the overall emotional tone. Neuroscientific research highlights the role of mirror neuron systems and shared neural circuitry in facilitating this contagion, while psychological studies show its impact on group cohesion, performance, and well-being.

Eldadi and colleagues showed that in team sports, this contagion affects the outcome of the game [94]. Hirsch and Boukarras further elucidate the mechanisms of spontaneous mimicry, where we unconsciously copy the smile or the frown of our neighbor [95, 96]. Collectively, these studies underscore the significance of emotional contagion for the health of the organization (see Figure 1.6). It supports the view that fostering positive feelings is a worthwhile pursuit.

From a psychological perspective, empathy is recognized as a social and cognitive skill that fosters the bonds between us. Anderson and Keltner argue that empathy is selectively activated to solidify social connections, supporting its evolutionary role in helping us survive the winter together [97]. Riess demonstrates that nonverbal empathic behavior enhances perceptions of warmth and competence, thereby promoting trust [98]. Miyazono and Inarimori propose that we are most kind when we identify with the group, suggesting that altruism depends on a sense of belonging [99]. Wilkinson highlights empathy's role as the "glue" of caring communities, emphasizing its capacity to reduce conflict and promote resilience [100].

The coherence between neural activations and empathic behavior is considered a marker of maturity. Rameson, Derntl, Singer, and Morelli employ paradigms to demonstrate that when the brain and the actions align, it predicts prosocial behavior and effective leadership [101–104].

However, life is hard, and chronic stress can disrupt this harmony. Levy and colleagues reveal that chronic trauma impairs the neural basis of empathy, with sad consequences for parenting and the abilities of the next generation [105, 106]. Nitschke and Bartz provide a review of the association between acute stress and empathy, highlighting the importance of resilience training so that leaders may maintain their kindness even when the world is heavy [107].

Converging evidence from neuroimaging, behavioral, and theoretical studies demonstrates that empathy is a multidimensional construct. Its development and expression are integral to the promotion of goodness. Its cultivation is both scientifically grounded and practically worthwhile.

> **Key Point:** Empathy is rooted in specific brain structures and neural networks, but chronic stress can impair these biological systems, highlighting the need for leaders to build resilience.

1.3 Ethical Leadership and Integrity

One often feels that the concept of ethical leadership stands like an old, reliable stove in the center of a cold room; it is widely acknowledged as the very foundation of goodness within the walls of an organization. It encompasses the demonstration and promotion of what scholars call normatively appropriate conduct, which is simply a fancy way of saying one must behave as a decent human being ought to behave, both in personal actions and when dealing with others [108].

At its heart, this form of leadership is defined by traits that seem almost old-fashioned in our hurried times: integrity, honesty, fairness, the clarity of transparency, and the heavy burden of accountability. Together, these virtues foster trust and credibility, warming the organizational climate [109–112]. These qualities are not merely desirable for the sake of the soul but are linked by the cold, hard facts of research to the long life and survival of the enterprise.

> **Key Point:** Ethical leaders act correctly and encourage others to do the same, which builds trust and helps the organization succeed.

1.3.1 Defining Ethical Leadership

It is a dual existence, this business of ethical leadership. It involves standing as a model of behavior while actively encouraging the same conduct in the flock. Stouten and colleagues remind us that such leaders must set clear standards, offering a sweet for the righteous deed and a stern word for the wicked, thereby shaping the very air the workers breathe [108]. This double burden, to be both the role model and the guide, distinguishes them from other sorts of leaders. Kazanskaia adds that such a soul must possess empathy, which is the ability to feel another's sorrow, and humility, along with a strong sense of responsibility [109]. They open the windows for conversation and create a space where a clerk feels psychologically safe, meaning they can speak their mind without fear of the whip, to voice concerns or report a wrong.

Key Point: A good leader acts as a role model and sets rules for good behavior, making sure everyone feels safe enough to speak up.

1.3.2   Building Trust and Organizational Culture

Trust arrives quietly, a guest invited by consistent acts of fairness. By acting with integrity, ethical leaders build credibility with their followers, which in turn makes the employees feel a sense of engagement and loyalty, perhaps even a little happiness in their work [111, 113]. Ughulu observes that this is especially vital when the world outside is a storm of change; the leader becomes a stabilizing force that demands the truth be seen and the ledgers be balanced [110]. The influence seeps into the floorboards, shaping the culture itself. Values are not just words but are written into the daily rituals and interactions, growing a garden of shared norms [109, 113]. In such air, the impulse to do wrong withers, replaced by a collective desire to serve the whole.

Key Point: When leaders are honest and fair, employees trust them more and work harder, which creates a better workplace for everyone.

1.3.3   Ethical Decision-Making Frameworks

To choose correctly is often a heavy burden. Leaders must facilitate sound decisions by leaning on established frameworks. They look to utilitarianism, which seeks the greatest happiness for the many, or deontology, which insists on duty above all, or virtue ethics, which asks one to be a good person rather than just do good acts. They use structures like the PLUS Model or the Six Lenses to ensure their hands remain clean and their reasons clear [114, 115]. These tools help the firm navigate the strange new waters of technology and the lonely distance of remote work [112]. Kazanskaia argues that we must weave these maps into the very education of the leader, for without a compass, how can the ship survive the uncertainty [114, 115]?

Key Point: Leaders use specific methods to make fair choices, which helps the company handle new problems and difficult situations.

1.3.4   Preventing Misconduct and Promoting Integrity

It is a sad truth that, given the chance, people may stray. Yet, research shows that a righteous leader is a strong wall against the darkness of fraud and corruption [116, 117]. Hussein and others have found that when a good leader stands beside strong rules of governance, the books are less likely to be cooked and the money less likely to be washed. Antunez tells us that the character of the captain matters more than the weather in preventing unethical behavior [116, 117]. They set the line that must not be crossed and provide a way to speak up when one sees a shadow, protecting the house from ruin and contributing to a culture where everyone shares the responsibility [113, 118].

Key Point: Strong ethical leaders stop employees from doing illegal or bad things by setting clear rules and consequences.

1.3.5   The Broader Impact of Ethical Leadership

The spirit of the leader flows down like water, touching the lowest clerk. When workers see goodness above them, they report a higher satisfaction with their lot and the desire to leave fades away [110, 111, 113]. It fosters a bravery to try new things, to innovate, for they know they are safe in an environment where trust is prioritized [111, 112]. And so, the literature converges on one truth: goodness is not a luxury. It is the bread and salt of survival. By living the truth, the leader builds a house that stands against the wind, proving that to be good is also to be wise [108–118].

Key Point: Ethical leadership makes employees happier and more loyal, which is necessary for the company to last a long time.

1.4   Established Leadership Theories

In the dusty libraries of management, two great philosophies stand out regarding the goodness of the soul in power: transformational leadership and servant leadership. Both theories emphasize the centrality of ethical conduct and prosocial motivation, which is the quiet desire to help others rather than oneself, aligning closely with the broader concept of goodness in the workplace.

> **Key Point:** Two main theories explain how good leaders focus on helping others and behaving ethically.

1.4.1   Transformational Leadership

Transformational leadership is characterized by a leader's ability to inspire the weary worker to look up from their desk and see a purpose greater than their own small wage. Originally conceptualized by Burns and expanded by Bass and Avolio, it rests on four pillars [119, 120]. There is idealized influence, where the leader acts with such grace they become a figure the followers long to copy. There is inspirational motivation, the painting of a picture of the future that stirs the blood. There is intellectual stimulation, asking the mind to wake up and think anew. And finally, individualized consideration, where the leader stops to ask about the follower's own dreams and needs.

Research confirms it works. Transformational leaders enhance engagement and innovation [119]. The mediating roles of motivation and stimulation amplify the effects of kindness and influence, leading to a sense of power and new ideas among the followers [120]. It is particularly effective when the sky is grey with crisis, fostering resilience. It walks hand in hand with ethical leadership, ensuring that the vision is grounded in integrity [109, 121].

> **Key Point:** Transformational leaders inspire employees to do more than expected by caring for them personally and giving them a clear vision to follow.

1.4.2 Servant Leadership

There is a quiet humility in the concept of servant leadership, first articulated by R.K. Greenleaf, which turns the usual order of things on its head [122]. It represents a shift away from the vanity of the general on the hill to a life centered on service to others. Servant leaders prioritize the needs, the growth, and the spiritual well-being of their followers, emphasizing empathy, the patience of listening, stewardship, and the building of a community [123–125]. Stewardship here is a fine word; it means caring for something that does not belong to you as if it were your own child. This approach is rooted in the simple belief that leadership is not about power but about serving, and that the success of the house is best achieved by lifting up those who dwell within it.

The core attributes of this gentle philosophy, such as humility and a commitment to helping others grow, have been linked by scholars to higher levels of engagement and trust [123–125]. These leaders create environments that are psychologically safe, meaning a place where a person can speak their truth without fear of retribution. In such air, people feel valued, which fosters collaboration and resilience. In the halls of hospitals and schools, where the work is human and fragile, servant leadership has been shown to improve both the soul of the worker and the outcome of the work [124].

It aligns with ethical leadership, for both walk the same path of moral behavior and integrity [115, 121]. To teach this method is to cultivate leaders who are equipped to navigate the complex moral dilemmas of our time and promote a success that endures [125].

The key similarities and differences between these two approaches are visually summarized in Figure 1.7.

> **Key Point:** A servant leader focuses on helping employees grow and feel safe, which makes the whole team work better together.

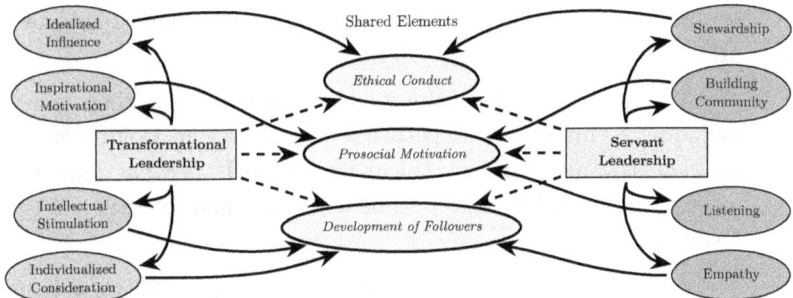

Figure 1.7: This diagram compares the foundational elements of transformational leadership and servant leadership, highlighting both their unique and shared attributes. Transformational leadership (left) is defined by four core components: idealized influence, inspirational motivation, intellectual stimulation, and individualized consideration. Servant leadership (right) is characterized by stewardship, community building, listening, and empathy. Both theories converge on three central principles (ethical conduct, prosocial motivation, and development of followers) which are depicted as shared elements at the center of the figure. Arrows indicate the relationships between each theory, their unique elements, and these common foundations, illustrating how both frameworks contribute to the broader understanding of ethical and goodness-oriented leadership.

1.4.3   Ethical Decision-Making

Life is full of fog and grey shadows, and so the convergence of these theories underscores the importance of having a map. Leaders need structured frameworks to navigate the complex ethical dilemmas that arise like sudden storms:

- The Rational Decision-Making Model provides a structured, step-by-step approach to solving problems, emphasizing cold logic, the gathering of evidence, and the careful weighing of alternatives [126].

- Rest's Model of Ethical Decision-Making outlines the journey of the conscience in four parts: moral awareness, moral judgment, moral intention, and finally, moral action. It highlights the hidden psychological processes and the development of the leader's soul [127].

- The PLUS Model (Policies, Legal, Universal, and Self) offers a practical lantern for evaluating decisions against the rules of the company, the laws of the land, universal values, and one's own private standards of integrity [115].

- The Markkula Center Framework offers a process for making choices, including seeing the issue, gathering the facts, and looking at the problem through various ethical lenses, such as what does the most good or what is most fair, before acting and reflecting on the result [115].

- The Six-Step Model expands on the rational approach by guiding leaders through a sequence [128]: (1) identifying the trouble, (2) gathering information, (3) evaluating the choices, (4) making the decision, (5) doing the deed, and (6) looking back to learn from what happened.

- Stakeholder Analysis involves systematically identifying every person who might be hurt or helped by a decision, ensuring that the leader considers the diverse consequences of their actions [129].

Adopting these models ensures that leaders are equipped not only with the heart to serve but with the tools to navigate difficulty with transparency. By drawing on these traditions, leaders can make decisions that uphold the integrity of the organization.

Thus, these theories provide robust frameworks for understanding goodness in leadership. As organizations face a world that grows more complex by the hour, the cultivation of leaders who embody these principles is both a moral duty and a necessity for survival [115, 119–121, 123–125].

> **Key Point:** Leaders use step-by-step guides to make fair choices, ensuring they consider the law, the rules, and how their actions affect others.

1.5   Cross-Cultural Perspectives

The way one leads is significantly shaped by the soil on which one stands. While some values are admired everywhere, the actual practices and expectations of leadership can differ markedly across the nations. Understanding these differences is vital, particularly when the work spans across borders.

Key Point: Leadership styles change depending on the country and culture, so it is important to understand these differences.

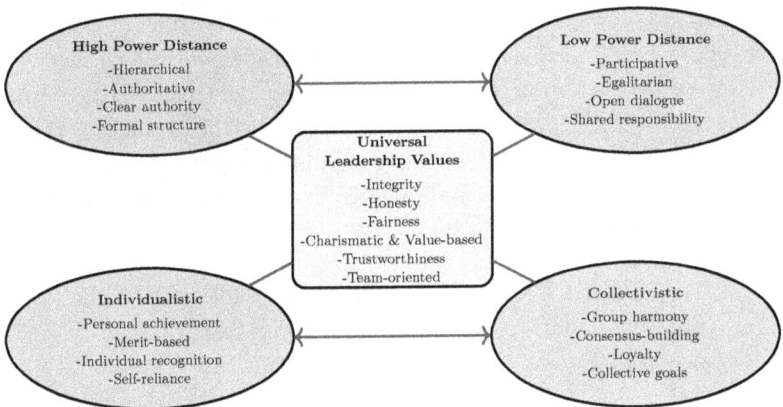

Figure 1.8: Visual representation of the relationship between universal leadership values and culturally specific leadership practices. The central rectangle highlights universal values (such as integrity, honesty, fairness, charisma, trustworthiness, and team orientation) that are widely endorsed across societies according to studies like GLOBE. Surrounding circles illustrate four contrasting cultural dimensions: high versus low power distance and individualistic versus collectivistic orientations. Lines connecting the universal values to each culture indicate that while foundational values are shared, their expression is shaped by each society's unique cultural context. Bidirectional arrows between the cultural dimensions represent interactions, overlaps, and tensions that can occur in multicultural environments.

1.5.1   Universal Leadership Values

Research has found that certain virtues, such as integrity, fairness, and honesty, are loved by people in all lands. Integrity, which is the harmony between what one says and what one does, is foundational to trust. Fairness, defined as treating all people with an equal hand, is expected of leaders, as is the clarity of honesty.

A major source of proof for this universality is the GLOBE (Global Leadership and Organizational Behavior Effectiveness) study. This was a massive undertaking, collecting data from 17,300 managers across 62 societies. It measured cultural practices and what people desire in a leader. The study identified six global behaviors and nine cultural dimensions, testing how culture links to leadership [130–132].

Key results indicate that attributes like being trustworthy, just, and encouraging are universally endorsed. This relationship is illustrated in Figure 1.8. Charismatic and value-based leadership, which involves inspiring others through a strong vision and personal sacrifice, was found to be effective everywhere, though the specific way it looks may vary. Similarly, team-oriented leadership is widely valued. The study found that trustworthiness and integrity are admired regardless of the language one speaks [130–132].

> **Key Point:** People all over the world want leaders who are honest, fair, and trustworthy, no matter where they are from.

1.5.2   Culturally Contingent Leadership Practices

Despite these universal truths, the expression of leadership often depends on the specific habits of a culture. Frameworks such as Hofstede's Cultural Dimensions help us understand how things like the distance of power or the fear of the unknown influence what is expected of a boss [130, 133, 134].

– Power Distance: Hofstede's research used surveys in over 70 countries to measure this dimension. Studies by Siddique (2020), Khatri (2009), and Janicijevic explore its implications. High power distance refers to cultures where people accept that authority is unequally distributed; they expect the leader to be a distant, authoritative figure. In these places, subordinates do not question the master. In contrast, low power distance cultures value equality, where the leader is more like a neighbor, encouraging open dialogue and shared responsibility [135–137].

– Individualism vs. Collectivism: Adamovic (2023) used experiments
to see how people react when thinking of themselves versus the group.
Individualistic cultures prioritize personal achievement, expecting
leaders to reward the specific person. Collectivist societies, however,
emphasize the harmony of the group, and leaders are expected to
foster loyalty among the whole. Scandura (2004) and Wendt confirm
that these orientations change how conflicts are resolved and how
work is done [138–141].

– Uncertainty Avoidance: This measures how much a culture fears
the unknown. High uncertainty avoidance cultures prefer clear rules
and structure; they do not like surprises or deviant ideas. They
demand leaders who provide guidance and stability. In contrast, low
uncertainty avoidance cultures are more comfortable with ambiguity
and are open to new, strange ideas. These findings highlight how
the fear of uncertainty shapes the behavior of the organization [142].

Key Point: Some cultures like strong bosses and strict
rules, while others prefer equality and flexibility, and leaders need to adapt to this.

1.5.3   Cultural Intelligence and Adaptive Leadership

There is a specific kind of wisdom required when one leaves the comfort
of one's own village and enters the house of a stranger. Scholars have
named this quality Cultural Intelligence, or CQ. It refers to the quiet
capability to function effectively when the songs, the sorrows, and
the unwritten rules of life differ from what one knows. Research on
this subject is vast and employs a variety of methodologies, ranging
from systematic literature reviews that gather the dust of previous
thoughts [143,144], to longitudinal surveys that track the changes in the
human soul over long periods, and structural equation modeling, which
is a mathematical way of seeing how hidden things connect [145]. There
are also qualitative interviews and case studies, where researchers
sit and listen to the stories of those who have lived through the
confusion [146,147].

For example, Ott reviewed the development of the Cultural Intelligence Scale, a tool designed to measure this sensitivity, and found it to be a robust predictor of how well a person might adjust to foreign soil and perform their duties. Sharma used longitudinal designs to watch how this intelligence grows like a slow tree over time, demonstrating that CQ predicts whether a team will succeed or fail in multicultural contexts. Kilduff found that this intelligence must dance with one's own personality traits to truly be effective [143, 145–148].

The key findings across these studies tell us a simple truth: leaders with high CQ are able to read the air in a room. They interpret behaviors that seem strange or rude to the uninitiated, they adapt their leadership style like a traveler changing coats for the weather, and they communicate so they are understood. This adaptability enhances the effectiveness of the organization, reduces the friction of conflict, and enables decisions that include everyone. It is not magic; it is learned through training, through the hardship of international experiences, and through the quiet reflection on one's own mistakes [139, 144]. The intricate web of these relationships, as well as the pathways through which this intelligence influences the outcome of our labors, are illustrated in Figure 1.9.

Adaptive leadership is the companion to this intelligence. It emphasizes flexibility and a responsiveness to the shifting clouds of cultural circumstances. Research by KKeung, who watched the youth play sports in Hong Kong, found that adaptive leadership involves tailoring strategies to the unique needs and cultural backgrounds of the participants, which fosters motivation and keeps their spirits high. Related studies using quantitative approaches show that this flexibility allows a leader to address complex challenges that would break a stiffer person, fostering innovation and supporting a willingness to learn. In a world that changes as quickly as the weather, this ability to adapt is particularly valuable, for leaders must navigate diverse expectations without losing their way [149, 150].

Key Point: Leaders need to understand different cultures and change their behavior to fit in, which helps everyone get along better and solve problems.

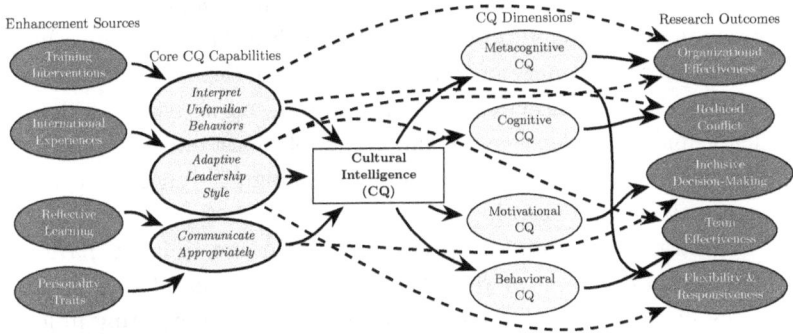

Figure 1.9: This diagram shows how Cultural Intelligence (CQ) develops from sources like training, international experiences, reflective learning, and personality traits. These sources build core CQ capabilities (interpreting unfamiliar behaviors, adapting leadership style, and communicating appropriately) which together form CQ and its four dimensions: metacognitive, cognitive, motivational, and behavioral. The diagram also shows how CQ and its dimensions lead to positive outcomes such as organizational effectiveness, reduced conflict, inclusive decision-making, team effectiveness, and adaptability. Full arrows represent relationships that are mediated through the CQ construct and its dimensions (i.e., the effect passes through CQ before reaching the outcomes). Dashed arrows indicate direct relationships found in research, where core CQ capabilities themselves (without mediation by CQ dimensions) have a direct impact on outcomes. This distinction highlights both the indirect (mediated) and direct pathways through which CQ and its core capabilities influence organizational results.

1.5.4   Ethical Dilemmas in Cross-Cultural Contexts

It is a painful thing when the conscience of a person collides with the customs of a place. Ethical dilemmas in international business frequently stem from divergent cultural norms, legal frameworks, and expectations regarding what is appropriate conduct [151]. Research highlights that these troubles often manifest in the shadows of bribery, in the treatment of laborers, in the care for the earth, and in the respect for diversity [152].

Consider the delicate matter of a gift. The boundary between a respectful gesture and a bribe is not universally defined. What is considered a polite offering in one culture, a necessary oil for the gears of friendship, may be interpreted as unethical or even illegal in

another. Studies examining perceptions of bribery and the distinction
between bribes and gifts reveal that the cultural context, the ethical
climate of the organization, and the presence of clear laws significantly
influence how such actions are understood and managed [153, 154].
These findings underscore the importance of robust ethical frameworks
and leadership that can navigate the ambiguity inherent in these
interactions without losing one's soul.

Multinational corporations, such as IKEA and Unilever, have felt
the heat of this scrutiny regarding labor practices in different regions.
They have responded not just with words, but by investing in local
education initiatives and implementing rigorous systems to monitor
their suppliers. These actions illustrate the ongoing challenge of
balancing global ethical standards with the need for local adaptation,
a process that requires both a sensitivity to local norms and a stubborn
commitment to universal ethical principles.

Leaders who effectively address these dilemmas employ a range
of strategies. They use cultural sensitivity training, they develop
and enforce inclusive codes of conduct that leave no room for doubt,
and they engage proactively with everyone involved. Educational
models that emphasize cultural competence; encompassing awareness,
knowledge, skills, and motivation; have been shown to foster ethical
integrity while respecting local values. Such approaches not only
enhance inclusivity but also support ethical decision-making in diverse
environments [155].

Cultural differences profoundly shape our perceptions of what
makes a leader effective [156]. While universal values such as integrity
and fairness provide a foundational guide, the specific expectations
for leaders and the ways in which ethical dilemmas are resolved are
deeply influenced by local habits [157]. Recent research demonstrates
that cultivating cultural intelligence and adaptive leadership skills is
essential for navigating these complexities. Leaders who develop these
competencies are better equipped to balance global standards with local realities, thereby promoting trust, effectiveness, and organizational
success [158, 159]. These studies collectively suggest that investing
in cultural intelligence and ethical leadership is not only worthwhile

but essential for achieving sustainable goodness in the international marketplace.

Key Point: What is considered right in one country might be wrong in another, so leaders must be careful and learn the local rules while still being honest.

1.6 Practical Implications and Strategies

And now, what is to be done? Life is short, and mistakes are expensive. This section suggests evidence-based strategies such as leadership training, mentorship, self-reflection, and the use of ethical decision-making frameworks [160]. Drawing on the extensive empirical and theoretical literature reviewed in this chapter, the following dos and don'ts provide practical guidance for individuals and organizations seeking to cultivate goodness in leadership. These recommendations are grounded in evidence and highlight both effective practices and the common pits into which one might fall.

1.6.1 Dos

- Do invest in ongoing leadership development. The mind must not be allowed to rust. Prioritize continuous learning through formal training, mentorship, coaching, and reflective practice. Programs should address not only technical skills but also emotional intelligence, empathy, and cultural competence, as these are consistently linked to leadership effectiveness and ethical conduct.

- Do integrate personality and emotional intelligence assessments into leadership selection and development. Use validated tools to identify and nurture traits such as conscientiousness, extraversion, honesty-humility, and emotional stability. Encourage leaders to leverage their unique strengths while addressing areas for growth.

- Do foster empathy and psychological safety. A leader should listen more than they speak. Encourage leaders to practice active listening, validate emotions, and create environments where team members feel safe to express concerns and ideas. Empathetic leadership builds trust, engagement, and resilience, and is especially vital in diverse or high-stress contexts.

- Do model and reinforce ethical behavior. Leaders should exemplify integrity, transparency, and fairness in all actions and decisions. Establish clear ethical standards, reward ethical conduct, and provide mechanisms for reporting and addressing misconduct.

- Do use structured ethical decision-making frameworks. Equip leaders with practical models (such as the PLUS Model, Markkula Center's Six Lenses, or stakeholder analysis) to guide complex decisions. Encourage reflection on the broader impact of choices and the inclusion of diverse perspectives.

- Do cultivate cultural intelligence and adaptive leadership. Provide training and experiences that enhance leaders' ability to interpret, adapt, and communicate effectively across cultures. Encourage openness to learning from different cultural norms and practices, and support adaptive strategies in global or multicultural environments.

- Do encourage self-reflection and feedback. Promote regular self-assessment and seek feedback from peers, subordinates, and mentors. Reflection helps leaders recognize biases, learn from mistakes, and align their behavior with organizational values.

- Do support organizational systems that reinforce goodness. Develop policies, reward systems, and cultures that prioritize ethical behavior, inclusivity, and the well-being of all stakeholders. Organizational support is essential for sustaining goodness-oriented leadership at all levels.

1.6.2 Don'ts

- Don't rely solely on technical or cognitive skills. Avoid the mistake of promoting leaders based only on analytical ability or subject-matter expertise. Neglecting emotional and cultural intelligence can undermine team cohesion, trust, and ethical standards.

– Don't ignore the impact of personality and situational fit. Overlooking the alignment between a leader's traits and the demands of their role or context can reduce effectiveness. Consider both individual differences and situational factors in leadership assignments.

– Don't tolerate unethical behavior or ambiguity. Failing to address misconduct, or sending mixed messages about ethical expectations, erodes trust and organizational integrity. Leaders must act decisively and transparently when ethical standards are breached.

– Don't assume one-size-fits-all approaches work across cultures. Applying leadership styles or ethical frameworks without regard for cultural context can lead to misunderstandings and resistance. Adapt strategies to local norms while upholding universal values such as integrity and fairness.

– Don't neglect the importance of psychological safety and trust. Environments where employees fear retribution or feel undervalued stifle engagement, innovation, and ethical behavior. Leaders must actively work to build and maintain trust.

– Don't overlook the need for ongoing support and accountability. Leadership development is not a one-time event. Without sustained organizational commitment, even well-intentioned leaders may revert to ineffective or unethical practices.

By adhering to these dos and avoiding the corresponding don'ts, organizations and individuals can more effectively cultivate goodness in leadership.

> **Key Point:** To be a good leader, one must keep learning, be kind to others, follow the rules, and avoid being arrogant or ignoring bad behavior.

1.7 So, Does "Being Good" Make You a Better Leader?

The question of whether "being good" truly makes one a better leader lies at the heart of this chapter's exploration. Drawing on a wealth of empirical research, theoretical frameworks, and cross-cultural perspectives, the evidence is clear: goodness is not merely an aspirational ideal, but a foundational element of effective leadership. Good-hearted leaders; those who embody empathy, integrity, and ethical conviction; consistently foster trust, engagement, and resilience within their organizations. As we consider the practical realities and complexities of ethical leadership, it is vital to recognize that the pursuit of goodness is both a moral responsibility and a strategic asset for leaders in every context.

1.7.1   Challenges and Trade-Offs in Ethical Leadership

However, we must not deceive ourselves; leaders who prioritize goodness and ethical integrity encounter a range of practical challenges and trade-offs in their daily decision-making. One of the most persistent dilemmas is the heavy burden of balancing the often competing interests of diverse stakeholders. There are the employees who rely on their wages, the customers who demand service, the shareholders who watch the ledger, and the broader community. An ethical leader must weigh these interests carefully, striving to build trust, enhance the reputation of the organization, and ensure sustainable business practices. This must be done even when the priorities of these groups conflict, or when sacrifices in the short term are required for a benefit that will only be seen in the distant future.

This balancing act is further complicated by the fog of ambiguity. Leaders are often forced to make decisions in situations where the right course of action is not clear, and where ethical frameworks such as utilitarianism and deontology may offer conflicting guidance. Utilitarianism asks us to calculate the greatest good for the greatest number, a cold sort of arithmetic, while deontology insists on strict adherence to duty and rules, regardless of the outcome. Caught between these two, a leader may feel lost.

Another significant challenge lies in managing the eternal tension between profitability and social responsibility. While ethical leadership is linked to long-term organizational success, leaders may face immense pressure to prioritize financial performance over ethical considerations, especially in environments that are highly competitive. Navigating this tension requires a stubborn commitment to core values and the courage to make difficult choices that may not yield immediate financial rewards but will foster trust and credibility over time.

Cultural complexity adds another layer of difficulty to this struggle. Leaders operating in global or multicultural contexts must navigate differing norms, expectations, and legal standards, making it essential to develop cultural intelligence and adaptive strategies. What is considered ethical in one culture may be viewed differently in another, requiring leaders to reconcile global standards with local realities while maintaining organizational integrity.

There are also risks associated with being overly agreeable or empathetic. While empathy and approachability are important qualities, excessive agreeableness can lead to ethical lapses, such as failing to hold others accountable or compromising on core values to avoid conflict. A leader must therefore cultivate moral courage and resilience, ensuring that empathy does not come at the expense of ethical standards or organizational effectiveness.

To address these challenges, effective strategies include establishing clear ethical guidelines, fostering open dialogue about values and expectations, and implementing structured decision-making frameworks that help leaders identify stakeholders, gather relevant facts, and apply ethical principles consistently. Building a culture of ethical leadership also involves ongoing education, modeling ethical behavior at all levels, and encouraging accountability throughout the organization.

Ultimately, while the pursuit of goodness in leadership is fraught with challenges and trade-offs, research and practice suggest that it is both worthwhile and essential for long-term organizational health and societal well-being. Leaders who navigate these complexities with integrity and adaptability are better positioned to create lasting value for all stakeholders.

Key Point: Being a good leader is hard because you have to make tough choices between making money and doing the right thing, and you cannot please everyone.

1.7.2 The Enduring Value of Goodness

Reflecting on the chapter's findings, it becomes evident that goodness in leadership is not only ethically commendable but also confers tangible, lasting benefits for organizations and society at large. Leaders who prioritize ethical conduct, empathy, and emotional intelligence create environments where trust and psychological safety flourish. This, in turn, leads to higher employee engagement, greater collaboration, and improved organizational performance. The empirical literature demonstrates that such leaders are more effective at navigating complex challenges, inspiring innovation, and sustaining long-term success; even in the face of adversity or uncertainty.

Moreover, the integration of goodness-oriented traits (such as honesty, humility, and conscientiousness) into leadership practice has been shown to enhance decision-making, reduce misconduct, and build resilient organizational cultures. Good-hearted leadership is associated with lower turnover, higher job satisfaction, and a stronger sense of shared purpose among team members. These outcomes are not limited to a single cultural or industry context; rather, they are observed across diverse settings, underscoring the universal value of ethical and empathetic leadership.

The positive influence of goodness in leadership also extends beyond organizational boundaries, contributing to broader societal welfare. Leaders who demonstrate integrity and compassion are instrumental in establishing ethical standards, fostering social trust, and advancing the collective good. In a globalized and increasingly complex environment, there is a heightened demand for leaders capable of uniting diverse constituencies, mediating divergent interests, and exemplifying principled conduct.

Thus, the answer to the question "Does being good make you a better leader?" is a resounding yes. Goodness in leadership is both a moral imperative and a practical advantage; one that yields sustainable organizational success, a positive workplace culture, and a meaningful impact on society. The enduring challenge for all leaders is to embody these principles with courage, consistency, and a genuine commitment to the well-being of others.

> **Key Point:** Being a good person helps you lead better because it makes employees feel safe and happy, which helps the company succeed and makes the whole world a little better.

Chapter 2

Goodness in Teaching

There is something quite simple, yet profound, in the observation that a teacher's personal qualities shape the very air of a classroom. One enters a room where a good teacher works, and there is a certain quality to the silence, a warmth in the interactions, an unspoken understanding that learning will happen here not through force but through genuine human connection. Recent research, of the sort that gathers data from many smaller studies and examines them together (i.e., a process called meta-analysis, a method by which scholars combine results from numerous independent investigations to discern larger patterns), has confirmed what many have long suspected through simple observation [161–163].

Kim and colleagues (2019) undertook such a comprehensive examination, collecting findings from many primary studies. They focused particularly on what psychologists call the Big Five personality traits, a framework that describes human personality through five broad dimensions: openness to experience (the tendency toward curiosity and creativity), conscientiousness (the quality of being thorough, careful, and disciplined), extraversion (the degree to which one draws energy from social interaction), agreeableness (the inclination toward cooperation and compassion), and neuroticism (the tendency toward emotional instability and anxiety). Using what researchers term random-effects

models (statistical approaches that account for variation across different studies, acknowledging that each study's context might produce
slightly different results) and moderator analyses (techniques that
examine which factors might strengthen or weaken the relationships
being studied), they discovered something both reassuring and important [161].

Teachers who demonstrate conscientiousness, that quality of being
dependable and organized; agreeableness, which encompasses kindness
and cooperation; and emotional stability, meaning low neuroticism or
a relative freedom from persistent anxiety and emotional turbulence,
these teachers proved more effective in their work. The measurement
of this effectiveness appeared in improved classroom management (the
ability to create and maintain an environment conducive to learning),
instructional quality (the skillfulness with which material is presented
and explained), and student outcomes (the tangible results in terms of
learning and achievement). The strength of these relationships, what
researchers call effect sizes (a standardized measure of how substantial
an observed relationship is, allowing comparison across different studies), ranged from small to moderate. While this might sound modest,
such consistency across many studies speaks to a genuine pattern
in human behavior. Moreover, the research revealed that neuroticism, that tendency toward worry and emotional instability, connected
strongly with teacher burnout (a state of emotional, physical, and
mental exhaustion caused by prolonged stress), while conscientiousness
and agreeableness served as protective factors, qualities that helped
teachers maintain their wellbeing and effectiveness over time [161].

> **Key Point:** Teachers who are organized, kind, and emo-
> tionally steady tend to teach more effectively and experi-
> ence less exhaustion from their work, while those prone to
> anxiety struggle more with the demands of teaching.

Digic (2018) approached the question from another angle, using
what scholars call a mixed-methods approach. This means combining
two different types of inquiry: quantitative research (which deals
with numbers, measurements, and statistical analysis) and qualitative

research (which explores experiences, meanings, and narratives through interviews and observations). The study gathered numerical data from teacher self-reports and student evaluations, then enriched this understanding through in-depth conversations with teachers across various educational settings. From this dual perspective emerged a central finding: good-heartedness, that quality encompassing empathy (the capacity to understand and share another's feelings), patience (the ability to remain calm and supportive despite frustration or difficulty), and authentic concern for students (a genuine investment in their wellbeing and growth), stood at the heart of teaching success. Teachers who consistently embodied these qualities created stronger relationships with their students, and these relationships in turn led to higher engagement (the degree to which students actively participate in and commit to their learning) and achievement (measurable success in academic tasks and learning objectives) [162].

Tobias and their research team (2025) carried this investigation further by employing validated assessment tools designed specifically to measure emotional intelligence, often abbreviated as EI. Emotional intelligence refers to the set of abilities through which individuals recognize, understand, and manage emotions in themselves and others. They used instruments such as the Mayer-Salovey-Caruso Emotional Intelligence Test, a carefully developed assessment that measures ability in emotional reasoning through problem-solving tasks rather than self-report questions. By correlating scores on these EI measures with various indicators of teaching performance, including classroom management, instructional quality, and feedback from both students and colleagues, the researchers found strong associations between high emotional intelligence and teaching effectiveness [163].

More specifically, they identified particular components of emotional intelligence as significant predictors of success. Self-awareness, the capacity to recognize one's own emotional states and their effects; self-regulation, the ability to manage disruptive emotions and impulses; motivation, an internal drive toward goals beyond external rewards; empathy, again that crucial ability to sense and understand others' emotional experiences; and social skills, the proficiency in managing

relationships and building networks. Each of these competencies contributed to creating what might be called a positive classroom climate,
an atmosphere characterized by mutual respect, psychological safety,
and productive engagement. This climate, in turn, related strongly to
student outcomes, both in objective measures such as test scores and
achievement metrics, and in subjective evaluations including student
satisfaction and peer assessments [163].

> **Key Point:** Teachers who understand and manage emo-
> tions well, both their own and those of their students,
> create better learning environments and achieve stronger
> results in the classroom.

2.1   The Meaning of Good-Heartedness

What does it mean, precisely, to be good-hearted in the context of
teaching? The research literature provides a clear picture, though one
that perhaps merely confirms what thoughtful observation has long
suggested [164,165]. Good-heartedness in teaching shows itself through
the consistent demonstration of empathy, patience, and authentic care
for students' development, both in their academic learning and in
their growth as individuals. These qualities are not merely pleasant
additions to technical teaching skill; empirical evidence establishes
them as essential for fostering those positive teacher-student relationships which, research has demonstrated repeatedly, serve as critical
predictors of student engagement, motivation, and achievement [166].

Bozkurt and Ozden (2010) conducted an early investigation into
how empathetic behaviors and teacher attitudes are defined across
different cultures. Using observational methods (systematic watching
and recording of classroom interactions) and survey-based approaches
(structured questionnaires that gather standardized information from
many participants), they assessed how empathy affects classroom climate, that intangible but palpable quality of the learning environment.
Their findings placed empathy at the center of creating supportive
learning spaces. Interestingly, they noted that culturally sensitive

approaches to empathy, recognition that different cultural contexts may shape how empathy is expressed and understood, are necessary for truly effective teaching [167].

Bijender and colleagues (2023) provided additional empirical support, which means evidence gathered through systematic observation and measurement rather than through theory alone. Their quantitative study explored the connection between teaching aptitude (the natural ability and fitness for teaching) and empathy. They used standardized instruments, carefully designed measurement tools that have been tested for reliability and validity, to assess both constructs among a diverse group of teachers. The statistical analyses, mathematical procedures for examining patterns in numerical data, revealed a strong positive relationship between empathy and teaching aptitude. This finding emphasized the practical necessity of including empathy training in teacher education programs, the courses and experiences through which individuals prepare for the teaching profession [168].

The nature of empathy in teaching receives deeper exploration in the work of Meyers and colleagues (2019). They proposed a multidimensional model, a framework that recognizes empathy not as a single quality but as comprising several distinct yet related components. These include cognitive empathy (the intellectual understanding of another's perspective), affective empathy (the emotional resonance or sharing of another's feelings), and behavioral empathy (the outward actions that demonstrate empathic understanding). Their research demonstrated that empathetic teaching fosters trust, engagement, and academic success through a mechanism both simple and profound: it enables teachers to understand students' experiences and needs, to resonate emotionally with students' struggles and joys, and to respond appropriately and supportively to what they perceive. This three-part process of understanding, feeling, and responding creates the conditions in which students can truly thrive [164].

Cooper (2004), through qualitative interviews (in-depth conversations that explore experiences and meanings) and classroom observations (systematic watching of actual teaching and learning as it unfolds), discovered that empathy does not exist as a fixed trait but emerges through ongoing, dialogic interactions. Dialogic refers to the back-and-forth nature of genuine conversation, where meaning is created together rather than transmitted from one person to another. Empathy manifests itself in what might seem like small gestures: everyday acts of kindness, patience with a struggling student, attentiveness to subtle signs of confusion or distress. Yet these apparently minor actions accumulate to create something substantial: a sense of belonging and motivation that students carry with them throughout their educational journey [165].

The importance of these relational qualities, the aspects of teaching that concern human connection rather than technical skill, receives strong support from the meta-analysis conducted by Roorda and colleagues (2011). Analyzing data from ninety-nine separate studies, they found that positive teacher-student relationships associate with medium to large effect sizes for student engagement. To put this in concrete terms, the impact of a good relationship between teacher and student on that student's active participation and investment in learning is substantial and measurable. The effects on academic achievement, while somewhat smaller, remain meaningful. Particularly in primary education, the years of early schooling, these relationships prove especially powerful [166].

Perhaps more striking still, the research revealed that negative relationships, particularly those characterized by conflict and antagonism, produce especially harmful effects on both engagement and achievement. This asymmetry, where negative relationships damage more than positive relationships help, suggests something important about the vulnerability of the learning process to emotional disruption [166].

Sherub Gyeltshen and Gyeltshen (2022) extended these findings by employing both quantitative and qualitative methods across all educational levels, from early childhood through higher education. Their comprehensive approach demonstrated that supportive teacher-student relationships enhance academic performance, increase student engagement and motivation, and reduce academic stress and anxiety. Academic stress refers to the psychological tension arising from educational demands, while anxiety in this context means the persistent worry and apprehension that can interfere with learning. The reduction of these negative states, it seems, matters as much as the promotion of positive ones [169].

Finally, Lozano Botellero and colleagues (2023) undertook an integrative review, a systematic examination and synthesis of research literature that spans nearly four decades. Their conclusions affirm what the accumulated evidence suggests: perceived teacher support, which encompasses several dimensions (social and emotional support, autonomy support meaning respect for students' independence and choices, and academic support including instructional help and guidance), relates strongly to students' academic motivation, achievement, and psychological wellbeing. Psychological wellbeing includes not just the absence of distress but the presence of positive mental states such as satisfaction, confidence, and a sense of purpose. The review also noted important methodological considerations, pointing out the need for more qualitative research (studies that explore depth and meaning rather than only measuring and counting) and greater contextual sensitivity (attention to how findings might vary across different settings and cultures). Yet despite these calls for nuanced future work, the review affirmed something universal: the importance of good-heartedness in teaching holds across diverse educational settings and cultural contexts [170].

> **Key Point:** When teachers consistently show empathy, patience, and genuine care, students feel more connected, try harder, achieve more, and experience less stress, with these benefits appearing across all ages and types of education.

2.2   Emotional Security as a Foundation

The psychological literature, that body of scientific work concerning mental processes and behavior, underscores something fundamental about learning: emotional security matters profoundly. Teachers who exhibit warmth (a quality of affectionate kindness), openness (receptivity to students' ideas and questions), and understanding (the capacity to grasp students' perspectives and difficulties) create environments in which students feel safe. This safety is not physical safety alone, though that matters too, but psychological safety: the sense that one can express oneself, ask questions that might seem foolish, make mistakes in the process of learning, and take intellectual risks without fear of humiliation or rejection.

Such emotional security serves as a foundation for learning motivation, that internal drive to engage with new material and master new skills, and for a sense of belonging, the feeling that one has a place in the classroom community and the wider educational institution. Both motivation and belonging prove necessary for sustained academic and professional growth, the kind of long-term development that extends far beyond any single lesson or course [166, 170].

The benefits of positive teacher-student relationships show themselves with particular clarity among certain groups of students. Those from disadvantaged backgrounds, meaning students who face economic hardship, limited educational resources in their homes or communities, or various forms of social marginalization, often rely especially heavily on the emotional support and encouragement that good-hearted educators provide. Similarly, students facing significant personal challenges (family difficulties, health issues, social struggles) or academic challenges (learning difficulties, gaps in prior knowledge, language barriers) may depend on teacher support as a crucial resource for perseverance and success. For these students, a teacher's good-heartedness may make the difference between continuing in education and giving up entirely [169, 170].

Empathy, that core component of good-heartedness discussed earlier, serves a practical function in teaching: it enables teachers to recognize and respond effectively to the diverse emotional and cognitive needs present in any group of students. Cognitive needs refer to requirements for intellectual development, including appropriate challenge, clear explanation, and scaffolding (structured support that is gradually removed as competence increases). Emotional needs include the requirements for safety, belonging, recognition, and encouragement.

In early childhood and primary education, those formative years when foundational skills and attitudes toward learning take shape, empathic teachers prove better equipped to create supportive environments that foster not only academic learning but also social and emotional development. Social development includes learning to interact cooperatively with peers, while emotional development encompasses recognizing and managing one's feelings and understanding those of others [164, 166].

In secondary education (the middle and high school years) and higher education (college and university), empathy facilitates what might be called diagnostic teaching: the identification of where students struggle and the adaptation of instructional strategies to meet individual needs. A teacher with strong empathic ability notices when a particular explanation has failed to connect, when a student's frustration signals not laziness but genuine confusion, when silence indicates not disinterest but anxiety about speaking up [165, 168].

In adult and professional education, contexts where learners bring diverse life experiences and often balance education with work and family responsibilities, empathy contributes to creating collaborative and inclusive learning climates. Collaborative learning environments are those in which participants work together and learn from each other, while inclusive climates are characterized by respect for diverse perspectives and backgrounds. These qualities have become increasingly valued in contemporary workplaces and training programs, which often emphasize teamwork and diversity as organizational strengths [170].

Neuroscientific studies, research using technologies that allow us to observe brain structure and activity, provide a biological foundation for understanding the role of empathy in teaching. Brain imaging research has identified specific neural networks, interconnected groups of brain regions that work together to perform particular functions, associated with both affective empathy (the emotional sharing mentioned earlier) and cognitive empathy (the intellectual perspective-taking also discussed above). These findings highlight that empathy has a biological basis in the brain's architecture, though this biological basis does not diminish the role of experience and learning in developing empathic capacity [164].

These neural mechanisms, the brain processes underlying empathic behavior, support the capacity for perspective-taking (the ability to imagine a situation from another's viewpoint) and emotional attunement (the synchronization of one's emotional state with another's, a kind of emotional resonance). Both capabilities prove essential for effective teaching across all contexts. Perspective-taking allows a teacher to anticipate where students might struggle based on their current knowledge and way of thinking. Emotional attunement enables a teacher to sense the emotional tone of a classroom, to notice when energy flags or anxiety rises, and to adjust accordingly [164, 165].

> **Key Point:** Teachers who can understand how students
> think and feel, both mentally and emotionally, create safer
> environments where students feel comfortable learning,
> with these skills being rooted in how our brains naturally
> work when we connect with others.

2.3   The Roles of Kindness and Patience

Kindness and patience, qualities closely related to empathy yet distinct in their expression, also play significant roles in teaching effectiveness. A kind teacher is one who demonstrates goodwill, generosity of spirit, and consideration for students' wellbeing. Kindness fosters trust, that fundamental confidence in another's benevolent intentions, and openness, the willingness to be vulnerable in the learning process. These qualities in turn create emotionally safe environments, settings where students feel secure enough to take the risks inherent in learning: asking questions, admitting confusion, trying difficult tasks despite the possibility of failure.

Patience, the ability to remain calm and supportive despite frustration, delay, or difficulty, allows educators to support students through their learning challenges without conveying exasperation or disappointment. Learning often involves struggle, the effortful working through of difficulties, and students need time to develop understanding and skill. A patient teacher conveys an important message: that struggle is normal and acceptable, that mistakes are part of learning, that the pace of learning matters less than the fact of learning. This message reinforces persistence (the quality of continuing despite difficulty) and resilience (the capacity to recover from setbacks), both of which prove crucial for long-term educational success [165, 167].

These qualities, kindness and patience, associate with several positive outcomes that have been measured and documented in research. Improved classroom management emerges, as students in environments characterized by kindness and patience tend to cooperate more readily and create less disruption. Higher student engagement follows, as students feel more comfortable participating and taking intellectual risks. More positive learning outcomes result, measurable in both achievement scores and in less tangible but equally important factors such as attitudes toward learning and sense of academic self-efficacy (confidence in one's ability to succeed in academic tasks) [161, 166].

In professional and adult education, contexts where learners often have extensive prior experience and well-formed identities, kindness and patience contribute particularly to the development of trust and a sense of community. Adult learners may bring vulnerability to educational settings, perhaps remembering past educational failures or feeling anxious about returning to formal learning after years away. They may struggle to balance learning with other life responsibilities. In such contexts, a teacher's kindness and patience signal respect for students' experiences and challenges, creating the psychological space necessary for engagement and growth. A sense of community, the feeling of belonging to a group with shared purpose and mutual support, proves vital for adult learners' engagement and success in ways that parallel but differ from the needs of younger students [170].

The impact of good-heartedness extends well beyond traditional academic settings, those familiar classrooms of schools and universities. In professional training, educational programs designed to develop specific job-related skills and knowledge, and adult education more broadly, empathy and kindness link to several valued outcomes. Enhanced learning occurs, as these qualities create conditions conducive to taking in new information and developing new capabilities. Better group dynamics emerge, with participants working together more effectively and supporting rather than competing with one another. Improved organizational outcomes follow, as individuals trained in environments characterized by empathy and kindness often bring these qualities into their work, affecting not just their own performance but the culture of their workplaces [170].

Interestingly, structured interventions, carefully designed programs with specific educational goals and methods, that explicitly teach empathy and compassion have shown promise. Research has demonstrated that these qualities can be increased through training among adult learners and professionals, though whether this represents the development of new capacities or the removal of barriers to existing ones remains an open question. Regardless of the mechanism, such training leads to more inclusive and supportive environments, settings where diverse individuals feel welcomed and valued [163].

In fields such as healthcare, where the quality of interpersonal interaction directly affects outcomes, empathy training has become increasingly common. Research associates such training with improved patient care (better health outcomes and patient satisfaction) and professional satisfaction (healthcare workers' sense of fulfillment and wellbeing in their work). These findings underscore a principle that extends beyond any single profession or context: good-heartedness, manifested through empathy, kindness, and patience, holds universal value in teaching and training across diverse settings and purposes [163, 164].

> **Key Point:** Kind and patient teachers help students learn better, feel more confident, and work together more effectively, with these benefits appearing not just in schools but also in workplace training and professional education.

While the preponderance of research supports the positive effects of good-heartedness on teaching effectiveness, intellectual honesty requires acknowledging certain methodological limitations, constraints inherent in how research is conducted that may affect the interpretation of findings. Much of the research relies on self-reported measures, data gathered by asking people about their own qualities, experiences, or behaviors. Such measures carry certain risks: people may not accurately assess themselves, may respond in socially desirable ways, or may lack insight into their own characteristics. Additionally, context-dependent effects, variations in how relationships hold across different settings or populations, suggest that the strength or even the presence of certain findings might differ depending on specific circumstances [161, 162].

Nevertheless, despite these important caveats, the convergence of evidence from multiple disciplines, including education, psychology, and neuroscience, using various methodological approaches, and examining diverse populations and contexts, provides strong support for a central claim: good-heartedness, manifested through empathy, kindness, and patience, constitutes a foundational element of effective teaching at all levels and in all settings. The consistency of findings across such varied approaches and contexts suggests that we are observing something genuine about human learning and teaching, not merely an artifact of particular measurement approaches or study designs [161–166, 169, 170].

Thus, after reviewing the scientific literature with care and attention to both its strengths and limitations, we may conclude with confidence that being a good-hearted person enhances teaching effectiveness across the lifespan and in diverse educational and professional contexts. The mechanism through which this occurs is neither mysterious nor complex: by fostering positive relationships, by creating supportive learning environments where students feel psychologically safe and valued, and by responding with sensitivity and appropriateness to the unique needs of individual learners, good-hearted educators play a pivotal role. Their influence extends to promoting academic achievement, supporting personal growth in dimensions that transcend any particular subject matter, and contributing to professional success both during and long after formal education concludes [161–170].

Key Point: Research from many different fields consistently shows that teachers who are genuinely kind, patient, and empathetic help their students learn better and grow more fully as people, with this truth holding across all ages and all types of teaching situations.

2.4 The Big Five Personality Traits

There exists in psychology a framework that has proven remarkably durable, one that attempts to map the vast terrain of human personality onto five broad dimensions. This framework, known as the Big Five personality traits, has over recent decades established itself as a foundational approach for understanding the differences between individuals in their teaching behaviors and effectiveness [161–163,171,172]. The five domains, openness to experience, conscientiousness, extraversion, agreeableness, and neuroticism, together capture what researchers believe are the major dimensions along which human personalities vary.

Openness to experience refers to the degree of intellectual curiosity, creativity, and preference for novelty and variety that a person exhibits. Those high in openness tend to be imaginative, willing to entertain new ideas, and interested in art, emotion, and unusual experiences. Conscientiousness describes the tendency toward self-discipline, orderliness, and achievement striving. Conscientious individuals are typically organized, dependable, and persistent in pursuing goals. Extraversion encompasses sociability, assertiveness, and the tendency to experience positive emotions and seek stimulation in the company of others. Extraverted people draw energy from social interaction and tend toward enthusiasm and expressiveness. Agreeableness reflects the quality of one's interpersonal relationships, including tendencies toward compassion, cooperation, and trust. Agreeable individuals are generally warm, considerate, and concerned with social harmony. Finally, neuroticism, sometimes labeled by its opposite pole as emotional stability, describes the tendency to experience negative emotions such as anxiety, depression, and vulnerability to stress [174,175].

These five dimensions have demonstrated remarkable stability, meaning they tend to remain relatively consistent across an individual's lifespan, though not entirely fixed. Research has documented this stability through longitudinal studies, investigations that follow the same individuals over many years to observe patterns of continuity and change [173, 176]. Moreover, these traits appear to hold across diverse cultural contexts, suggesting they represent something fundamental about human personality organization rather than merely reflecting Western psychological concepts [174].

In the specific context of teaching, scholars have employed the Big Five model as a tool for predicting various outcomes. These include classroom management, the complex set of skills and strategies teachers use to create and maintain an orderly, focused learning environment; instructional quality, the effectiveness with which material is presented and pedagogical techniques are employed; teacher-student relationships, the quality and nature of interpersonal connections between educators and learners; and susceptibility to burnout, that state of physical, emotional, and mental exhaustion resulting from prolonged occupational stress [161, 177, 178].

Meta-analyses, those comprehensive studies that synthesize findings from many individual research investigations to identify overall patterns, and systematic reviews, detailed examinations of existing research literature according to explicit criteria, have yielded fairly consistent findings [161]. Conscientiousness and agreeableness emerge repeatedly as the most robust predictors of positive teaching outcomes. Robust here means reliable and consistent across different studies, samples, and measurement approaches. Meanwhile, neuroticism appears as what researchers term a risk factor, a characteristic that increases the likelihood of negative outcomes, in this case teacher stress and reduced effectiveness.

The relationship between conscientiousness and teaching success manifests in several observable ways. Conscientious teachers demonstrate strong classroom management abilities, creating environments where learning can proceed with minimal disruption. They show reliability, consistently meeting obligations and maintaining standards. These qualities associate with higher student achievement, that measurable progress students make in their learning [161]. Agreeableness, meanwhile, underpins those interpersonal qualities discussed earlier: empathy, patience, and the capacity to build supportive teacher-student relationships. An agreeable teacher more naturally creates an atmosphere of warmth and acceptance, qualities that facilitate student engagement and wellbeing [161].

Extraversion and openness to experience also contribute to teaching effectiveness, though their effects prove more context-dependent, meaning the strength and nature of their influence varies depending on the specific teaching situation, subject matter, or educational level. Extraversion facilitates what might be called the performance aspects of teaching: classroom engagement, dynamic communication, the creation of an energetic learning atmosphere. An extraverted teacher often finds it easier to command attention, encourage participation, and maintain an animated classroom presence [179]. Openness to experience supports a different set of qualities: innovative teaching methods, the willingness to experiment with new pedagogical approaches, and adaptability in responding to unexpected situations or diverse student needs. Teachers high in openness tend to view teaching as an evolving practice requiring continual learning and adjustment rather than as a fixed set of techniques to be applied uniformly [179].

In contrast, high neuroticism creates difficulties. Teachers scoring high on this dimension experience increased stress, that psychological and physiological response to demanding situations; emotional exhaustion, a depleted feeling resulting from excessive emotional demands; and tend to create a less positive classroom climate, an atmosphere that may communicate anxiety or negativity to students. These patterns can undermine both teacher wellbeing and student outcomes, creating a concerning cycle where teacher distress affects teaching quality, which may in turn increase teacher distress [161,180–182].

> **Key Point:** Research has identified five main personality dimensions that affect teaching, with organized and kind teachers generally doing better, outgoing and curious teachers adapting well to different situations, and anxious teachers struggling more with the demands of their work.

2.4.1 Conscientiousness

Of all the personality traits examined in educational research, conscientiousness emerges with particular consistency as a predictor of effective teaching. One encounters this finding again and again across empirical studies, those investigations based on systematic observation and measurement, and meta-analyses, those comprehensive syntheses mentioned earlier. The trait itself encompasses several related qualities: organization, the capacity to arrange one's work and materials systematically; reliability, the tendency to follow through on commitments and maintain consistent standards; self-discipline, the ability to regulate one's behavior in service of goals despite distractions or difficulties; and goal-directed behavior, the persistent pursuit of objectives through planned action [161, 171].

These qualities connect to several important teaching outcomes. Superior classroom management appears consistently in studies of conscientious teachers. Classroom management, that complex skill mentioned earlier, involves not merely maintaining order but creating a structured environment conducive to learning, where expectations are clear, routines are established, and disruptions are minimized through proactive organization rather than reactive discipline. Higher student achievement, measurable progress in learning as assessed through various evaluation methods, also associates with teacher conscientiousness. Perhaps most relevant for teacher wellbeing, conscientiousness links to reduced burnout, suggesting that the organizational and self-regulatory capacities associated with this trait help teachers manage the considerable demands of their profession [161, 178].

To understand the research findings, we must briefly consider how researchers measure the strength of relationships between variables. A key metric employed in these studies is the correlation coefficient, typically denoted by the letter r. This statistical measure quantifies both the strength and direction of the linear relationship between two variables, in this case between conscientiousness and various teaching outcomes. The value of r ranges from negative one to positive one. A value of positive one indicates what statisticians call a perfect positive relationship, meaning that as one variable increases, the other

increases in perfect proportion. A value of negative one indicates
a perfect negative relationship, where as one variable increases, the
other decreases in perfect proportion. A value of zero means no linear
relationship exists between the variables; knowing one tells you nothing
about the other [161].

In practical terms, higher absolute values of r, those closer to
either positive one or negative one, indicate stronger associations
between variables. Values closer to zero indicate weaker associations.
In educational and psychological research, scholars have developed
conventional interpretations for the magnitude of correlation coefficients. An r value around 0.1 is considered small, suggesting a weak
but potentially meaningful relationship. A value around 0.3 is considered moderate, indicating a relationship of medium strength. A
value of 0.5 or above is considered large, representing a strong association. However, very high correlation values are quite rare in studies
of complex human behaviors, where multiple factors always operate
simultaneously. Even correlations in the small to moderate range can
represent important and meaningful relationships, particularly when
they appear consistently across many studies [161].

The meta-analysis conducted by Kim and colleagues in 2019 provides perhaps the most comprehensive examination of conscientiousness in teaching. This synthesis drew together data from twenty-five
separate studies, encompassing 6,294 teachers in total. Such aggrega-
tion of data allows researchers to overcome the limitations of individual
studies, which may be affected by particular samples or contexts, and
to identify patterns that hold across diverse situations. The analysis revealed that conscientiousness stood as the strongest Big Five predictor
of teacher effectiveness, with effect sizes (that measure of relationship
strength discussed above) in the moderate range, approximately r
equals 0.3 to 0.4, when teaching effectiveness was measured through
evaluations of teaching performance rather than student achievement
alone [161].

Interestingly, the association proved particularly pronounced when
personality was rated by others, colleagues or supervisors who observed
the teacher's work, rather than by teachers themselves through self-

report questionnaires. This pattern highlights what researchers call the observable nature of conscientious behaviors in educational settings. Conscientiousness manifests in visible actions: organized lesson plans, punctual arrival, consistent grading practices, systematic classroom procedures. Others can readily perceive these behaviors, and their perceptions may in some ways provide more objective assessments than teachers' own views of themselves, which may be colored by various biases inherent in self-evaluation [161].

Kim's earlier study from 2018 approached the question from a different angle, examining student perceptions of their teachers. This investigation involved 2,082 secondary school students, young people in middle and high school years, and their 75 teachers. The students rated their teachers on various dimensions, and these ratings were analyzed in relation to teacher personality traits. The study demonstrated that teachers rated as highly conscientious by their students were perceived as providing more academic support, meaning help with learning tasks, clear instruction, and assistance with academic challenges. However, and this proves noteworthy, this perception did not directly translate into higher student academic achievement after controlling for prior performance (students' achievement levels before the study period) and other covariates (additional variables that might influence outcomes, such as socioeconomic background or school resources) [172].

This finding reminds us that the relationship between teacher qualities and student outcomes operates through complex pathways. The perception of support matters for student experience and engagement, even if its effect on achievement proves difficult to isolate from other influential factors. Moreover, achievement itself represents only one dimension of educational success, important certainly, but not exhaustive of what education aims to accomplish [172].

The meta-analysis published by Liu and colleagues in 2022 examined a different but related question: the relationship between personality traits and teacher burnout. This synthesis encompassed twenty-eight studies involving over 12,000 teachers. The analysis confirmed that conscientiousness correlates negatively with emotional exhaustion and depersonalization, these being the core dimensions of burnout as measured by standard instruments such as the Maslach Burnout Inventory. Emotional exhaustion refers to feeling emotionally drained and depleted by one's work, while depersonalization involves developing cynical, detached attitudes toward students and treating them as objects rather than individuals. The correlation coefficient of approximately negative 0.2 indicates a modest but meaningful protective effect [178].

To understand what a negative correlation means in this context, consider that as conscientiousness increases, burnout symptoms decrease. The organized, disciplined, goal-directed nature of conscientiousness appears to help teachers manage their workload and emotional demands more effectively, reducing the likelihood of the exhaustion and cynicism that characterize burnout. This protective effect, while not large enough to entirely prevent burnout regardless of circumstances, nevertheless represents an important resource that conscientious teachers bring to their work [178].

Studies focusing on specific subject areas echo these broader findings. Research examining mathematics teachers, for instance, has found that conscientiousness associates with better lesson planning (the systematic preparation of instructional activities), persistence (continued effort despite difficulties), and student outcomes (learning results in mathematical understanding and skill) [171]. Mathematics teaching, with its emphasis on logical sequencing, careful explanation, and systematic practice, may particularly benefit from the organizational and disciplined qualities that conscientiousness provides.

Taken together, the accumulated evidence underscores what we might call the centrality of conscientiousness in fostering effective, resilient, and high-achieving teaching professionals. A conscientious teacher brings to the classroom not merely technical knowledge of subject matter but also the personal qualities necessary to organize that knowledge into coherent lessons, to maintain the structured environment in which learning can occur, to persist through the inevitable difficulties of teaching work, and to sustain professional effectiveness over time without succumbing to burnout [161, 171, 178].

Key Point: Teachers who are organized, reliable, and self-disciplined manage their classrooms better, support their students more effectively, and handle the stress of teaching more successfully than those who lack these qualities.

2.4.2   Agreeableness

Agreeableness as a personality dimension encompasses several interrelated qualities: interpersonal warmth (the capacity to convey genuine friendliness and caring), empathy (that ability discussed at length earlier to understand and share the feelings of another), patience (the capacity to remain calm and supportive despite frustration), and cooperativeness (the tendency to work harmoniously with others and to prioritize relationship harmony). Together, these qualities shape what researchers call the social and emotional climate of the classroom, the atmosphere of interpersonal relationships and emotional tone that pervades the learning environment [161, 172].

The research on agreeableness presents a somewhat more nuanced picture than that for conscientiousness. Kim's 2019 meta-analysis, that comprehensive synthesis described earlier, found that agreeableness was not a significant predictor of teacher effectiveness when effectiveness was measured specifically by student achievement or by formal teaching evaluations, the ratings provided by supervisors or through standardized evaluation instruments. This finding might initially seem surprising, given the emphasis placed on interpersonal qualities in discussions of good teaching [161].

However, qualitative studies, investigations that explore experiences and meanings through methods such as interviews and observations, and correlational studies, research that examines relationships between variables, consistently highlight the importance of agreeableness for teacher-student relationships and classroom climate. The distinction here matters: agreeableness may not predict the specific outcome of student achievement as measured by test scores, but it profoundly affects the quality of relationships and the emotional atmosphere in which learning occurs [161].

Kim's 2018 study illuminates this distinction. In that investigation

of secondary school students and their teachers, students perceived
teachers who scored high in agreeableness as providing more personal
support, meaning emotional support, encouragement, and care for
students as individuals beyond their academic performance. This
perceived personal support, in turn, associated with higher student
self-efficacy, that crucial sense of confidence in one's ability to succeed
in academic tasks. Self-efficacy, a concept developed by psychologist
Albert Bandura, refers to one's belief in their capability to organize and
execute the courses of action required to produce given attainments. In
educational contexts, students with higher self-efficacy tend to persist
longer at difficult tasks, set more challenging goals, and ultimately
achieve more [172].

Thus, while agreeableness may not directly predict achievement
in the immediate sense, it affects psychological variables such as
self-efficacy that themselves influence achievement over time. The
pathway from teacher personality to student outcomes proves indirect
but nonetheless real and important [172].

This finding aligns with integrative reviews, comprehensive examinations that synthesize both quantitative and qualitative research,
and meta-analyses demonstrating that affective teacher-student relationships, connections characterized by positive emotions and mutual
care, link to greater student engagement (active participation in and
commitment to learning) and wellbeing (psychological health and life
satisfaction). The research by Roorda and colleagues (2011) and the
integrative review by Lozano Botellero and colleagues (2023), both
discussed in the previous section, support this understanding [166,170].

Regarding teacher wellbeing, meta-analytic evidence from Liu
and colleagues (2022) indicates that agreeableness correlates negatively with emotional exhaustion and depersonalization, those core
dimensions of burnout described earlier. The correlation coefficient of
approximately negative 0.14 suggests a modest but meaningful protective effect. To interpret this negative correlation, as agreeableness
increases, burnout symptoms tend to decrease, though the relationship
is not as strong as that observed for conscientiousness. Nevertheless,
the finding suggests that agreeable teachers, perhaps through their

tendency to form positive relationships and to approach interpersonal difficulties with patience and understanding, experience somewhat less of the emotional depletion that burnout represents [178].

Studies examining empathetic classroom climates provide additional support for the role of agreeableness. Research has shown that classrooms characterized by empathy, where teachers demonstrate understanding of students' perspectives and feelings, tend to have less conflict and more cooperation. Students in such environments report feeling more valued and understood, which promotes their engagement and success. The work by Bozkurt and Ozden (2010) and Meyers and colleagues (2019), discussed in detail in the previous section, documents these patterns [164, 167].

In sum, the research on agreeableness presents what might be called a mixed but ultimately positive picture. While agreeableness may not directly predict academic achievement as measured by test scores or formal teaching evaluations, it proves instrumental in fostering supportive relationships, positive classroom climates, and teacher resilience. These outcomes matter profoundly for education conceived broadly, as a process concerned not only with cognitive development but also with students' social and emotional growth and with the sustainability of teaching as a profession. An agreeable teacher may not necessarily produce the highest test scores, but they create the kind of humane, supportive environment in which students can develop not only intellectually but also as whole persons [161, 164, 166, 167, 170, 172, 178].

> **Key Point:** Teachers who are warm, patient, and cooperative create classrooms where students feel cared for and confident, even though these qualities may not directly show up in test scores, they matter deeply for how students experience school and develop as people.

2.4.3   Openness to Experience

Openness to experience, that dimension of personality characterized by intellectual curiosity, creativity, and receptivity to new ideas, occupies an interesting position in educational research. For many years, its relevance to teaching received less attention than traits such as conscientiousness or extraversion, perhaps because its connection to teaching effectiveness seemed less obvious. However, contemporary educational contexts, characterized by rapid change, diverse student populations, and evolving pedagogical approaches, have brought openness to experience into sharper focus [161, 179].

What does it mean, in practical terms, for a teacher to be high in openness to experience? Such individuals tend to be intellectually curious, actively seeking out new information and ideas beyond what their immediate duties require. They show creativity, the capacity to generate novel and appropriate solutions to problems, in their teaching methods and their responses to challenges. They demonstrate receptivity to new ideas, a willingness to consider perspectives and approaches different from those they currently hold. They often have broad interests, finding value in art, literature, philosophy, and other domains beyond their specific subject matter [174, 175].

Kim's 2019 meta-analysis found that openness associated positively with teacher effectiveness, particularly in contexts that value innovation and adaptability. Innovation refers to the introduction of new methods or ideas, while adaptability means the capacity to adjust to new conditions or demands. In educational systems or schools that emphasize these qualities, where teachers are encouraged to experiment with new approaches and to adjust their methods to meet changing needs, openness to experience emerges as an asset. The correlation between openness and effectiveness in these contexts, while still modest, suggests that curious, creative teachers have advantages in environments that value these qualities [161].

The study by Bledsoe and colleagues (2025) examined student responses to active learning pedagogies, instructional approaches that engage students in the learning process through activities and discussion rather than through passive reception of information. Active learning might include group problem solving, class discussions, hands-on experiments, or project-based work. The study demonstrated that both teachers and students high in openness adapted more readily to these novel instructional methods. They exhibited greater creativity in their roles, whether those roles involved teaching or learning, and this creativity facilitated deeper engagement and learning [179].

This finding connects to a broader observation about professional development in teaching. Many individuals, in teaching as in other professions, reach what might be called a plateau early in their careers. A plateau represents a leveling off, a period where growth and development cease or slow dramatically. Such individuals rely primarily on the knowledge and methods they acquired during their first few years of professional experience. From that point forward, they may spend decades essentially repeating the same routines, applying the same approaches, without actively seeking growth or new learning. The work continues, certainly, and may even be performed competently according to established standards. Yet there is no longer that active engagement with development, that seeking of new understanding and capability.

In contrast, consider a less experienced but highly open individual, someone characterized by curiosity and eagerness to learn. Such a person continues to grow throughout their career, actively seeking new knowledge, reflecting on practice, experimenting with new methods, learning from successes and failures. Within a relatively short time, this person may attain the same level of wisdom, and even surpass the expertise, of someone with significantly more years of experience. The chronologically less experienced but intellectually more active teacher possesses a kind of practical wisdom that the plateaued veteran, despite more years in the classroom, may lack.

This observation highlights something critical about openness and what psychologists call a growth mindset in teaching. A growth mindset, a concept developed by psychologist Carol Dweck, refers to the belief that abilities and intelligence can be developed through effort, learning, and persistence, in contrast to a fixed mindset that views these qualities as static traits. Openness to experience naturally aligns with a growth mindset, as both involve the belief that change and development are possible and desirable. In the dynamic environment of contemporary education, where student populations change, technologies evolve, research reveals new insights about learning, and societal expectations shift, continuous learning and adaptability prove vital for remaining relevant and effective [179].

Methodologically, research examining openness typically employs validated Big Five inventories, standardized questionnaires that have been tested for reliability (consistency of measurement) and validity (accuracy in measuring what they claim to measure). Researchers then relate scores on these inventories to various measures of instructional innovation (the introduction of new teaching methods), flexibility (the capacity to adjust approaches as needed), and professional development (engagement in learning activities to enhance teaching capability). Effect sizes for openness generally fall in the small to moderate range, approximately r equals 0.1 to 0.3, suggesting relationships that, while not as strong as those for conscientiousness, nevertheless prove meaningful [161, 179].

Importantly, the impact of openness may be amplified in particular contexts, specifically in educational systems or schools that actively encourage pedagogical experimentation. In more traditional or constrained environments, where teachers must adhere closely to prescribed curricula and standardized methods, the advantages of openness may find less expression. In more innovative or autonomous settings, where teachers have freedom to experiment and adapt, openness becomes a more significant asset [161].

The meta-analysis by Liu and colleagues (2022) reported a negative correlation between openness and emotional exhaustion, one dimension of burnout, with r approximately negative 0.11. This suggests that openness may provide some buffer against burnout, perhaps because open individuals find their work more intellectually stimulating and are better able to see challenges as interesting problems rather than merely as frustrations. The correlation is modest, indicating a small protective effect, but it contributes to the overall picture of openness as generally beneficial for teachers [178].

In the specific context of mathematics education, openness has been linked to the adoption of creative teaching strategies, approaches that go beyond routine drill and practice to engage students' mathematical thinking in deeper ways, and to responsiveness to diverse student needs, the capacity to adjust instruction for students with different backgrounds, preparation levels, and learning styles [171].

Thus, openness to experience supports the development of what might be called stimulating, flexible, and innovative learning environments. Teachers high in openness bring an intellectual vitality to their work, a willingness to try new approaches, and an adaptability that serves both themselves and their students well, particularly in educational contexts that value these qualities [161, 171, 178, 179].

> **Key Point:** Curious and creative teachers who remain
> open to new ideas adapt better to change and continue
> growing throughout their careers, making them especially
> valuable in modern education where flexibility and innova-
> tion matter increasingly.

2.4.4   Extraversion

Extraversion encompasses a cluster of related tendencies: sociability (the inclination to seek and enjoy the company of others), assertiveness (the capacity to express oneself confidently and take charge when appropriate), and energetic engagement (high energy levels and enthusiasm in social situations). These qualities manifest clearly in teaching contexts, shaping the dynamic and interactive dimensions of classroom life [161, 179].

Kim's 2019 meta-analysis identified extraversion as a positive predictor of teacher effectiveness. The relationship proves particularly apparent in measures that capture classroom dynamics: student engagement (active participation and investment in learning), teacher-student interaction quality (the skillfulness and warmth of interpersonal exchanges), and what might be called the energy level or vitality of the learning environment. Extraverted teachers, drawing on their natural sociability and energy, tend to create more animated, interactive classrooms [161].

The study by Bledsoe and colleagues (2025) provides concrete illustrations of how extraversion operates in educational settings. In their examination of active learning environments, contexts requiring substantial student participation and interaction, they found that extraverted individuals, whether teachers or students, were more active in group discussions. They contributed more frequently, spoke with greater ease, and seemed to derive energy from the interactive process rather than finding it draining. Moreover, extraverted individuals more readily assumed leadership roles, those positions involving coordination of group efforts and public representation of ideas. They contributed to what observers described as a lively classroom atmosphere, an environment characterized by energy, enthusiasm, and active exchange [179].

These patterns appear particularly pronounced in active learning settings, those instructional approaches mentioned earlier that emphasize discussion, collaboration, and hands-on engagement rather than passive listening. In such contexts, an extraverted teacher's natural inclinations align well with pedagogical goals. However, it is worth noting that extraversion may prove less central in more traditional, lecture-based instruction, where the primary mode involves one-way transmission of information. Even there, though, an extraverted teacher may bring energy and enthusiasm that engage students' attention [179].

Regarding teacher wellbeing, extraversion shows a negative association with burnout, meaning that as extraversion increases, burnout symptoms tend to decrease. The meta-analysis by Liu and colleagues (2022) reported this relationship particularly for emotional exhaustion, with a correlation coefficient of approximately negative 0.18. This suggests a modest protective effect. One might speculate about the mechanism: perhaps extraverted teachers, deriving energy from social interaction, find the inherently social nature of teaching less draining than do more introverted individuals. Where an introvert might find continuous interaction with students exhausting, requiring recovery time alone, an extravert might experience those same interactions as energizing [178].

Kim's 2018 study, examining student perceptions of their teachers, noted that extraversion, while not directly linked to student academic achievement in the statistical models, associated with higher levels of perceived teacher support and classroom engagement. Students experienced extraverted teachers as more accessible, more enthusiastic, and more engaged with the class as a whole. These perceptions matter for the subjective quality of educational experience, even when their connection to achievement remains difficult to establish definitively [172].

It is important to acknowledge that the findings on extraversion, like those on other traits, represent central tendencies and correlations rather than absolute requirements for effective teaching. Highly effective teachers can be found at all points along the extraversion-introversion continuum. Introverted teachers may bring different strengths: depth of reflection, careful listening, comfort with silence and individual work. The research suggests that extraversion confers certain advantages, particularly in interactive contexts, but not that it is essential for teaching success [161, 179].

These findings suggest that extraversion enhances what might be called the social and participatory dimensions of teaching. An extraverted teacher naturally creates an environment of active exchange, drawing students into discussion and participation. The energy and enthusiasm characteristic of extraversion prove contagious, often elevating the overall vitality of classroom life. These qualities support both instructional effectiveness, at least in contexts valuing interaction and engagement, and teacher resilience, as extraverted teachers seem somewhat less vulnerable to the emotional exhaustion that threatens teacher wellbeing [161, 172, 178, 179].

Key Point: Teachers who are outgoing, energetic, and comfortable with social interaction create more lively and engaging classrooms, and they tend to handle the social demands of teaching with less exhaustion than quieter, more reserved teachers.

2.4.5   Neuroticism

If the other Big Five traits represent resources or assets for teachers, neuroticism stands as what researchers consistently identify as a liability or risk factor. Neuroticism, characterized by emotional instability, anxiety (persistent worry and apprehension), and susceptibility to stress (a tendency to experience psychological and physiological distress in response to demands), creates difficulties across multiple dimensions of teaching [161, 177, 178, 180, 181].

Kim's 2019 meta-analysis, that comprehensive synthesis of research discussed throughout this section, along with subsequent reviews, established that neuroticism associates strongly and positively with teacher burnout. A positive correlation in this context means that as neuroticism increases, burnout increases as well. The relationship appears particularly strong for the core dimensions of burnout: emotional exhaustion and depersonalization. The correlation coefficient of approximately r equals 0.3 represents a moderate effect size, one of the stronger relationships documented in this literature. To put this in concrete terms, teachers high in neuroticism face substantially elevated risk of experiencing the emotional depletion and cynical detachment that characterize burnout [161, 178].

The study by Pishghadam and Sahebjam (2012) corroborates and extends these findings. Their research demonstrated that teachers high in neuroticism prove more prone not only to emotional exhaustion but also to creating negative classroom climates. A negative classroom climate might be characterized by tension, irritability, or emotional unpredictability on the teacher's part, which students often sense and respond to with their own anxiety or disengagement. Such climates undermine both teacher wellbeing, as the stress and negativity feed back into the teacher's own emotional state, and student outcomes, as students learn less effectively in anxious, tense environments [181].

The research by Bilal and colleagues (2022) provides additional and concerning evidence. Their study found that neuroticism not only increases vulnerability to stress and burnout but may also contribute to negative classroom behaviors. These might include impaired student-teacher relationships, where the teacher's anxiety or emotional instability interferes with forming positive connections with students. In more extreme cases, neuroticism has been associated with what researchers carefully term inappropriate conduct, behavior falling outside professional standards. This association does not suggest that most neurotic teachers engage in such conduct, but rather that the emotional dysregulation and stress associated with high neuroticism create risk factors that, in combination with other circumstances, may lead to problematic behaviors [180].

Methodologically, studies examining neuroticism typically employ self-report inventories, questionnaires where teachers assess their own tendencies toward anxiety, worry, and emotional instability. Some studies also use observer-rated Big Five inventories, where colleagues or supervisors rate the teacher's personality characteristics based on observed behavior. These assessments are then analyzed alongside validated burnout measures, most commonly the Maslach Burnout Inventory, a widely used instrument that assesses emotional exhaustion, depersonalization, and reduced personal accomplishment, the three dimensions of burnout as conceptualized in the dominant model [161, 177, 178].

Researchers use various statistical techniques to quantify the associations between neuroticism and teaching outcomes. Regression analysis, a method that examines how one or more predictor variables relate to an outcome while controlling for other factors, allows researchers to estimate the unique contribution of neuroticism to burnout or teaching effectiveness. Meta-analytic techniques, mentioned earlier, allow for the combination of results across multiple studies to derive overall effect size estimates [161, 178].

The study by Ruggieri and colleagues (2022) highlights a specific aspect of the neuroticism-burnout relationship. They found that neuroticism serves as the strongest predictor of teacher disillusionment, a component of burnout involving loss of idealism, disappointment with the teaching profession, and questioning of one's career choice. Disillusionment represents a particular kind of demoralization, where the gap between one's aspirations for teaching and the experienced reality becomes painful and potentially unbearable. Teachers high in neuroticism, perhaps because of their tendency toward negative emotional states and their heightened stress reactivity, prove especially vulnerable to this form of professional disappointment [177].

The research underscores something important: the need for targeted interventions to support teachers with high neuroticism. Such interventions might include stress management training, programs that teach techniques for regulating emotions and coping with demands; cognitive-behavioral approaches, methods for identifying and modifying unhelpful thought patterns that contribute to anxiety and stress; mindfulness practices, techniques for maintaining present-moment awareness and acceptance; and adequate organizational support, including reasonable workloads, supportive administration, and access to mental health resources [177, 178].

The evidence does not suggest that individuals high in neuroticism cannot become effective teachers. Rather, it indicates that they face additional challenges and require additional support. Teaching is inherently demanding work, involving constant social interaction, high responsibility, frequent evaluation, and emotional labor, the effort required to manage one's emotions in professional contexts. For individuals predisposed to anxiety and emotional reactivity, these demands create heightened risk of distress and burnout [161, 177, 178, 180, 181].

Collectively, the accumulated evidence positions neuroticism as a central risk factor for teacher stress, emotional exhaustion, and diminished classroom effectiveness. This finding carries implications for teacher education, suggesting the value of helping prospective teachers develop emotional regulation skills; for hiring and placement, suggesting the importance of ensuring adequate support systems; and for professional development and teacher wellbeing programs, suggesting the need for interventions specifically designed to help teachers manage stress and maintain emotional equilibrium [161, 177, 178, 180, 181].

> **Key Point:** Teachers who tend toward anxiety and emotional instability face greater risk of burnout and struggle more with the emotional demands of teaching, highlighting

the importance of providing strong support systems and stress management resources for teachers who experience these challenges.

Figure 2.1 provides a visual synthesis of these relationships, illustrating how the five personality dimensions relate to teaching effectiveness, with conscientiousness and agreeableness emerging as foundational assets, openness and extraversion contributing contextually valuable qualities, and neuroticism standing alone as a consistent source of vulnerability requiring deliberate support and intervention.

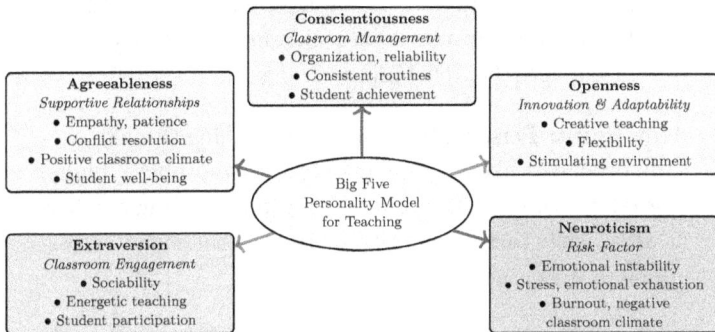

Figure 2.1: The Big Five Personality Model applied to teaching effectiveness. Research demonstrates that conscientiousness and agreeableness are the strongest predictors of positive teaching outcomes, while neuroticism is a consistent risk factor. Openness and extraversion also contribute to effective teaching, particularly in fostering innovation and classroom engagement.

2.5   Mechanisms and Practical Implications

One might observe that personality traits do not operate in some mysterious or magical fashion to affect teaching. Rather, they exert their influence through identifiable psychological and relational mechanisms, the specific processes and pathways through which personality characteristics translate into observable outcomes. These mechanisms include classroom climate (the overall emotional and social atmosphere of the learning environment), instructional quality (the skillfulness and effectiveness with which teaching is conducted), teacher-student relationships (the nature and quality of interpersonal connections between educators and learners), and teacher wellbeing (the psychological, emotional, and physical health of teachers themselves). These mechanisms, it should be noted, operate not merely in isolated or particular settings but across educational levels, from early childhood through higher education, and across cultural contexts, in diverse societies with varying educational traditions and values. They shape both the immediate, day-to-day experiences of teachers and students, those moment-to-moment interactions and feelings that constitute the lived reality of education, and the broader outcomes of educational systems, the long-term results measurable in achievement, wellbeing, and societal impact [161, 166, 178].

> **Key Point:** Personality traits affect teaching through specific processes like creating classroom atmosphere, building relationships with students, and maintaining teacher health, with these effects appearing consistently across different ages, subjects, and cultures.

2.5.1   Mechanisms

Research, in this case, that systematic investigation through which we attempt to understand patterns in human behavior, consistently demonstrates that specific personality traits contribute to teaching effectiveness through distinct pathways. A pathway here means a particular route or process through which an influence travels, much as a river follows a particular course from source to sea. The traits do not all work in the same way or affect the same outcomes; rather, each operates through its own characteristic mechanisms [161, 172, 179].

High agreeableness and high extraversion, for instance, foster what researchers describe as supportive and engaging classroom environments. To foster means to encourage or promote the development of something, much as a gardener fosters plant growth through proper care. Agreeable teachers, those individuals characterized by empathy (the capacity to understand and share others' feelings), patience (the ability to remain calm and supportive despite frustration), and cooperativeness (the tendency to work harmoniously with others), demonstrate particular skill at building strong, positive relationships with students. They excel at managing conflicts constructively, meaning they address disagreements and tensions in ways that resolve problems while preserving and even strengthening relationships. They create a classroom climate, that overall atmosphere mentioned earlier, which supports student wellbeing (psychological and emotional health) and engagement (active participation in and commitment to learning) [161, 166, 172].

Extraverted teachers, meanwhile, bring a different but complementary set of qualities to their work. They contribute energy, that quality of vigor and vitality; sociability, the inclination to seek and enjoy interaction with others; and assertiveness, the capacity to express oneself confidently and take charge when appropriate. These qualities facilitate lively discussions, creating exchanges of ideas characterized by animation and active participation. They encourage what researchers term active participation, the engaged involvement of students in classroom activities and discourse, which can enhance student motivation (the internal drive to learn) and classroom dynamics (the patterns of interaction and energy that characterize classroom life) [161, 179].

Figure 2.2 provides a visual representation of these empirical relationships, illustrating the varying strength of correlations across the Big Five dimensions. Empirical relationships refer to associations observed through systematic data collection and analysis rather than merely theorized or assumed. The figure demonstrates through visual means what the research literature establishes through statistical analysis: that the five personality dimensions relate to teaching effectiveness with different strengths and in different ways [161].

Conscientiousness, that trait discussed at length in an earlier section, ensures structure, reliability, and consistency in the classroom. To ensure here means to make certain or guarantee, suggesting that conscientiousness reliably produces these qualities. Teachers high in conscientiousness excel in several interconnected areas. Planning, the process of preparing and organizing instructional activities in

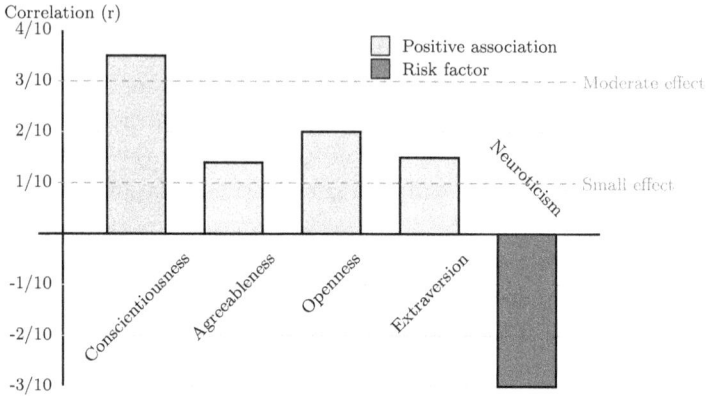

Figure 2.2: Correlation coefficients (with 95% confidence intervals) between Big Five personality traits and teaching effectiveness. Conscientiousness shows the strongest positive association ($r \approx 0.35$), while neuroticism is the primary risk factor ($r \approx -0.30$). Error bars represent the range of effect sizes reported across studies. Positive values indicate beneficial associations with teaching effectiveness, while negative values for neuroticism indicate increased risk of burnout and reduced effectiveness.

advance, receives their careful attention. Organization, the systematic arrangement of materials, time, and activities, characterizes their work. The maintaining of clear expectations, meaning the establishment and consistent communication of standards for behavior and performance, creates a framework within which learning can proceed smoothly. Together, these capacities support effective classroom management (creating and maintaining an orderly, focused learning environment) and student achievement (measurable progress in learning) [161, 171].

The dependability of conscientious teachers, their reliability in meeting commitments and maintaining standards, and their attention to detail, their careful noticing of small but important aspects of their work, enable them to deliver structured lessons (instructional sessions with clear organization and logical progression), provide timely feedback (responses to student work given promptly enough to support learning), and uphold consistent routines (regular patterns of activity that create predictability and stability). All of these prove critical for student learning, meaning they are essential rather than merely helpful [161, 171].

Openness to experience, that trait characterized by intellectual curiosity and receptivity to new ideas, enables teachers to adapt to new challenges, those unexpected problems or changing circumstances that inevitably arise in educational work, and to incorporate innovative practices, teaching methods or approaches that represent departures from traditional or established techniques. Open teachers demonstrate greater likelihood of experimenting with creative teaching methods, trying approaches that involve imagination and originality; integrating new technologies, incorporating contemporary tools and digital resources into their instruction; and responding flexibly to diverse student needs (the varying requirements of students with different backgrounds, abilities, and learning styles) and curriculum changes (modifications to what is taught or how it is organized). This adaptability, the capacity to adjust to new conditions or demands, fosters a stimulating learning environment, one that arouses interest and encourages intellectual curiosity, which in turn encourages critical thinking (the careful, reflective consideration of ideas and claims) and curiosity (the desire to learn and understand) among students [161, 179].

Low neuroticism, which means the same thing as high emotional stability (the tendency to remain calm and even-tempered rather than anxious and emotionally reactive), supports teachers' resilience (the capacity to recover from difficulties and maintain functioning under stress) and emotional regulation (the ability to manage one's emotional responses) in the face of occupational stress (the psychological and physical strain arising from work demands). Teachers with low neuroticism prove better able to maintain composure (remaining calm and in control of oneself), to manage stress (employing effective strategies for coping with demands), and to create a positive classroom climate (an atmosphere characterized by warmth, support, and emotional safety). These capacities reduce the risk of burnout (that state of emotional, physical, and mental exhaustion discussed earlier) and emotional exhaustion (feeling emotionally drained and depleted by work) [161, 177, 178].

	Conscientiousness	Agreeableness	Openness	Extraversion	Emotional Stability
Conscientiousness	Same Trait	Supportive + Organized Environment	Structured + Creative Methods	Reliable + Dynamic Delivery	Organized + Emotionally Stable
Agreeableness	Caring + Well-Planned	Same Trait	Empathetic + Flexible Approach	Warm + Engaging Interaction	Supportive + Calm Climate
Openness	Innovative + Systematic Planning	Creative + Student-Centered	Same Trait	Novel + High-Energy Methods	Creative + Emotionally Consistent
Extraversion	Energetic + Well-Structured	Enthusiastic + Caring Style	Dynamic + Innovative Teaching	Same Trait	Engaging + Emotionally Stable
Emotional Stability	Low Anxiety + Organized Approach	Calm + Nurturing Environment	Stable + Open to New Ideas	Confident + Socially Active	Same Trait

Figure 2.3: Matrix showing all possible pairwise combinations of Big Five personality traits in teaching contexts. Each cell represents how two traits combine to create specific teaching advantages, with medium gray cells indicating positive trait combinations that enhance teaching effectiveness, dark cells with white text showing interactions with emotional stability, i.e. low neuroticism. Note that low neuroticism represents emotional stability, which serves as a multiplicative factor that enhances other personality traits' contributions to teaching success.

In contrast, and this contrast proves important, high neuroticism associates with increased stress (heightened experience of psychological and physiological strain), negative classroom climate (an atmosphere characterized by tension, unpredictability, or emotional discomfort), and a higher risk of teacher burnout. These outcomes can undermine, meaning gradually weaken or damage, both teacher wellbeing (the psychological and physical health of the teacher) and student outcomes (the results students achieve in their learning and development) [161, 178, 180, 181].

It proves essential to recognize that these mechanisms are not isolated, meaning they do not operate independently or in separation from one another. Rather, they interact dynamically, influencing one another in ongoing, complex ways. Figure 2.3, the trait interaction matrix, illustrates this interactive quality. A matrix in this context refers to a structured arrangement showing how different elements relate to or combine with one another. Consider an example to make this concrete: a teacher who scores high in both agreeableness and conscientiousness possesses a particularly favorable combination. Such a teacher is likely to create a classroom that is both supportive (warm, caring, emotionally safe) and well-organized (structured, orderly, with clear routines and expectations). This combination maximizes, meaning brings to the highest possible level, both student engagement (active participation and investment in learning) and achievement (measurable learning progress) [161, 172].

The relative strength of these associations, meaning how powerful the relationships are compared to one another, may vary depending on several factors. Specific teaching outcomes matter: the personality traits that most strongly predict classroom management (maintaining order and focus) may differ from those that most strongly predict instructional innovation (introducing new teaching methods). The methods used to measure personality and effectiveness also influence results. Self-report questionnaires (where teachers assess their own traits) may yield somewhat different findings than observer ratings (where colleagues or supervisors assess teacher personality based on observed behavior). Teaching effectiveness assessed through student achievement tests produces different patterns than effectiveness assessed through classroom observations or student satisfaction surveys [161, 172, 178].

Key Point: Different personality traits help teaching in different ways: being kind and outgoing creates warm, lively classrooms; being organized ensures clear structure; being curious enables adaptation; and being emotionally steady prevents burnout, with these qualities working together rather than separately.

2.5.2   Practical Implications

The practical implications, the real-world applications and consequences, of these findings extend across multiple domains of educational practice. They touch on teacher selection, the processes by which
individuals are recruited and hired for teaching positions; training,
the initial preparation of teachers through formal education programs;
and professional development, the ongoing learning and growth of
teachers throughout their careers. These implications deserve careful
consideration, as they suggest concrete ways in which research findings
might inform and improve educational practice [161, 163, 178].

Educational institutions, the schools, colleges, universities, and
other organizations engaged in teaching and learning, can use personality assessments, standardized instruments designed to measure
personality traits, as one component in the recruitment and selection
of teachers. Such assessments might help to identify candidates who
possess traits associated with effective teaching, those characteristics
that research has linked to positive outcomes. However, and this
qualification proves vital, such assessments should be used ethically,
meaning in accordance with moral principles of fairness and respect
for persons. Careful attention to fairness, treating all candidates
justly without bias or discrimination, to privacy, protecting personal
information and respecting individuals' right to control information
about themselves, and to the avoidance of discrimination, ensuring
that selection processes do not unfairly disadvantage individuals based
on characteristics unrelated to teaching ability, must guide any use of
personality assessment in hiring [161].

Professional development programs, structured learning opportunities designed to enhance teachers' knowledge and skills, can be tailored
to cultivate and support beneficial personality traits. To tailor means
to adapt or adjust to fit particular needs, much as a tailor adjusts
clothing to fit an individual. To cultivate means to develop or improve
through deliberate effort, suggesting that personality traits, while
relatively stable, are not entirely fixed and can be influenced through
appropriate interventions [163, 178].

Consider specific examples of such tailored programs. Stress management training, instruction in techniques for recognizing and reducing stress, and resilience training, programs designed to strengthen the capacity to cope with adversity, may prove particularly valuable for teachers high in neuroticism. Such training might help them develop coping strategies (specific techniques for managing difficult situations) and emotional regulation skills (abilities to recognize, understand, and manage emotional responses). The aim would be not to change fundamental personality but to provide tools and techniques that help individuals manage the challenges associated with their temperamental tendencies [177, 178].

Creativity workshops, structured sessions designed to enhance creative thinking and practice, and training in innovative pedagogical methods, instruction in new or unconventional teaching approaches, can support teachers lower in openness. Such programs might encourage these teachers to experiment with new approaches, trying methods outside their usual practice, and to adapt to changing educational demands, adjusting their teaching as circumstances require. Again, the goal is not personality transformation but rather the development of skills and comfort with practices that might not come as naturally to less open individuals [179].

Moreover, interventions specifically designed to foster empathy (the capacity to understand and share others' feelings), patience (the ability to remain calm and supportive), and authentic concern for students (genuine investment in students' wellbeing and growth), those core components of good-heartedness discussed extensively in earlier sections, can enhance teacher-student relationships and classroom climate. Empathy training, structured programs designed to develop empathic capacity, has been shown through empirical research to improve teaching aptitude (natural ability and fitness for teaching) and student engagement (active participation in and commitment to learning). Programs that promote emotional intelligence, structured interventions designed to develop the abilities to recognize, understand, and manage emotions in oneself and others, can strengthen teachers' self-awareness (recognition of one's own emotional states and their effects), motivation (internal drive toward goals), and social skills (proficiency in managing relationships), all of which further support effective teaching [163, 164, 168].

It proves important to recognize, however, a fundamental limitation of this entire line of inquiry: personality is only one of many factors influencing teaching effectiveness. This acknowledgment matters because it guards against what might be called personality determinism, the mistaken belief that personality alone determines outcomes. Situational factors (aspects of the immediate context), institutional factors (characteristics of the school or educational organization), and contextual variables (broader environmental and cultural conditions) also play significant roles [161, 170].

Consider what these other factors might include: school climate (the overall atmosphere and culture of the educational institution), including whether it is supportive or stressful, collaborative or competitive; administrative support (the quality and extent of assistance provided by school leadership), including whether administrators value and assist teachers; class size (the number of students in a class), which affects how much individual attention teachers can provide; and cultural expectations (socially shared beliefs about what teaching should involve and what students should achieve), which vary across societies and communities. All of these factors interact with teacher personality to shape outcomes [161, 178].

Effective educational policy, the guidelines and decisions that govern educational systems, and practice, the actual methods and approaches used in teaching, should therefore adopt what might be called a holistic approach, one that considers the whole situation rather than focusing narrowly on single factors. This approach would integrate personality development, efforts to support beneficial personality-related characteristics and skills, with broader organizational and contextual supports, improvements in working conditions, resources, administrative practices, and institutional culture [161, 178].

A teacher high in beneficial personality traits such as conscientiousness and agreeableness will still struggle in a school with inadequate resources, unsupportive administration, excessive class sizes, or a toxic institutional culture. Conversely, even teachers with less optimal personality profiles can succeed when provided with strong organizational support, reasonable working conditions, and effective mentoring. The goal, then, should be to attend to both individual characteristics and systemic conditions [161, 170, 178].

Finally, ethical considerations, concerns about what is morally right and fair, prove paramount, meaning of supreme importance, in the use of personality data. Institutions must ensure that personality assessments are used to support, rather than limit, teachers' professional growth. This means that assessment results should inform developmental opportunities and support rather than serving as rigid barriers to employment or advancement. Privacy and fairness must be maintained throughout the process, with personal information protected and all individuals treated justly [161].

The goal, fundamentally, should be to create environments in which all teachers can thrive, not merely those with particular personality profiles. Thriving means not just surviving but flourishing, growing, and experiencing wellbeing and success. This requires drawing on teachers' unique strengths, recognizing that different personality configurations bring different valuable qualities, and supporting their ongoing development as educators through appropriate professional learning opportunities, reasonable working conditions, and organizational cultures that value and support teaching work [161, 163, 170, 178].

> **Key Point:** Schools can use personality information to help teachers grow and succeed, such as providing stress management training for anxious teachers or creativity workshops for more traditional ones, but this should always be done fairly and as part of broader efforts to improve working conditions and support for all teachers.

2.6   So, Does "Being Good" Make You a Better Teacher?

One arrives, after examining all this accumulated evidence, at a question both simple and profound. Does being good, in the everyday sense of that word, genuinely make one a better teacher? The question might seem almost naive, the sort of thing one hesitates to ask in academic discourse, preferring more technical formulations. Yet it lies at the heart of all the research discussed in the preceding sections. The accumulated evidence, that body of findings drawn from psychological research (the scientific study of mind and behavior), educational research (systematic inquiry into teaching and learning), and neuroscientific research (investigation of the brain and nervous system), provides an answer that is both clear and robust, meaning reliable and strongly supported: yes, being good, understood here as possessing and consistently demonstrating prosocial qualities (characteristics that benefit others and support positive social interaction), does indeed make one a better teacher [161–165].

What do we mean precisely by being good in this context? The term encompasses several interrelated qualities: empathy (the capacity to understand and share another's feelings), kindness (the quality of being friendly, generous, and considerate), patience (the ability to remain calm and supportive despite frustration or delay), and conscientiousness (the tendency toward organization, reliability, and goal-directed behavior). Together, these constitute what might be called good-heartedness, that quality of genuine care and benevolent intention toward others [161, 162, 164].

Meta-analyses, those comprehensive syntheses of research discussed earlier that combine findings from many studies to identify overall patterns, and large-scale studies, investigations involving substantial numbers of participants that provide statistical power to detect meaningful relationships, consistently show certain patterns. Teachers who score high in traits such as conscientiousness and agreeableness, these being core components of the good-heartedness under discussion, demonstrate greater effectiveness across multiple dimensions of their work [161, 178].

These more effective teachers excel in classroom management, that complex set of skills for creating and maintaining an orderly, focused learning environment. They foster stronger teacher-student relationships, connections characterized by mutual respect, trust, and positive regard. Perhaps most importantly for their own sustainability in the profession, they experience less burnout, that state of emotional, physical, and mental exhaustion resulting from prolonged occupational stress. The experience of less burnout means not merely that these teachers feel better, though that matters, but that they can sustain effective practice over longer periods, maintaining their capacity to serve students year after year rather than leaving the profession or continuing while depleted and ineffective [161, 178].

Consider conscientiousness more specifically. This trait demonstrates what statisticians call a moderate correlation with teaching effectiveness, particularly when effectiveness is measured through peer or supervisor evaluations (assessments provided by colleagues or administrators who observe the teacher's work) rather than through student achievement alone (test scores or other measures of student learning outcomes). The correlation is moderate, meaning neither weak nor overwhelmingly strong, with correlation coefficients typically in the range of r equals 0.3 to 0.4. Yet even moderate correlations represent meaningful relationships when they appear consistently across diverse studies and contexts [161].

Why might conscientiousness correlate more strongly with effectiveness as judged by professional observers than with student achievement per se? Perhaps because observers can directly perceive the organizational qualities, the careful planning, the reliability and consistency that conscientiousness produces. These qualities create the conditions for effective teaching, but the translation of those conditions into measurable student achievement depends on many additional factors: student characteristics, curriculum quality, available resources, and countless other variables that intervene between teacher behavior and student outcomes [161, 172].

Agreeableness presents a somewhat different pattern, one discussed earlier. While not always directly linked to academic outcomes as measured by achievement tests, agreeableness proves vital, meaning absolutely necessary, for building supportive classroom climates (atmospheres characterized by warmth, safety, and positive emotional tone) and resilient teacher-student bonds (relationships characterized by trust and capable of weathering difficulties). These qualities matter profoundly for students' experience of education and for outcomes beyond test scores: engagement, motivation, sense of belonging, social and emotional development [161, 166, 172].

Among all the qualities associated with good-heartedness, empathy emerges with particular importance. Empathy, that capacity discussed extensively in earlier sections to understand and share another's emotional experience, enables teachers to perform several crucial functions. Empathetic teachers prove better able to recognize the diverse needs of their students, perceiving not only academic struggles but also emotional states, social difficulties, and personal challenges that affect learning. They can respond effectively to what they perceive, adjusting their approach to meet individual requirements. They adapt their instructional strategies, modifying teaching methods to suit different learning styles, preparation levels, and circumstances [164, 168].

Perhaps most fundamentally, empathetic teachers create emotionally secure environments, classroom atmospheres in which students feel psychologically safe. Psychological safety, a term coined by organizational researcher Amy Edmondson, refers to the belief that one can express oneself, ask questions, admit mistakes, and take interpersonal risks without fear of negative consequences to self-image, status, or career. In educational contexts, psychological safety means students can participate actively in learning, acknowledge confusion, make errors in the process of developing understanding, and express their thoughts without fear of humiliation or rejection [164, 165].

This emotional security, in turn, enhances several important outcomes. Student engagement increases, meaning students participate more actively and invest more fully in learning activities. Motivation strengthens, that internal drive to learn and achieve that ultimately matters more than any external pressure. Achievement improves, as students in psychologically safe environments learn more effectively. These effects prove especially pronounced for students facing adversity or disadvantage, those individuals dealing with poverty, family difficulties, learning challenges, social marginalization, or other obstacles to educational success. For such students, the teacher's emotional support can be transformative, genuinely changing life trajectories rather than merely providing modest benefit [164–166, 170].

The mechanisms, the specific processes and pathways, by which being good enhances teaching prove multifaceted, meaning they operate through multiple channels simultaneously. Good-hearted teachers build trust, that fundamental confidence in another's benevolent intentions and reliable behavior, and rapport, a close and harmonious relationship in which people understand each other well. Trust and rapport serve as foundations for student engagement and for students' willingness to take intellectual risks, to venture beyond what they already know and can do comfortably. Without trust, students remain guarded, reluctant to reveal confusion or struggle, unwilling to attempt challenging tasks where failure might occur [165, 166].

Kindness and patience foster what might be called a safe, inclusive, and motivating environment. Safe means emotionally secure, as discussed above. Inclusive means welcoming to all students regardless of background, ability, or characteristics, creating a sense that everyone belongs and has value. Motivating means inspiring the internal drive to learn and achieve. Such environments naturally reduce conflict, as students feel less threatened and more cooperative. They promote positive behaviors, as students respond to kindness with prosocial conduct rather than defensiveness or aggression [165, 167].

Students who feel cared for, who perceive that their teacher genuinely values and is concerned for them, demonstrate several positive patterns. They participate more actively, contributing to discussions, asking questions, engaging with learning activities. They persist through challenges, continuing to work at difficult tasks rather than giving up when understanding does not come immediately. They achieve academically, learning more and performing better on various measures of educational success. The sense of being cared for meets a fundamental human need for connection and belonging, freeing psychological energy that can then be directed toward learning [166, 169, 170].

Prosocial traits, those qualities that benefit others and support positive interaction, also protect teachers themselves against burnout and emotional exhaustion. This protective function matters not only for teacher wellbeing but also for sustained teaching effectiveness. A burned-out teacher, depleted emotionally and perhaps questioning the value of their work, cannot maintain the energy, enthusiasm, and care that effective teaching requires. Teachers with strong prosocial qualities seem better able to sustain their engagement with teaching work, perhaps because the positive relationships they form provide emotional rewards that balance the inevitable stresses and frustrations of the profession [161, 177, 178].

Neuroscientific studies, investigations using technologies that allow observation of brain structure and function, provide additional support for these findings from a biological perspective. Research employing brain imaging techniques such as functional magnetic resonance imaging, often abbreviated as fMRI (a method that measures brain activity by detecting changes in blood flow), has identified specific neural networks underlying empathy and emotional regulation. Neural networks refer to interconnected groups of brain regions that work together to perform particular functions [164].

These studies show that the neural networks associated with empathy and emotional regulation exhibit activation, meaning they show increased activity, in effective teachers during teaching-related tasks. This activation enables teachers to attune to students' needs, to synchronize their understanding with students' emotional and cognitive states, and to respond adaptively, adjusting their behavior appropriately based on what they perceive. The biological evidence thus converges with the behavioral and psychological evidence, all pointing toward the importance of empathy and related qualities in teaching [163, 164].

The practical implications, the real-world applications of these research findings, appear clear. Cultivating prosocial qualities in teachers, through selection (choosing individuals for teaching positions), training (initial preparation programs), and ongoing professional development (continued learning throughout careers), can yield significant benefits for both educators and students. To cultivate means to foster the development of something through deliberate effort, suggesting that while personality traits show some stability, they are not entirely fixed and can be influenced through appropriate interventions [161, 163].

Interventions, structured programs or activities designed to produce specific changes, that foster empathy, emotional intelligence (the set of abilities through which individuals recognize, understand, and manage emotions), and stress resilience (the capacity to maintain functioning and recover from difficulties under stress) prove particularly valuable. Such interventions might include empathy training programs, workshops on emotional intelligence, mindfulness practices (techniques for maintaining present-moment awareness), and stress management instruction. Evidence suggests that these programs can enhance the relevant qualities and skills, leading to improved teaching effectiveness and teacher wellbeing [163, 168, 178].

However, and this qualification matters, it proves important to recognize that personality is only one piece of the puzzle, one element in a complex system. The puzzle metaphor suggests that many elements must fit together to create the complete picture of teaching effectiveness. Institutional support, the assistance and resources provided by schools and educational organizations; school climate, the overall culture and atmosphere of the educational institution; and contextual factors, broader environmental and social conditions, all play vital roles alongside teacher personality [161, 170, 178].

A teacher possessing ideal personality traits will still struggle in an unsupportive institution with inadequate resources, excessive demands, poor leadership, or a toxic culture. Conversely, teachers with less optimal personality profiles can succeed when provided with strong organizational support, effective mentoring, reasonable working conditions, and positive institutional culture. The goal, therefore, should be to attend to both individual characteristics and systemic conditions, recognizing that both matter and that neither alone suffices [161, 178].

While the evidence proves compelling, meaning strongly persuasive and difficult to dismiss, it is not absolute in the sense of being perfect or beyond all question. Some methodological limitations persist, constraints inherent in research design that affect interpretation of findings. These include reliance on self-report measures, where individuals assess their own characteristics and behaviors, which may be affected by limited self-awareness or desire to present oneself favorably. Another challenge involves isolating personality effects from contextual influences, determining how much observed outcomes result from teacher personality versus from the many other factors simultaneously operating [161, 162].

Moreover, the impact of being good may vary across different situations. Educational levels, whether one teaches young children, adolescents, or adults, may influence which personality qualities matter most and how strongly they relate to effectiveness. Cultural contexts, the particular societies and communities in which teaching occurs, shape both how personality qualities are expressed and how they are perceived and valued. Specific teaching roles, whether one teaches mathematics or literature, works with mainstream or special needs students, teaches in affluent or disadvantaged communities, all may influence the relationship between personality and effectiveness [161, 167, 170].

Nonetheless, despite these important qualifications, the convergence of findings, the fact that multiple types of studies using different methods and examining different populations all point in the same direction, affirms something fundamental. The central role of good-heartedness in effective teaching appears genuine and important. This convergence comes from across disciplines, from education, psychology, and neuroscience, and across methodologies, including meta-analyses, experimental studies, observational research, and qualitative investigations [161–166, 170, 178].

Goodness in teaching, then, is not merely a moral ideal, a vision of what would be nice but perhaps impractical or unnecessary. Rather, it is an empirically supported foundation, a basis confirmed through systematic observation and measurement, for multiple valued outcomes: academic success (achievement in learning), personal growth (development as a whole person beyond academic skills), and professional fulfillment (satisfaction and meaning in one's work as a teacher). Being a good person, possessing and enacting qualities of empathy, kindness, patience, and conscientiousness, truly does make one a better teacher, better in ways that matter both for students' immediate experience and learning and for their long-term development and flourishing [161–166, 169, 170, 178].

Key Point: Research clearly shows that being a genuinely good person, someone who is kind, patient, empathetic, and conscientious, makes you a more effective teacher in ways that matter for both student success and your own wellbeing, though this works best when combined with good working conditions and institutional support.

Chapter 3

Goodness in Driving

Individuals with a fundamentally good disposition often learn from a single initial mistake and become more vigilant drivers, thus not repeating such infractions. In contrast, others may follow a different trajectory. Research in psychology and organizational behavior consistently demonstrates that a single unethical act, such as a minor traffic violation, can increase the likelihood of further unethical behavior; not just in driving, but across many domains of life. This phenomenon is often described as the "slippery slope," where small transgressions (like rolling through a stop sign or exceeding the speed limit) can gradually pave the way for more serious violations over time. For example, Dai et al. found that individuals who cheated in lab-based tasks were also more likely to commit fare-dodging on public transportation in the field [183]. Similar patterns are seen in workplaces, where minor acts like taking office supplies can predict later, more serious fraud, and in academics, where students who cheat on small assignments are more likely to escalate to major violations [184,185]. Welsh et al. described how individuals who commit minor ethical breaches are more likely to escalate their misconduct, as each small infraction lowers the psychological barrier to the next, more significant act [186]. Their studies showed that when unethical behavior increases incrementally, people are less likely to notice or feel guilty about their actions, making it easier to justify further rule-breaking. Similarly, Reek and Ariely [187] observed that both perpetrators and observers are less likely to recognize or intervene in unethical behavior when it develops gradually, allowing standards to erode unnoticed.

This escalation is driven by several psychological mechanisms. One key factor is moral rationalization, where individuals justify their initial bad acts (perhaps telling themselves that "everyone speeds a little") which reduces feelings of guilt and makes it easier to repeat or intensify the behavior. Over time, repeated minor violations can lead to moral disengagement, a process in which drivers detach from their internal moral standards and become desensitized to the consequences of their actions. Another important mechanism is self-control depletion, or ego depletion: after exerting self-control in one area (such as resisting the urge to check a phone while driving), individuals may have less willpower to resist other temptations, increasing the risk of further unethical acts like aggressive driving or running red lights.

Additionally, the concept of moral licensing plays a significant role. Meta-analytic evidence by Blanken et al. [188] shows that after engaging in a good deed (such as letting another driver merge) individuals may feel they have earned "moral credits," which can paradoxically make them more likely to justify subsequent bad behavior, like cutting someone off in traffic. This effect, while modest, is robust across a range of contexts and highlights how our sense of moral self-regulation can sometimes backfire, leading to inconsistent or even contradictory patterns of conduct.

Real-world case studies further illustrate these dynamics. For example, research on workplace misconduct and criminal psychology shows that initial minor rule-breaking, if left unchecked, can normalize unethical behavior and create a culture where more serious violations become increasingly likely [189]. In the context of driving, this means that tolerating small infractions (whether by individuals or within a broader driving culture) can set a precedent that encourages more dangerous and unethical behavior on the road.

Hence, a growing body of research underscores that character and ethical decision-making are not static traits but are shaped by a dynamic interplay of psychological mechanisms and situational factors. Initial minor unethical acts, such as small driving violations, can set off a chain reaction that increases the likelihood of further, and potentially more serious, misconduct. Recognizing and addressing these early transgressions is therefore vital for promoting safer and more ethical driving behavior.

3.1 Predictors of Unethical Driving

3.1.1 Personality Traits and Psychological Dispositions

A growing body of research highlights the role of personality traits in predisposing individuals to unethical driving behaviors. Traits such as aggressiveness, sensation-seeking, low conscientiousness, and moral disengagement are consistently associated with a greater likelihood of engaging in such behaviors. For instance, drivers who perceive themselves as highly skilled or who downplay the risks of their actions are more likely to justify and engage in violating the rules of traffic. Recent psychological studies have demonstrated that personality traits, including those described by Zuckerman's and Gray's models (described below), as well as individual decision-making styles, are significant predictors of risky driving behaviors [190].

A substantial body of evidence now supports the association between the Big Five personality traits and a wide range of driving behaviors. A recent systematic review and meta-analysis found that low conscientiousness and high neuroticism are particularly strong predictors of risky and unethical driving, while agreeableness and openness tend to be protective factors [191]. These findings suggest that personality assessment could play a valuable role in identifying individuals at higher risk for persistent traffic violations.

Longitudinal studies have further demonstrated that certain personality factors, such as impulsivity and sensation-seeking, are predictive of persistent risky driving and increased crash involvement, especially among young adults [192]. This evidence highlights the importance of

early interventions targeting personality-related risk factors in order
to reduce the likelihood of repeated violations and accidents.

Moreover, research has shown that personality traits not only
influence the likelihood of engaging in risky driving but also affect
emotional responses behind the wheel. One such trait, known as trait
anger, refers to a stable tendency within individuals to experience
anger frequently and intensely across a variety of situations, rather
than as a fleeting reaction to a specific event. Drivers with high levels
of trait anger are more likely to become irritated or enraged in response
to common driving frustrations, such as traffic congestion or perceived
slights from other motorists. This heightened predisposition to anger
can lead to more frequent and severe episodes of driving-related anger,
which in turn increases the risk of aggressive behaviors in traffic
situations [193]. These findings underscore the complex interplay
between enduring personality characteristics (such as trait anger or
low agreeableness) and situational triggers in shaping unethical or
dangerous driving conduct. Research further suggests that trait anger
can impair executive function and hazard perception, making drivers
more vulnerable to risky decisions and impulsive actions on the road
[194].

Attitudes and perceived behavioral control, which are closely related to personality traits like impulsivity and risk-taking, have also
been identified as significant predictors of violating the rules of traffic.
Furthermore, moral disengagement mechanisms (such as rationalizing
or minimizing the ethical implications of one's actions) facilitate the
justification of aggressive or rule-breaking driving. Additional research
has shown that socioeconomic status interacts with personality and
attitudes, further influencing the likelihood of engaging in risky or
unethical driving behaviors [195].

3.1.2   The Big Five Personality Traits and Driving

A substantial body of psychological research has converged on the
Big Five personality traits (openness to experience, conscientiousness,
extraversion, agreeableness, and neuroticism) as a robust framework

for understanding individual differences in behavior, including those relevant to driving [174,175,196–198]. Each trait represents a spectrum along which individuals may vary, and these dimensions have been shown to be relatively stable across the lifespan and cultures [174,175]. The Big Five model is widely used in both research and applied settings to predict a range of outcomes, including ethical decision-making and risk-related behaviors [174,199].

As stated above, meta-analyses have found that agreeableness and neuroticism are the most robust predictors of risky and aggressive driving behaviors, with agreeableness being protective and neuroticism a risk factor [200,201]. However, a more recent and comprehensive meta-analysis by Luo et al. (2023) found that conscientiousness and openness to experience are also significantly, though more weakly, associated with safer and more positive driving behaviors [200]. Thus, individuals high in agreeableness, conscientiousness, and openness are less likely to engage in risky or aggressive driving and more likely to display positive, prosocial driving behaviors.

Conscientiousness

While conscientiousness (reflecting self-discipline, organization, and reliability) has often been considered a protective factor against risky driving, the evidence is mixed. Individuals high in conscientiousness are generally thought to obey traffic laws, avoid impulsive maneuvers, and demonstrate lower rates of traffic violations and accidents. However, a large meta-analysis by Akbari et al. (2019) found no significant association between conscientiousness and risky driving behaviors [201]. In contrast, a more recent and comprehensive meta-analysis by Luo et al. (2023) did find a significant negative association, indicating that higher conscientiousness is linked to less risky and aggressive driving, as well as more positive driving behaviors [200]. Conversely, low conscientiousness is associated with increased driving errors and a greater propensity for unethical or risky behaviors, but the strength of this relationship may depend on the specific driving outcomes measured and the analytic approach used [200,201].

Neuroticism

Neuroticism, characterized by emotional instability and proneness to negative emotions, is a robust risk factor for unsafe driving. Drivers high in neuroticism are more susceptible to anger, frustration, and stress behind the wheel, which can lead to impulsive decisions, errors, and traffic violations [200]. The effect of neuroticism is often mediated by impulsivity and trait anger, increasing the likelihood of aggressive responses to driving stressors [201]. Both Akbari et al. (2019) and Luo et al. (2023) found significant positive associations between neuroticism and risky or aggressive driving behaviors, confirming its role as a consistent risk factor [200, 201].

Agreeableness

Agreeableness, encompassing traits such as empathy, cooperativeness, and trust, is associated with fewer risky and aggressive driving behaviors. Highly agreeable drivers are more likely to be patient and considerate, reducing the risk of road rage and promoting prosocial driving practices [200, 201].

A recent systematic review and meta-analysis of over 11,000 drivers worldwide found that agreeableness (a personality trait encompassing empathy, kindness, and cooperativeness) was the strongest protective factor against risky and unethical driving behaviors. Individuals high in agreeableness were significantly less likely to engage in behaviors such as speeding, aggressive maneuvers, or ignoring traffic rules, supporting the view that a fundamentally 'good heart' is a key ingredient in ethical driving conduct. In contrast, traits such as neuroticism, sensation seeking, and driving anger were associated with increased risk, while conscientiousness and openness showed no significant relationship with risky driving in this large-scale analysis [201]. Luo et al. (2023) further confirmed that agreeableness is negatively associated with both risky and aggressive driving, and positively associated with positive driving behaviors [200].

Openness to Experience

The relationship between openness to experience (which includes cognitive flexibility and willingness to try new approaches) and driving behavior is less clear. Open individuals are more likely to learn and apply new traffic rules and respond effectively to novel situations on the road [200]. Akbari et al. (2019) found no significant association between openness and risky driving [201], while Luo et al. (2023) reported a small but significant negative association with risky and aggressive driving, and a positive association with positive driving behaviors [200]. Thus, openness may play a modest protective role, particularly for positive driving conduct, but findings are not entirely consistent across studies.

Extraversion

The relationship between extraversion and driving behavior is less consistent. Some studies suggest that high extraversion may be linked to increased errors or violations, particularly in professional driving contexts, while others find no significant association. Both Akbari et al. (2019) and Luo et al. (2023) found no significant overall association between extraversion and risky or positive driving behaviors, indicating that extraversion is not a reliable predictor in this domain [200, 201].

Mechanisms and Practical Implications

Hence, while earlier meta-analyses found only agreeableness and neuroticism to be robust predictors of risky driving behaviors [201], a recent meta-analysis synthesizing findings from 34 studies summarized these associations as follows: conscientiousness and agreeableness are the strongest protective factors, neuroticism is the most consistent risk factor, and openness is generally linked to positive driving behaviors, while extraversion shows weaker or more variable associations (as depicted in Figure 3.1). These patterns are observed across diverse cultural and demographic groups, though the strength of associations may vary by age, gender, and measurement approach [199].

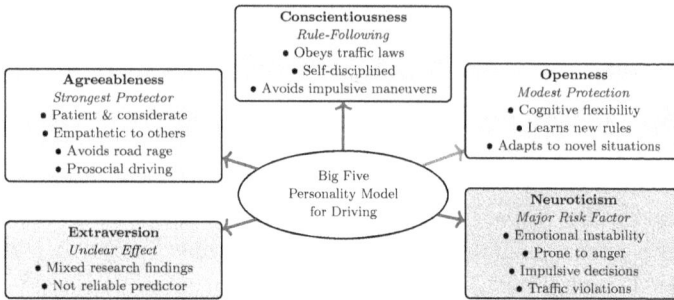

Figure 3.1: The Big Five Personality Model applied to driving behavior. Research demonstrates that agreeableness serves as the strongest protective factor against risky and unethical driving, while neuroticism is the most consistent risk factor. Conscientiousness and openness provide modest protection, whereas extraversion shows unclear associations with driving outcomes.

The influence of the Big Five on driving is mediated by mechanisms such as emotional regulation, moral disengagement, adaptability, and empathy. For example, high neuroticism and trait anger can impair emotional control, increasing the likelihood of aggressive or impulsive driving. Low conscientiousness and agreeableness may facilitate rationalization of unethical behaviors, such as justifying speeding or queue-jumping. In contrast, openness supports adaptability to new traffic environments, and agreeableness fosters prosocial behaviors such as yielding and avoiding conflict [200, 201].

These findings have practical implications for road safety interventions. Personality assessment may help identify individuals at higher risk for unsafe driving, enabling targeted interventions such as stress management training for high-neuroticism drivers or rule-following education for those low in conscientiousness. Personality-informed approaches are also increasingly used in professional driver selection and training, as well as in the design of public safety campaigns and in-vehicle feedback systems [174, 201].

It is important to note, however, that personality is only one factor among many influencing driving behavior; situational and environmental factors also play major roles. Furthermore, ethical use of personality data is essential to avoid privacy violations or discrimination [174].

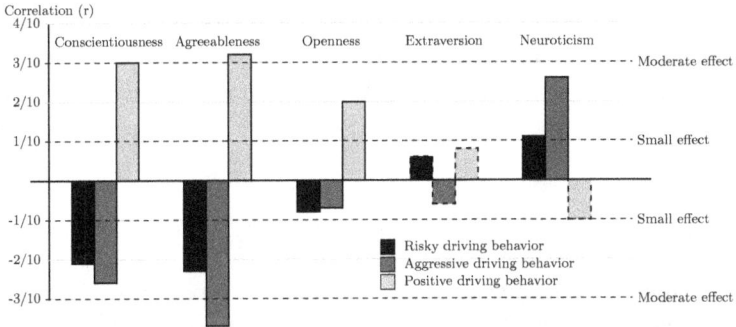

Figure 3.2: Correlation coefficients (r) between Big Five personality traits and driving behaviors, based on recent meta-analyses [199–201]. Each trait shows three bars: risky driving, aggressive driving, and positive driving. Positive values indicate positive correlations, negative values indicate protective effects. Bars with dashed outlines indicate non-significant associations (ns).

Figure 3.2 presents a quantitative summary of the associations between each of the Big Five personality traits and three categories of driving behavior: risky, aggressive, and positive (safe/prosocial) driving. The figure displays meta-analytic correlation coefficients (r-values) derived from large-scale studies and systematic reviews [199–201]. For each trait, three bars are shown: one for risky driving (left), one for aggressive driving (center), and one for positive driving (right). Negative r-values indicate that higher levels of the trait are associated with less risky or aggressive driving (i.e., a protective effect), while positive r-values indicate a greater propensity for the behavior in question.

The results reveal that agreeableness and conscientiousness are the strongest protective factors, with moderate negative correlations for both risky and aggressive driving, and moderate positive correlations for positive driving behaviors. Openness to experience shows a small but significant protective effect, particularly for positive driving. In contrast, neuroticism is a consistent risk factor, with positive correlations for risky and aggressive driving, and a negative (though non-significant) association with positive driving. Extraversion, as indicated by the dashed bars, shows no significant associations with any driving outcomes. The figure also includes reference lines to help interpret the magnitude of the effects, and a legend clarifying the color coding for each behavior type. This visual summary underscores the differential impact of personality traits on driving conduct and highlights the traits most relevant for interventions and risk assessment [199–201].

3.1.3   Zuckerman's Model of Personality

Zuckerman's alternative five-factor model is a prominent framework in personality psychology, particularly noted for its emphasis on traits directly related to risk-taking and sensation-seeking behaviors. Unlike the traditional Big Five, Zuckerman's model includes dimensions such as Impulsive Sensation Seeking, Aggression–Hostility, Activity, Sociability, and Neuroticism–Anxiety. Empirical research indicates that individuals who score highly on Impulsive Sensation Seeking and Aggression–Hostility are more likely to engage in risky and unethical driving behaviors. For example, sensation-seeking drivers may display a greater propensity for speeding, abrupt lane changes, or other forms of aggressive maneuvering. Similarly, elevated Aggression–Hostility is associated with a higher likelihood of road rage and confrontational driving incidents. These associations suggest that Zuckerman's model provides valuable insights into the personality-driven mechanisms underlying persistent risky driving and the escalation of minor infractions into more serious violations. The model's focus on impulsivity and sensation seeking aligns with observed patterns in repeat offenders and individuals prone to moral disengagement while driving [190].

3.1.4   Gray's Reinforcement Sensitivity Theory

Gray's model, often referred to as Reinforcement Sensitivity Theory (RST), offers a biologically grounded account of personality by focusing on individuals' sensitivity to rewards and punishments. Central to this model are two neurobiological systems: the Behavioral Inhibition

System (BIS) and the Behavioral Activation System (BAS). The BIS is responsive to signals of punishment, novel stimuli, and non-reward, thus promoting avoidance and cautious behavior, which can manifest as risk aversion in driving contexts. Conversely, the BAS is activated by signals of reward and escape from punishment, fostering approach-oriented and impulsive behaviors. Individuals with a highly active BAS are typically more susceptible to engaging in rule-breaking and reckless driving in pursuit of excitement or perceived gains. In contrast, those with a dominant BIS may display more reserved and law-abiding driving conduct. Gray's framework has been instrumental in linking individual differences in reward and punishment sensitivity to the likelihood of unsafe driving practices, providing a nuanced understanding of how personality influences ethical and risk-related decision-making on the road [190].

3.1.5 Attitudes, Social Norms, and Cognitive Factors

Attitudes toward traffic safety, social norms, and cognitive factors are central to understanding and predicting driving behavior. A substantial body of research demonstrates that drivers with negative or lax attitudes toward traffic safety are more likely to engage in violations, errors, and lapses, while positive attitudes are associated with safer driving practices. Attitudes are not static; they are shaped by a combination of individual skills, demographic factors, and broader cultural and social influences.

Recent empirical work has clarified the relationship between self-perceived driving skills and attitudes toward traffic safety. For example, Bayat et al. found that drivers with higher self-reported safety skills tend to have less favorable attitudes toward rule violations, speeding, careless driving, and drinking and driving, whereas those with higher decisional skills may paradoxically show more favorable attitudes toward risky behaviors, possibly due to overconfidence in their ability to manage hazardous situations. This highlights the importance of targeting both attitudes and skill development in road safety interventions, as well as the need to address overconfidence and self-assessment biases among drivers [202].

Social norms, both descriptive (beliefs about what others do) and injunctive (beliefs about what others approve or disapprove), play a significant role in shaping driving behavior. If drivers perceive that violations such as queue-jumping or speeding are common or socially tolerated, they are more likely to engage in these behaviors themselves. This effect is amplified in environments where enforcement is weak or inconsistent, and where cultural norms are tolerant of aggressive or unethical driving. Cross-cultural research by Yousaf and Wu demonstrates that in countries with stricter enforcement and less social tolerance for violations, drivers report fewer aggressive and risky behaviors compared to countries with weaker enforcement and more lenient norms. These findings underscore the moderating effect of cultural context and enforcement on the relationship between attitudes, norms, and actual driving behavior [203].

Cognitive factors such as risk perception, self-regulation, and executive function also contribute to driving behavior. Drivers who underestimate the risks associated with violations, or who have deficits in executive function (such as poor impulse control or decision-making), are more prone to errors and risky actions. Bayat et al. further show that safety skills (encompassing risk perception and rule compliance) are inversely related to favorable attitudes toward violations, while decisional skills (the ability to make quick judgments in complex situations) can sometimes foster overconfidence and risk-taking if not balanced by a strong safety orientation [202].

The interplay between personality, attitudes, and social norms is further moderated by demographic and cultural factors. For instance, younger drivers and males are generally more likely to hold lenient attitudes toward violations and to engage in risky driving, a pattern observed across diverse cultural contexts [202, 203]. Cultural values, such as how much people respect and follow authority figures and rules, individualism, and uncertainty avoidance, also shape the prevailing social norms and attitudes toward traffic safety, influencing the acceptability of aggressive or unethical driving behaviors [204].

One influential framework for understanding these cultural differences is Hofstede's Cultural Dimensions Theory, developed by Dutch social psychologist Geert Hofstede [205]. This theory identifies several key dimensions along which cultures can vary, including power distance (the extent to which less powerful members of a society accept and expect unequal power distribution), individualism versus collectivism (the degree to which people prioritize individual goals over group goals), and uncertainty avoidance (how comfortable a culture is with ambiguity and uncertainty). These dimensions help explain why behaviors and values differ between societies and provide insight into how social norms are formed. For example, in countries with high power distance, people may be more likely to accept strict enforcement of traffic laws by authorities, while in more individualistic societies, personal freedom and self-expression might lead to different attitudes toward road rules. Similarly, cultures with high uncertainty avoidance may develop stricter traffic regulations to minimize unpredictability on the roads. Thus, these cultural values, as described by Hofstede's theory, shape prevailing social norms and attitudes toward traffic safety, influencing the acceptability of aggressive or unethical driving behaviors.

Moreover, the relationship between attitudes and behavior is bidirectional and dynamic. Interventions that improve safety skills and foster stricter attitudes toward violations can reduce risky driving, but these must be supported by consistent enforcement and culturally sensitive public messaging. Conversely, environments that tolerate minor infractions may inadvertently normalize more serious violations over time. Hence, attitudes, social norms, and cognitive factors interact in complex ways to shape driving behavior. Effective road safety strategies must address not only individual attitudes and skills but also the broader social and cultural context in which driving occurs, recognizing the powerful influence of perceived norms, enforcement practices, and demographic factors on the likelihood of violations and crashes [202–204].

3.1.6   Situational and Environmental Influences

Situational and environmental factors exert a substantial influence on the prevalence of unethical or aggressive driving. High levels of traffic congestion, long queues, and poorly designed intersections are consistently associated with an increased likelihood of queue-jumping, as these conditions heighten frustration and impatience among drivers. The presence or absence of enforcement measures (such as police patrols or surveillance cameras) also plays a critical role. When enforcement is visible, drivers are more likely to comply with traffic norms; conversely, in the absence of such deterrents, violations become more frequent as the perceived risk of sanction diminishes [206, 207].

Environmental stressors, including noise, crowding, and adverse weather or road conditions, further elevate the risk of aggressive driving behaviors. For example, agent-based simulations and empirical studies have demonstrated that factors such as poor pavement conditions and inclement weather can interact with human characteristics (such as age and experience) to influence both the likelihood of infractions and overall traffic performance. These external stressors can exacerbate impatience and reduce the threshold for rule-breaking, particularly in high-density urban environments [206].

Time pressure is another robust situational factor: when drivers are under pressure to arrive quickly, their intention to commit violations increases, regardless of their level of driving experience [208]. Special events and peak hours that increase traffic density also intensify the incidence of traffic violations, as the increased volume of vehicles and resulting delays can lead to a higher frequency of aggressive maneuvers as drivers seek to minimize their own inconvenience [206, 207].

Importantly, the impact of situational and environmental factors is not uniform across all drivers. Individual differences in personality traits and moral dispositions moderate the response to these external pressures. Research consistently shows that drivers with higher levels of agreeableness (characterized by empathy, cooperativeness, and a tendency to consider the welfare of others) are less likely to engage in aggressive or unethical driving, even under stressful or frustrating conditions. This suggests that a fundamentally "good heart" or prosocial disposition acts as a buffer against situational triggers for unethical behavior [193, 200, 201].

As mentioned above, studies using the Big Five personality framework have found that agreeableness and conscientiousness are protective factors, reducing the likelihood of aggressive responses to situational stressors such as congestion or provocation by other drivers. In contrast, individuals high in neuroticism or with Type A personality traits (marked by impatience, competitiveness, and a sense of time urgency) are more susceptible to situational triggers and more likely to resort to violations when frustrated [193, 209]. Evolutionary game-theoretic models further support these findings, showing that drivers with Type A personalities are more likely to prioritize personal gain (such as reduced travel time) over the collective good, especially in competitive or high-pressure environments, whereas those with more patient and risk-averse dispositions (Type B) are more likely to adhere to orderly and prosocial driving behaviors [209].

Moreover, the influence of situational factors is shaped by the interaction between individual moral norms and the immediate social environment. When drivers perceive that unethical behaviors such as queue-jumping are common or socially tolerated (i.e., when negative descriptive norms prevail), they are more likely to rationalize and adopt such behaviors themselves, particularly if enforcement is lax [207, 208]. However, drivers with strong internalized moral standards, i.e., those who would feel guilt or view such actions as uncivilized, are less likely to succumb to these pressures, highlighting the moderating role of personal ethics and "good-heartedness" in the face of adverse situational cues [207].

Thus, while situational and environmental factors can create conditions that foster unethical or aggressive driving, the propensity to engage in such behaviors is significantly moderated by individual differences in personality and moral disposition. Drivers with a fundamentally prosocial orientation are more resilient to situational pressures and less likely to violate traffic norms, even when external stressors are present. Conversely, those with traits associated with impatience, competitiveness, or low empathy are more vulnerable

to the influence of adverse situational factors, increasing the risk of
unethical driving conduct [193, 206–209].

3.1.7   Type A and Type B Personality Types in Driving Behavior

The theory of Type A and Type B personality types originated in
the 1950s and 1960s from the work of cardiologists Meyer Friedman
and Ray Rosenman, who observed that certain behavioral patterns
were associated with an increased risk of coronary heart disease. They
identified two contrasting personality profiles: Type A and Type B.
Type A individuals are characterized by competitiveness, impatience,
a pronounced sense of time urgency, and a tendency toward hostility
and aggression. In contrast, Type B individuals are described as more
relaxed, patient, non-competitive, and less driven by time pressure or
external stressors [209].

In the context of driving, these personality types have been shown
to influence both attitudes and behaviors on the road. Type A drivers
are more likely to experience frustration in congested traffic, become
impatient during delays, and exhibit aggressive or risky driving behaviors such as queue-jumping, abrupt lane changes, and violations
of traffic rules. Empirical studies and evolutionary game-theoretic
models demonstrate that Type A drivers are more likely to prioritize
personal gain (such as reduced travel time) over collective road safety,
especially in competitive or high-pressure environments [209]. These
drivers tend to focus on the immediate benefits of actions like queue-
jumping, often underestimating or discounting the potential risks to
themselves and others.

Conversely, Type B drivers are generally more patient and risk-
averse. They are less likely to engage in aggressive maneuvers or
violate traffic norms, even when faced with situational stressors such
as congestion or time pressure. Type B individuals tend to weigh the
potential risks of their actions more heavily and are more likely to
adhere to orderly and prosocial driving behaviors, such as waiting
their turn in traffic queues and yielding to others when appropri-

ate [209]. This cautious approach is consistent with their broader personality profile, which emphasizes calmness, cooperation, and a lower propensity for anger or hostility.

The distinction between Type A and Type B personalities is not absolute; rather, individuals may exhibit traits from both categories to varying degrees. Some research also recognizes intermediate or mixed types, though these are less commonly studied in the context of driving behavior [209]. Additionally, the influence of personality type on driving is shaped by the interaction with situational factors, such that even Type B drivers may occasionally engage in risky behaviors under extreme circumstances, while some Type A individuals may moderate their actions in the presence of strong social or legal deterrents.

Importantly, the relationship between personality type and driving behavior is supported by a substantial body of research. Studies consistently find that Type A drivers have higher rates of traffic violations, accidents, and aggressive incidents compared to their Type B counterparts [209]. These findings align with broader psychological literature, which links Type A traits to increased stress, impatience, and a lower threshold for frustration, all of which can manifest as unsafe driving practices.

3.1.8   Cross-Cultural Considerations

Cross-cultural research consistently demonstrates that, while psychological and demographic predictors of unethical driving behaviors such as queue-jumping are broadly universal, the prevalence, expression, and social acceptability of these behaviors are strongly shaped by cultural norms, enforcement practices, and the broader traffic safety climate [203, 204, 210–212].

Large-scale comparative studies reveal that countries differ markedly in their tolerance for traffic violations, aggressive driving, and acceptance of road safety regulations. For example, in some societies, minor violations and aggressive maneuvers are more socially tolerated, which can increase the frequency of behaviors like queue-jumping and speeding. In contrast, cultures with stricter social norms and lower tolerance for such behaviors tend to report lower rates of violations and traffic crashes [210–212]. The perceived likelihood of social or legal sanction (shaped by both formal enforcement and informal community expectations) plays a critical moderating role in these cross-cultural differences [204, 210].

Empirical evidence from multi-country surveys indicates that drivers' attitudes toward violations and dangerous driving are closely linked to the prevailing traffic safety culture, which encompasses shared values, beliefs, and norms about acceptable behavior on the road [210, 212]. For instance, a recent international study found that speeding was more commonly tolerated in North America and Europe, while mobile phone use while driving was most prevalent in Africa, often due to underestimation of risk and strong social expectations to remain connected [210]. Similarly, drinking and driving behaviors were more frequently reported in Asia/Oceania and Africa, with regional differences attributed to variations in legislation and enforcement, such as the likelihood of police checkpoints [210].

Cross-cultural differences are also evident in risk perception and willingness to take risks in traffic. For example, drivers in Sub-Saharan Africa reported higher risk perceptions and sensitivity, but also a greater willingness to take risks, compared to drivers in Norway, Russia, and India [211]. Notably, respondents from Sub-Saharan Africa and India expressed safer attitudes toward speaking out against unsafe driving and greater support for traffic rules and sanctions, yet actual behaviors did not always align with these attitudes, highlighting the complex interplay between cultural values, enforcement, and individual conduct [211].

The role of governance quality and economic development further moderates these cultural effects. Recent research shows that high-quality governance (characterized by effective legislation, consistent enforcement, and low corruption) can reduce the influence of cultural norms that might otherwise promote violations, especially in high- and middle-income countries [204]. For example, the Power Distance dimension (the extent to which inequality and authority are accepted) is associated with higher rates of non-speeding violations in high-income countries with weaker governance, but this effect is diminished where governance is strong and enforcement is consistent [204]. Similarly, cultural values such as embeddedness (emphasis on group cohesion and social status) are linked to increased speeding in countries with high GDP but low governance quality, suggesting that cultural tendencies toward rule-breaking are most pronounced when institutional controls are weak [204].

Comparative studies using the Driver Behaviour Questionnaire (DBQ) have found that the structure of aberrant driving behaviors (such as aggressive violations, ordinary violations, and errors) is generally stable across cultures, but the frequency and social meaning of these behaviors vary significantly [203, 212]. For example, aggressive violations are more prevalent in Southern European and Middle Eastern countries, while ordinary violations (such as speeding) are more common in Western and Northern Europe. These differences are partly attributed to variations in enforcement, infrastructure, and the informal rules that govern everyday driving [212].

Importantly, cross-cultural research also highlights the protective role of positive driving behaviors and prosocial attitudes. Studies show that positive driving (such as yielding, courteous behavior, and adherence to rules) is more common in cultures with strong traffic safety norms and effective enforcement, and is associated with lower accident rates [203, 210]. Conversely, environments that tolerate minor infractions or lack consistent enforcement may inadvertently normalize more serious violations over time.

Hence, while individual psychological traits and demographic factors are important predictors of unethical driving, their expression is profoundly shaped by the cultural, institutional, and normative context. Effective road safety interventions must therefore be culturally sensitive, combining education, enforcement, and community engagement to shift social norms and reduce tolerance for risky or aggressive driving. Strengthening governance quality and ensuring consistent enforcement are particularly critical in translating cultural values into safer driving behaviors across diverse societies [204, 210, 212].

3.1.9   Demographic Factors

Empirical research demonstrates that demographic factors (including gender, age, and socioeconomic status) are associated with patterns in traffic violations and risky driving behaviors. For example, studies consistently find that male drivers are more likely than female drivers to commit certain types of traffic violations, a trend observed across various cultural contexts [213]. Age also plays a significant role, with younger drivers generally exhibiting a greater propensity for risky driving and higher accident rates [213]. This is reflected in global statistics, where road traffic injuries are the leading cause of death for children and young adults aged 5–29 years [214]. These trends may be partially explained by differences in attitudes toward risk and perceptions of danger, as research suggests that young male drivers are more likely to underestimate the risks associated with unsafe driving [215].

Socioeconomic status (SES) is another factor that can influence driving behaviors. However, it is important to recognize that higher rates of traffic violations among drivers from lower socioeconomic backgrounds often reflect broader structural challenges. Lower-income areas experience an increased incidence of traffic crashes, injuries, and deaths compared to more affluent ones, a pattern attributed to factors such as reduced access to comprehensive driver education, increased daily stressors, and greater exposure to high-risk traffic environments [216, 217]. Additionally, populations with lower SES are particularly vulnerable to environmental stressors like air pollution and hazardous road conditions, which can compound the risk of traffic-related injuries and fatalities [214, 217].

Socioeconomic and demographic factors may impact not only the likelihood of engaging in risky driving but also the outcomes following traffic incidents, such as access to medical care and recovery resources [216]. For example, lower-income and minority populations are disproportionately affected by traffic crashes, with research showing that Black and Hispanic Americans experience higher motor vehicle-related death rates than White or Asian Americans, even after accounting for miles traveled [217, 218]. This increased risk is frequently linked to external factors, including neighborhood infrastructure, environmental exposure, and limited access to resources that support safe mobility [216, 217].

Rather than reflecting inherent differences between groups, these patterns underscore the influence of broader social and environmental contexts on driving behavior. For instance, lower-income neighborhoods often have poorer infrastructure, fewer safety features, and less enforcement, leading to higher crash rates and worse outcomes for residents [217]. Furthermore, certain demographics, such as pedestrians and cyclists in under-resourced areas, face disproportionately higher risks, highlighting the need for age- and context-appropriate policy and design strategies [214, 216].

Hence, socioeconomic status and other demographic factors interact with individual characteristics and external circumstances, shaping patterns in traffic infractions and outcomes [213, 217]. These disparities are well-documented in both peer-reviewed research and official government statistics, and they persist across different regions and demographic groups [214, 218].

3.2 So, Does "Being Good" Make You a Better Driver?

The extensive research reviewed in the preceding sections reveals a clear and compelling relationship between prosocial characteristics (what we might simply call having a "good heart") and safe, ethical driving behavior. The evidence consistently demonstrates that drivers with fundamentally prosocial dispositions are significantly less likely to engage in risky, aggressive, or unethical driving practices.

The overarching message from this research synthesis is that prosocial individuals, i.e., those characterized by empathy, patience, conscientiousness, and genuine concern for others' wellbeing, consistently demonstrate safer and more ethical driving behavior across diverse situations and cultures. This detailed relationship is illustrated in Figure 3.3, which provides a visual framework showing how prosocial factors, antisocial factors, and contextual factors all interact to influence driving behavior.

Figure 3.3: Framework illustrating the relationship between having a 'good heart' and driving behavior. The central concept branches into three key domains with multiple contributing factors: 'Prosocial Factors' that promote safe and ethical driving, including high agreeableness as the strongest protective factor; 'Antisocial Factors' that increase risky and unethical driving behaviors, with high neuroticism as a major risk factor; and 'Contextual Factors' that moderate these relationships through demographic, environmental, and situational influences.

As summarized in Table 3.1, prosocial drivers exhibit several key characteristics that translate directly into better road behavior. Most notably, high agreeableness emerges as the strongest protective factor, with empathetic and cooperative individuals showing remarkable patience and consideration for other road users. These drivers are naturally inclined to avoid road rage incidents and engage in prosocial driving behaviors such as yielding and courteous merging. Additionally, drivers with high conscientiousness demonstrate strong self-discipline and rule-following tendencies, while those with high openness show cognitive flexibility that helps them adapt to new traffic rules and novel driving situations.

Table 3.1: Prosocial factors that contribute to good driving attitudes and behaviors

Feature / Factor	Notes / Mechanism
Learning from mistakes	Good-hearted drivers learn from errors, become more vigilant.
High Agreeableness	Empathy, patience, cooperativeness; strongest protective factor.
High Conscientiousness	Self-discipline, rule-following; protective, but evidence is mixed.
High Openness	Cognitive flexibility, adapts to new rules; modest protection.
High Behavioral Inhibition System (BIS)	Cautious, risk-averse, law-abiding.
Positive attitudes toward traffic safety	Associated with fewer violations and safer driving.
Perceived social norms (pro-safety)	Strong norms against violations reduce risky behaviors.
Risk perception (high/accurate)	Underestimating risk increases violations; accurate risk perception is protective.
Executive function/self-regulation	Poor impulse control increases errors and risky actions.
Type B personality (patient, relaxed)	More likely to wait, yield, and avoid aggressive maneuvers.
Cultural norms (strict enforcement)	Societies with strict norms/enforcement see fewer violations.
Governance quality (high)	Strong governance/enforcement reduces violations, even in cultures with high risk tolerance.
Exposure to prosocial driving	Encourages courteous, rule-abiding behavior.

In stark contrast, Table 3.2 illustrates how antisocial traits create a pathway toward dangerous and unethical driving. The research reveals a troubling "slippery slope" phenomenon where minor violations can escalate into more serious infractions if left unchecked. Drivers prone to moral rationalization and disengagement find it increasingly easy to justify bad behavior, while traits like high neuroticism, impulsivity, and sensation-seeking create a robust risk profile for persistent dangerous driving.

Similarly, Table 3.3 demonstrates that the expression of prosocial or antisocial driving tendencies is moderated by various contextual factors. While some demographic and socioeconomic factors show associations with driving behavior, these relationships often reflect structural and environmental influences rather than inherent personal dispositions.

Table 3.2: Antisocial factors that contribute to bad driving behaviors

Feature / Factor	Notes / Mechanism
Slippery slope of unethical acts	Minor violations escalate to more serious ones if unchecked.
Moral rationalization	Justifying bad acts reduces guilt, increases repeat offenses.
Moral disengagement	Detachment from moral standards, desensitization to consequences.
Self-control depletion (ego depletion)	Less willpower after exertion increases risk of further unethical acts.
High Neuroticism	Emotional instability, anger, impulsivity; robust risk factor.
Trait Anger	Increases risk of aggressive driving, impairs hazard perception.
Impulsivity / Sensation-seeking	Predicts persistent risky driving, especially in youth.
Aggression–Hostility (Zuckerman)	Linked to road rage, confrontational driving.
High Behavioral Activation System (BAS)	Reward-seeking, impulsive, rule-breaking.
Negative/lax attitudes toward safety	Predicts more violations, errors, and lapses.
Overconfidence in driving skill	Can lead to risk-taking and rule violations.
Perceived social norms (pro-violation)	If violations are seen as common/tolerated, more likely to occur.
Type A personality (impatient, competitive)	More likely to violate rules, aggressive under stress.
Cultural norms (tolerant of violations)	Societies with lenient norms see more violations.
Governance quality (low)	Weak governance allows cultural risk tolerance to translate into more violations.
Exposure to aggressive driving	Normalizes violations, increases likelihood of imitation.

Together, these findings underscore that safe and ethical driving is not merely a matter of knowledge or technical skill, but is deeply rooted in the underlying moral and psychological makeup of the driver. Prosocial characteristics (such as empathy, patience, and a willingness to consider the wellbeing of others) serve as powerful safeguards against risky or aggressive behaviors on the road. Conversely, antisocial traits and adverse contextual factors can create a fertile ground for dangerous driving, especially when left unaddressed by social norms or enforcement. Ultimately, promoting a culture of "good-hearted" driving requires not only fostering positive individual dispositions, but also shaping supportive environments and community standards that reinforce prosocial conduct and discourage ethical lapses behind

the wheel. By integrating psychological insights with practical interventions and policy, it is possible to create safer roads and healthier
driving cultures for all.

Table 3.3: Contextual factors with variable or mixed effects on driving behaviors

Feature / Factor	Notes / Mechanism
Socioeconomic status (low SES)	Negative effect: Linked to higher violations due to structural/environmental factors, not inherent disposition.
Situational stressors (congestion, time pressure)	Negative effect: Increase likelihood of violations, especially for those with antisocial traits.
Environmental stressors (noise, poor roads)	Negative effect: Elevate risk of aggressive driving, especially in high-density areas.
Demographics: Young age	Negative effect: Young drivers more likely to take risks, underestimate danger.
Demographics: Male gender	Negative effect: Males more likely to commit certain violations.
Demographics: Minority/low-income status	Negative effect: Higher crash rates due to environmental/infrastructural factors.
Moral licensing	Mixed effect: Good deeds can paradoxically justify later bad acts.
High Extraversion	Unclear effect: Mixed findings; not a reliable predictor.

Chapter 4

Goodness in Religion

The matter of whether a devout spirit is also a feeling one has been the subject of much scholarly examination, with the results, it must be confessed, proving quite inconsistent. Certain studies suggest a clear and positive connection, that religiousness and empathy walk hand in hand. Yet others find them to be strangers, or even, under certain unfortunate circumstances, adversaries. Here, we shall review these recent accounts, first turning our attention to those which report a benevolent union, and then to those which find no such thing.

4.1 Studies Reporting Positive Associations

Indeed, a good many accounts lend weight to the idea that a religious life is connected to a deeper capacity for empathy. This is not so much the intellectual act of understanding another's predicament, but what is called emotional or affective empathy, which is to say, the simple, unbidden feeling of another's sorrow or joy in one's own breast.

4.1.1   Personality Structure and Empathy

Let us consider the work of Łowicki and Zajenkowski, who in 2017 presented an inquiry involving some 661 Polish adults, mostly young women, who responded to questions online [219]. These scholars sought to measure not only general religiousness and empathy, but also to make finer distinctions. They sought to distinguish between two sorts of piety, the intrinsic, which is a faith held for its own sake, as a private and central meaning to one's life, and the extrinsic, which is a faith used for other ends, for community, for comfort, or for social standing. They also measured what modern psychology, with a certain flair for the dramatic, calls the Dark Triad of personality. These are three rather lamentable traits: psychopathy, which is a chilling lack of feeling for others; Machiavellianism, a tendency toward manipulation and cunning; and narcissism, a grand and often fragile preoccupation with oneself.

What they discovered was that both empathy and a general sense of religiousness were quite at odds with the coldness of psychopathy and the cunning of Machiavellianism. It was as if empathy itself formed a bridge, for it helped to explain why those who lacked these dark qualities were more likely to possess religious beliefs. And a very telling detail emerged. That faith held for its own sake, the intrinsic kind, was contrary to both psychopathy and Machiavellianism, while the faith used for social ends, the extrinsic, was found to keep company with narcissism. The authors put forward a rather profound idea, that a capacity for empathy, and what they term mentalization, which is the very human talent for imagining the minds of others, is fundamental to faith itself. For how, they ask, can one believe in a God, in a supernatural agent, without first being able to conceive of a mind, a consciousness, separate from one's own? These discoveries, they propose, suggest that empathy may be the very psychological soil from which a religious disposition and a more balanced personality can grow [219].

Key Point: Empathy, especially when combined with intrinsic religiousness, is linked to lower levels of manipulative and callous personality traits, suggesting that a feeling heart and genuine faith often go hand in hand.

4.1.2   Self- and Other-Reports of Empathy

One might, with a certain worldly cynicism, wonder if a religious person merely reports themself to be more empathetic out of a desire to appear virtuous. The same scholars, Lowicki and Zajenkowski, addressed this very doubt in a later study [220]. They did not simply take the word of 236 adults. No, they also sought the opinions of those who knew them best, their partners, friends, or parents, asking these acquaintances for their honest assessment. They measured that emotional empathy, the kind felt in the heart, and asked a simple question about the subject's religiousness.

The findings were quite clear. The more religious individuals not only saw themselves as having higher emotional empathy, but they were also seen as more empathetic by their close relations. It was a perception shared by both the self and the other. And this connection was specific. It was tied to that emotional empathy we spoke of, to the feelings of compassion and sympathy for another, and not to cognitive empathy, which is the more detached ability to understand another's point of view. It seems, then, that religiousness is bound up with the heart's capacity for compassion, more so than the mind's capacity for analysis. The authors concluded from this that the link between religious feeling and empathy is no mere self delusion, no trick of social presentation, but a genuine phenomenon, visible to all who look closely [220].

Key Point: Religious people are seen as more emotionally empathetic not only by themselves but also by those close to them, indicating that the link between faith and compassion is genuine and observable.

4.1.3   Neural Correlates and Mechanisms

A most curious and, one must say, poignant piece of evidence comes
from the work of Cristofori and colleagues, who looked into the very
seat of these feelings, the brain itself [221]. Their study was with
a group of veterans who had returned from the war in Vietnam,
individuals who had suffered what are called penetrating traumatic
brain injuries, terrible wounds to the head, and they were compared
to healthy people of a similar background. The scholars had these
participants complete inventories about their feelings of empathy and
about their inner relationship with God.

They paid special attention to a region of the brain known as the
ventromedial prefrontal cortex, or vmPFC, an area understood to
be involved in the complex tapestry of social emotion and decision
making. And here they found something quite unexpected. The
patients whose injuries were located in this very region, the vmPFC,
reported a stronger sense of belonging with God, a more intimate
internalized relationship with the divine. A wound to the brain, it
seemed, could somehow intensify a person's feeling of closeness to the
divine. What is more, this feeling of closeness to God was tied to their
scores on the measure of empathic concern, that same compassionate
empathy. Through a careful statistical analysis, the scholars showed
that religious cognition, this inner image of God, acted as a mediator.
That is to say, the brain lesion seemed to affect empathy through
the mechanism of religious belief, as if the beliefs themselves were
amplifying the empathic response. From this, the authors propose
that our mental picture of God, this internal representation, might
serve to magnify our natural human capacity for empathy. It is a
striking thought, that religious ideas, born of the mind, could in turn
nurture one of our most vital social feelings, a feeling which serves
as a great engine for cooperation among people who would otherwise
remain strangers [221].

> **Key Point:** A close relationship with God, shaped by
> brain processes, can enhance a person's capacity for com-
> passion, showing that religious belief may amplify empathy

at a neural level.

4.1.4   Empathy and Religiosity in a Non-Western Society

A great deal of our knowledge on this matter, it must be said, has been gathered from the Western world, from countries steeped in a particular religious history. But one must ask, does the human heart behave in the same way in other corners of the globe? A recent inquiry from Japan offers a glimpse of an answer [222]. Japan is a land where formal piety is said to be on the wane, where few, when asked directly, will profess to be religious in the way a European might understand the term. And yet, many of its people continue to hold a quiet belief in supernatural forces, in spirits or gods, even without the structure of an organized church. This peculiar spiritual climate allowed certain scholars to explore whether empathy, which is the soul's capacity to feel for and to comprehend another, is connected to such beliefs outside the familiar confines of the West.

To this end, the investigators posed their questions to more than 1,800 Japanese souls, some university students, others adults from across the nation, in two large studies. They inquired about their belief in what are called supernatural agents, a rather clinical term for the gods, spirits, and unseen forces that one might feel preside over human affairs. And they measured empathy in its two aspects, one being that tender feeling of concern and compassion for another's plight, and the other being the more intellectual exercise of guessing what another might be thinking or feeling. The results were quite telling. Those who reported a greater measure of empathic concern, that is, those whose hearts were more readily moved to compassion and sympathy, were also more likely to believe in these supernatural powers. This connection held firm even though the majority of these people would not call themselves religious. It was present in the young and in the old, suggesting it is some fundamental feature of the Japanese character, not merely a quirk of a particular generation.

It is a curious thing to note that the simple ability to understand another's thoughts, a skill sometimes called "mentalizing," was not so strongly tied to religious belief as was the simple feeling of concern. In other words, it was the warmth of the heart, you see, not the cold calculation of the mind, that was most closely bound to this sense of the spiritual.

These findings from Japan suggest that the bond between a feeling heart and a believing spirit is no mere Western peculiarity. Even in a society where one does not often see public displays of faith, those who are more compassionate seem more open to the possibility of a world beyond what the eye can see. The connection was, to be sure, a modest one. It tells us that while empathy plays its part, other things, such as the way one is taught to think or the stories one learns from one's culture, are also of great importance.

Such insights from the East are echoed in other lands. Consider the work of Abu Al Ghanam, who in 2024 conducted what is known as a cross sectional study, a kind of snapshot in time, among 380 young Muslim university students in Jordan [223]. He used carefully prepared scales to measure their religiosity, their empathy, their tendency toward prosocial behavior, which is to say, their inclination to act for the good of others, and the quality of their friendships. He then employed a rather intricate statistical method, structural equation modeling, by which one can trace the various threads of influence, both direct and indirect, much like mapping the currents in a complex river. His analysis showed that both religious devotion and empathy had a significant and direct effect on good deeds. They also improved the quality of the students' friendships, which in turn led to even more prosocial acts. Every indirect path he examined, for instance, the path from religiosity to good friendships and then onward to good deeds (religiosity → peer relationships → prosocial behavior), proved to be significant. The scholar concluded that religion provides these young people with a clear moral compass and encourages virtuous values, while empathy helps them to manage their own feelings and to form the warm attachments to others that are the very soil of a good and helpful life [223].

Key Point: Even outside the West, people with greater

empathic concern are more likely to believe in supernatural agents, suggesting that the empathy–religion link is a cross-cultural phenomenon, though modest in strength.

4.1.5   Computational and Theoretical Models

We turn now from the study of living, breathing people to a rather different sort of inquiry, one conducted not in the field or the laboratory, but within the silent, logical confines of a machine. These are computational studies, in which scholars build mathematical models to simulate the hidden psychological processes that might connect piety and empathy. Van Ments, Roelofsma, and Treur, for example, constructed in 2018 what they call an adaptive temporal causal network model, a kind of mechanical theatre of the mind, to simulate how religion might influence a person's capacity for empathy or, indeed, for its opposite, disempathy [224]. This model is a complex affair, weaving together what is known from the study of the brain, from theories about our earliest attachments to our parents, and from the study of religion itself. It represents mental states as interconnected points, and it learns, it adapts over time, just as a person might.

The simulations run on this machine produced a fascinating drama. They showed that a person who holds an empathic God image, who conceives of God as loving, is far more likely to behave with empathy. On the other hand, a person with a disempathic or authoritarian God image, who imagines God as a great and punitive judge, is more likely to show a lack of empathy, or even hostility, particularly toward those they consider outsiders. The model can even simulate a state of mind like religious fundamentalism, showing how an anxious attachment to a severe image of God can curdle into hostility. It provides a formal, logical framework for a very old idea, that the way we imagine our God, whether as a figure of love or of wrath, can either open our hearts or close them [224].

Key Point: How a person imagines God (i.e., loving or punitive) can shape whether their faith fosters empathy or hostility, highlighting the power of religious imagery in guiding social feelings.

4.2   Studies Reporting Negative Associations

And yet, as is so often the case in the affairs of people, the story is not
so simple. Other scholars have found that the relationship between a
religious soul and a feeling heart is more complicated, depending on
the sort of piety, the kind of empathy, or toward whom that empathy
is directed.

4.2.1   Conditional Effects

Duriez, in 2004, looked at 375 young psychology students in Flanders
[225]. He used a clever instrument called the Post Critical Belief
Scale, which does not simply ask if one is religious, but how one is
religious. It distinguishes between the simple fact of belief, what he
calls Exclusion versus Inclusion of Transcendence, and the manner in
which one holds that belief, which he calls Literal versus Symbolic.
It is the difference, you see, between one who reads a sacred text
as a book of plain facts and one who reads it as a book of poetry,
of metaphor, of deeper meaning. Empathy was measured, and the
desire to appear socially virtuous was accounted for. The results
were striking. Empathy had no connection to whether a person was
religious or not. It was, however, positively related to the way they
held their beliefs. Those who approached their faith in a symbolic,
open, and metaphorical way were more empathetic. It was not belief
itself, but the quality of that belief, its flexibility and poetry, that
seemed to nurture the empathetic soul [225].

> **Key Point:** It's not religious belief itself, but how flexibly
> and symbolically it's held, that predicts greater empathy;
> rigid, literal faith shows no such benefit.

4.2.2   Motivational Basis of Prosociality

Saslow and his colleagues, in 2013, asked a slightly different question: what is it that moves a person to a generous act? They suspected that compassion might be the prime mover for some, but not for all [226]. In a large survey of over 1,300 Americans, they found that compassion was a very strong predictor of generosity, but only among the less religious. Then, they brought 101 people into their laboratory and performed what is called a compassion induction, which is to say, they showed them a moving video of children suffering in poverty. This appeal to the heart increased generosity among the less religious individuals, but had no such effect on the more religious. In a third study, they had over 200 people play peculiar sorts of games, played for money, designed to measure a person's trust and generosity toward a stranger. Again, for the less religious, a feeling of compassion directly led to greater generosity. For the more religious, it did not. The authors concluded that the goodness of less religious people seems to spring directly from the well of compassion. For the more devout, it seems generosity flows from a different spring, perhaps from a sense of duty, from the teachings of their doctrine, or even from a concern for their standing in the community [226].

> **Key Point:** For less religious people, compassion directly drives generosity, while for the more religious, good deeds may stem from duty or doctrine rather than heartfelt empathy.

4.2.3   Empathy Toward Outgroups

Finally, we come to a sad and important qualification. Both Duriez and the creators of that computational model, van Ments and his colleagues, observe that religion may nurture empathy chiefly for one's own people, for the in group, but not for the out group, for the stranger, the outsider [224, 225]. The model of van Ments simulates with a chilling logic how an authoritarian or punitive image of God, or a fundamentalist turn of mind, can lead to a distinct lack of empathy for those outside the circle of faith. Religious texts themselves, it is noted, often draw a sharp line between one's community member and the foreigner. It seems that this great force of religion, depending on the form it takes in a human heart, can either expand that heart to embrace all of mankind, or build walls around it, leaving it warm for those inside, but cold to the world without [224, 225].

> **Key Point:** Religiosity often boosts empathy for one's own group but can reduce concern for outsiders, meaning faith may sometimes limit universal compassion.

4.2.4   Null Findings for Specific Empathy Domains

And yet, the picture remains clouded. Other inquiries find no such clear connection, or even, in certain corners, a troubling inverse. Consider the work of Wilson and Clements, who in 2017 looked into the matter of empathy for the victims of crime, surveying some 84 university students [227]. They used one scale to measure not just religious belief, but the translation of that belief into action, and another to gauge the students' feelings for those who had suffered a crime. The investigators found no clear thread connecting a person's general religious involvement with their capacity for empathy toward a victim.

But here a curious, even contradictory, picture emerged when they looked more closely. Certain religious practices seemed to have a negative effect on what we have called cognitive empathy, that is, the clear headed understanding of a situation. For instance, those who gave more of their time to volunteering in religious settings were indeed less likely to blame a victim for their misfortune, which is a good thing, to be sure. And yet, these same people were found to have less knowledge of the simple facts surrounding victims and their plight. It is a strange thing to consider. It suggests that certain religious activities, while perhaps softening the heart, may at the same time cloud the mind's understanding. Even more perplexing, those who gave a greater portion of their income to religious causes were found to hold perpetrators less accountable for their actions. The authors note, with a certain scholarly reserve, that these findings may point to a lower cognitive empathy among the more religious participants, for a clear awareness of facts is a necessary prelude to such understanding [227].

Key Point: Some studies find no clear link between religiosity and empathy, and certain religious practices may even reduce understanding of others' suffering, especially in cognitive domains.

4.2.5 Types of Empathy and Their Relationship to Religiosity

Before we proceed, it is necessary to pause, for this word, empathy, is not so simple as it seems. It is not a single instrument, but a whole orchestra of feeling and thought within the human soul, with each part playing its own distinct role. Many of the studies we have examined take care to distinguish between these parts, namely, emotional empathy, cognitive empathy, and that sad, self regarding feeling of personal distress. Let us take a moment to understand them, as a doctor must understand the different organs of the body.

Emotional (Affective) Empathy refers to the empathy of the heart. It is the capacity to feel a resonance with another's emotional state, to share in their feeling. It manifests as compassion, as sympathy, as a simple, unbidden concern for another. This feeling is directed outward, a feeling for another in their time of need. Across the many studies we have considered, it is this component, this emotional empathy, that is most reliably found in the company of a religious disposition. We have seen how Lowicki and Zajenkowski found that religious people were seen, both by themselves and by their friends, as possessing more of this empathic concern [220]. We have seen it in Japan, where a compassionate heart was more likely to believe in spirits, even without a formal church. It seems that a religious life, especially one lived from an inner conviction, may both nurture and be nurtured by this capacity for feeling with another.

Cognitive Empathy, on the other hand, is a different faculty altogether, the empathy of the mind. It is the capacity to understand another's thoughts, to see from their perspective, to grasp their intentions. This process is sometimes called mentalizing, or perspective taking. It is a more intellectual act, less driven by the passions. It is to know what another feels, which is quite different from feeling it oneself. The connection of this cognitive empathy to a religious life is far less certain. The study from Japan, you will recall, found only a weak link here. Other studies suggest a connection may exist only under specific conditions, as when a person approaches their faith not as a book of rules to be taken literally, but as a collection of symbols and stories to be interpreted with an open mind [225]. And so, this empathy of the mind shows no steady or universal friendship with religiosity.

Outgroup Empathy brings us to a sad and difficult matter, that of empathy for the stranger, for the one who is not of our own kind. It is sometimes called universal concern. It is the capacity to extend one's feeling and concern to those outside one's own religious, ethnic, or social circle. While the empathy of the heart may burn brightly for one's own, outgroup empathy asks it to shine on all, on those who are different or far away. And here, it must be said, several studies have found a negative association. A higher degree of religiosity is sometimes linked to a lower level of empathy for these outsiders. This lamentable pattern may arise because a strong religious identity can foster a favoritism for one's own group, which can, without any evil intent, diminish one's concern for those outside it. Research has shown that highly religious people may prioritize the needs of their own community, sometimes at the expense of a more universal compassion.

Personal Distress is not truly empathy at all, but its pale, self regarding cousin. It is a reaction to another's suffering that is focused only on the self. It is to see another's pain and to feel not for them, but to feel only one's own anxiety, one's own unease and sense of being overwhelmed. It is a feeling that centers on one's own discomfort and often leads not to helping, but to turning away. The studies we have reviewed here generally find no consistent link, either positive or negative, between a religious life and this feeling of personal distress. Duriez, for example, reported that religiosity was not related to it, in contrast to the other forms of empathy [225]. This suggests that a life of faith does not necessarily make a person more prone to this particular kind of self absorption when faced with the suffering of their fellow human being.

Table 4.1: Types of empathy and their relationship to religiosity.

Type	Association	Mechanism
Emotional / Affective Empathy	Strong positive association	The empathy of the heart, a feeling of compassion and sympathy for others, is found to be most consistently tied to a religious life. This is seen in what people say of themselves and what others say of them, in lands both East and West, and is strongest when faith is held for its own sake.
Cognitive Empathy	Weak / conditional association	The empathy of the mind, the understanding of another's thoughts, shows an inconsistent relationship with a religious life. A connection may appear only when religious ideas are treated not as literal fact but as symbol and metaphor. The bond is far less robust than with emotional empathy.
Outgroup Empathy	Negative association	Empathy for the stranger, for those outside one's own religious or social circle, is sometimes found to be weaker among more religious people. This may be an unfortunate consequence of loyalty to one's own group, which can unintentionally diminish a more universal concern for all.
Personal Distress	No consistent association	This self focused discomfort in the face of another's suffering shows little relation to religious belief. It is a feeling of anxiety and being overwhelmed, rather than outward concern, and a life of faith seems neither to increase nor decrease it.

Thus, modern science tells us that the type of empathy is of the utmost importance when we consider its relation to a life of faith. The empathy of the heart, that is, compassion and concern, is most consistently and positively tied to religiousness. The empathy of the mind shows a more fickle and conditional relationship. Empathy for the outsider, tragically, often shows a negative bond. And that self centered feeling of personal distress appears to have no connection at all. This more nuanced picture helps to clarify the great complexity of how religion and empathy interact to shape our social lives.

The distinctions among these different types of empathy, these different chambers of the heart and mind, and their complicated dance with a life of faith, are summarized in Table 4.1. This table provides a concise overview of each type, the nature of its association with religiosity, and the underlying reasons proposed in these scholarly works. As can be seen, emotional empathy shows the strongest positive bond, while cognitive empathy shows a weaker, more conditional one. Empathy for the outsider is often negatively associated, and personal distress shows no consistent link at all.

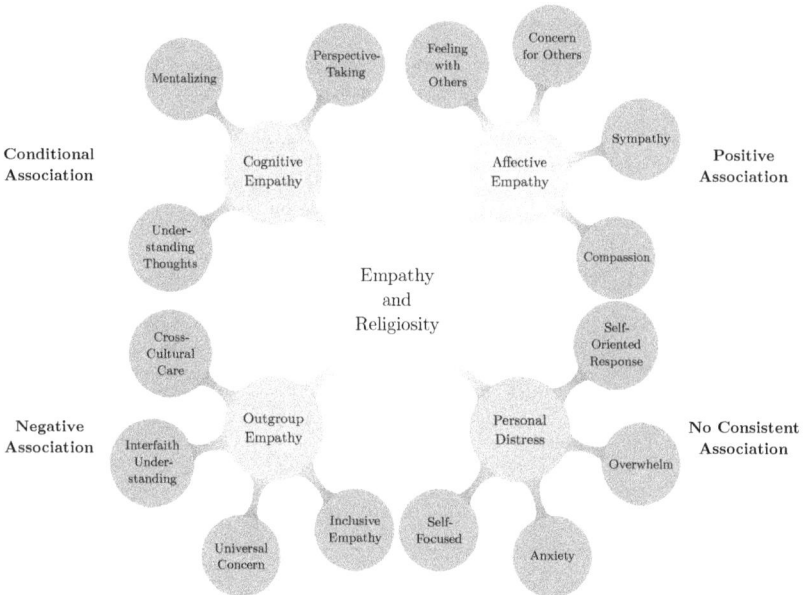

Figure 4.1: A map of the soul, illustrating the tangled relationship between a life of faith and the four types of empathy. The central idea branches out into its four great provinces. Affective Empathy, the empathy of the heart, shows the strongest and most positive bond, born of compassion, sympathy, and concern. Cognitive Empathy, the empathy of the mind, shows but a weak or conditional attachment, involving the intellectual act of perspective taking. Outgroup Compassion, or care for the stranger, often shows a sad, negative attachment. And finally, Personal Distress, that self focused and anxious response, shows no consistent bond at all, for it is a feeling for oneself, not for another.

To help our minds grasp this tangled business, let us look at the drawing presented in Figure 4.1. It is a kind of map, if you will, a conceptual framework, which lays out these four provinces of empathy in their relation to a life of faith. The figure arranges these domains of the soul visually, and highlights the direction and the strength of their supposed attachments to religious belief. Together, the earlier Table 4.1 and this Figure 4.1 provide a summary of what the scholars have so far discovered, clarifying, one hopes, the distinct ways in which these different facets of the human heart interact with a life of piety.

> **Key Point:** Emotional empathy is most strongly tied to religiousness, cognitive empathy shows a weaker link, out-group empathy can be negatively associated, and personal distress is unrelated; highlighting the complexity of the faith–empathy connection.

4.3   And So, Does a Good Heart Make for a Pious Soul?

The relationship between a devout life and a feeling heart, we must confess, is a thing of many sides and cannot be answered with a simple yes or no. On the one hand, a great chorus of scholarly voices, drawing evidence from what people say of themselves and what others say of them, from lands near and far, and even from peering into the very workings of the brain, tells us that a religious life, particularly when that faith is a private and central matter of the heart, is found in the company of a deeper emotional empathy. Religious people, it seems, often possess, and are seen by others to possess, a greater measure of compassion and concern for those in need. This pattern appears in different cultures and is even supported by those mechanical models which suggest that a benevolent idea of God can indeed foster a tender heart and good deeds.

And yet, this benevolent union is not found everywhere or for everyone. The bond depends entirely on the kind of empathy one speaks of, on the way a person holds their beliefs, and on the social situation in which they find themself. The empathy of the mind, for instance, that intellectual capacity to understand another's view, shows a much weaker and more conditional friendship with a religious life, appearing only when beliefs are held in a symbolic, poetic way, not a literal one. What is more, the very spring from which kindness flows may differ. For those who are less religious, it seems compassion itself is the prime mover of their generosity. For the more devout, good deeds may arise from a different source, from a sense of moral duty, from the word of their doctrine, or from a concern for their good name, rather than from a simple feeling for their fellow human being.

Most crucially, when we turn our gaze to the matter of empathy for the stranger, for those who do not belong to one's own flock, the picture grows darker still. Multiple studies indicate that a greater piety is sometimes tied to a lesser feeling for the outsider. This lamentable pattern likely reflects the human tendency to favor one's own kind, a loyalty to one's circle which can, without malice, build a wall around the heart and reduce a more universal concern. Both the empirical findings and those computational models alike suggest that certain kinds of religious feeling, especially those that draw strict boundaries or imagine a punitive God, may even give rise to a coldness of heart, or worse, toward those on the outside.

And so, to be religious is not, in any straightforward sense, to be more empathetic in all things. For many, a life of faith is indeed tied to a greater tenderness of heart, but this tenderness is often reserved for one's own. Toward the stranger, the religious person may show no more feeling, or even less, than their worldly peer. The matter is best understood as a nuanced and delicate affair. Religion, it seems, can both nurture and limit the empathetic soul, depending entirely on how its beliefs are held, how they are understood, and how they are lived out in the brief and complicated drama of a human life.

> **Key Point:** Religion can nurture compassion, especially for one's own group, but does not guarantee universal empathy; its effects depend on the type of empathy, the nature of belief, and social context.

Chapter 5

Goodness in Politics

The interface between personality and politics has emerged as a central focus in recent leadership science. Political leaders, by virtue of their positions, wield significant influence over the ethical, cultural, and institutional directions of societies. Increasingly, empirical research has sought to elucidate the ways in which dispositional factors (particularly the Big Five personality traits and the so-called Dark Triad) shape not only leadership effectiveness, but also the ideological orientation and style of political leaders. This chapter synthesizes the current state of evidence regarding the association between personality traits and political leadership, with a particular focus on the magnitude of these relationships (as indexed by correlation coefficients, r-values), their differentiation across left- and right-leaning orientations, and their expression in diverse cultural contexts.

5.1 Left vs. Right

Leadership in the political domain is a multifaceted construct shaped by a confluence of personal attributes, ethical norms, and contextual factors. The Big Five model (comprising openness to experience, conscientiousness, extraversion, agreeableness, and neuroticism) remains the predominant framework for investigating individual differences relevant to leadership and political behavior. Recent research has extended this focus to include the Dark Triad traits: Machiavellianism, narcissism, and psychopathy.

Empirical studies employing direct surveys of politicians have revealed that, compared to the general public, elected officials tend to be more extraverted, agreeable, emotionally stable, and conscientious, but slightly lower on openness/intellect [228]. For example, Hanania (2017) administered a 50-item Big Five questionnaire to 278 American state legislators and a large control group from the general public, finding statistically significant differences on all traits except openness among female legislators. These findings suggest that the personality profile of politicians is distinct from that of the broader population, likely reflecting both self-selection and the demands of political office.

Building on this, Dietrich et al. (2012) conducted a comprehensive study of U.S. state legislators using established Big Five inventories, confirming significant variation in personality traits among legislators and highlighting that politicians are not a homogenous group [229]. Their results showed that legislators, on average, scored higher on extraversion and conscientiousness compared to the general public, and that these traits were linked to legislative behavior: higher agreeableness predicted more collaborative approaches, while higher openness was associated with support for innovative policies. This underscores the importance of considering personality in understanding legislative politics, as these traits can influence not only individual behavior but also broader legislative outcomes and institutional dynamics.

5.1.1   Interpreting r-values in the Context of Political Bipolarity

Political ideology is often conceptualized as a bipolar spectrum, with left-leaning (liberal or progressive) and right-leaning (conservative) orientations at opposite ends [230]. In this framework, a negative correlation (r) between a personality trait and right-wing ideology implies a positive association with left-wing ideology, and vice versa. For example, if Openness to Experience is negatively correlated with conservatism, it is positively correlated with liberalism.

The r-value, or Pearson correlation coefficient, quantifies the strength and direction of the linear relationship between two variables. In the context of personality and politics, r-values typically range from -1 (perfect negative association) to +1 (perfect positive association), with 0 indicating no linear relationship. In bipolar political systems, a negative r-value for a trait with conservatism means that individuals higher in that trait are more likely to identify as left-leaning, and a positive r-value means the trait is more common among right-leaning individuals.

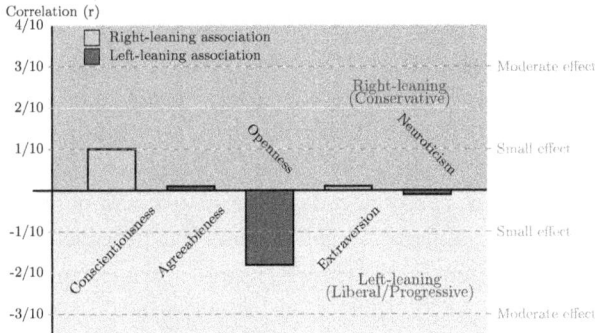

Figure 5.1: Correlation coefficients between Big Five personality traits and political orientation (left–right spectrum) based on Sibley et al. (2012) meta-analysis [232]. All r-values are scored so that negative means more left-leaning (liberal/progressive), positive means more right-leaning (conservative). Among the Big Five, Openness to Experience shows the strongest association with left-leaning ideology (r = −0.18), while Conscientiousness is associated with right-leaning ideology (r = +0.10). Correlations for Agreeableness, Extraversion, and Neuroticism are close to zero, indicating minimal or no reliable association with left–right political orientation.

A substantial body of research supports the assertion that openness to experience is the most salient personality trait distinguishing left-leaning (liberal or progressive) political leaders. Openness encompasses intellectual curiosity, receptivity to new ideas, aesthetic appreciation, and a preference for novelty and complexity. In a cross-national study of 303 elected politicians from Canada and Belgium, Joly et al. (2018) used the Ten-Item Personality Inventory (TIPI) and expert-coded party ideology scores to examine the relationship between personality and partisanship. Their results showed that openness to experience was negatively correlated with right-wing ideology (r = -0.14 in the full sample, r = -0.23 in Canada, r = -0.15 in Flanders), indicating that higher openness is associated with more progressive orientations [231]. Regression analyses controlling for age and gender confirmed that openness was the only Big Five trait to consistently predict left-right ideology among politicians (see Figure 5.1).

These findings are consistent with the congruency model, which posits that individuals gravitate toward political ideologies that align with their dispositional traits. Politicians high in openness are more likely to be found in progressive parties and to advocate for innovation, inclusivity, and social change. The effect size, while modest, is robust across different political systems and measurement approaches.

Meta-analytic evidence further clarifies these relationships. Sibley et al. (2012) synthesized 73 studies (N = 71,895) and found that Openness to Experience was negatively correlated with political conservatism (r = -0.18), while Conscientiousness was positively correlated (r = 0.10) [232]. Importantly, because the political spectrum is bipolar, these r-values can be interpreted as follows: a negative r for openness means that higher openness predicts more left-leaning (liberal) views, and a positive r for conscientiousness means that higher conscientiousness predicts more right-leaning (conservative) views. The meta-analysis also found that the strength of these associations can vary by context; for example, the negative correlation between openness and conservatism was much stronger in low-threat environments (r = -0.42), but nearly vanished under moderate threat (r = -0.07) [232]. This demonstrates that the personality-ideology link is not fixed, but can be moderated by societal conditions.

De Neve (2011) further substantiates this pattern using a large, nationally representative U.S. sample and sibling fixed-effects models to control for family background [233]. He finds that higher openness to experience is robustly associated with more liberal or left-leaning political views, even after accounting for shared environmental and genetic factors. Importantly, De Neve also demonstrates that early life experiences, such as childhood trauma, can moderate the effect of openness on political ideology, suggesting that both inherited personality traits and formative experiences contribute to the development of political beliefs. This highlights the complex interplay between genetic predispositions and environmental factors in shaping the roots of political ideology.

Gerber et al. (2010) also confirm that the effect of Big Five traits, especially openness, is often as large as that of education or income in predicting ideology, and that these relationships can differ across issue domains and social contexts [234]. This underscores the importance of interpreting r-values not as absolute determinants, but as indicators of probabilistic tendencies that interact with context.

In contrast, the relationship between agreeableness and political orientation is less robust. Joly et al. (2018) found no significant association between agreeableness and ideology among politicians, and the correlation fluctuated near zero across different national contexts. This suggests that, while agreeableness may play a role in collaborative or prosocial leadership styles, it is not a reliable marker of ideological orientation in political elites.

5.1.2   Summary of r-value Interpretation

To summarize, in a bipolar political context:
- A negative r between a trait and conservatism means the trait is more common among left-leaning individuals.
- A positive r means the trait is more common among right-leaning individuals.
- The magnitude of r indicates the strength of the association, but most effects are modest (e.g., $|r| < 0.3$), reflecting the multifactorial nature of political orientation.
- Contextual factors (e.g., societal threat, issue domain) can moderate these associations, sometimes strengthening or weakening the observed relationships [232, 234].

Right-leaning or conservative political leaders are most reliably characterized by higher conscientiousness. Conscientiousness involves

orderliness, self-discipline, reliability, and a strong orientation toward
duty and adherence to established structures. Hanania (2017) found
that Republican legislators in the United States scored higher on
conscientiousness and lower on openness and agreeableness compared
to their Democratic counterparts [228]. These differences persisted
after controlling for demographic variables.

However, the relationship between conscientiousness and ideology
among politicians is not always as strong as in the general population.
Joly et al. (2018) reported no significant association between conscientiousness and party ideology in their sample of Canadian and Belgian
politicians, suggesting that the effect may be context-dependent or
attenuated among political elites [231]. This may be due to range
restriction, as politicians as a group tend to be relatively high in
conscientiousness, as also shown by Dietrich et al. (2012) [229].

De Neve (2011) also finds that higher conscientiousness is associated with more conservative or right-leaning ideologies, and that this
relationship is robust to controls for family background and early life
experiences [233]. This convergence across studies strengthens the
evidence for a dispositional basis for ideological orientation, while also
highlighting the importance of context and selection effects in shaping
the personality profiles of political elites.

Extraversion, while a robust predictor of leadership emergence
and effectiveness, does not consistently differentiate between left-
and right-leaning orientations. Both Hanania (2017) and Joly et al.
(2018) found no systematic differences in extraversion by ideology
among politicians. Neuroticism (emotional instability) is generally
negatively associated with leadership effectiveness, but its relationship
with political ideology is weak or inconsistent.

5.2   The Dark Triad and Political Leader-
ship

Beyond the Big Five, recent research has examined the role of the
Dark Triad traits in political ambition and behavior. Studies indicate

that Machiavellianism and narcissism are positively associated with political ambition and self-perceived qualifications for office, while psychopathy is linked to more aggressive or provocative forms of political participation [235–237]. For example, Peterson and Palmer (2019) found that individuals higher in Machiavellianism and narcissism were more likely to express political ambition and to believe they would be successful candidates. Rogoza et al. (2022) demonstrated that narcissism and psychopathy, but not Machiavellianism, were consistently related to political participation in both Polish and British samples.

Mackin and Roese (2024) further showed that psychopathy, among the Dark Triad traits, was the strongest predictor of "ideological poking," i.e., the public display of products aimed at insulting political opponents. Across two studies, psychopathy was significantly associated with willingness to display offensive political products, even after controlling for demographic variables, while Machiavellianism and narcissism were not significant predictors [237].

5.3   Cross-Cultural Perspectives

The associations between personality traits and political orientation are generally robust in Western, Educated, Industrialized, Rich, and Democratic (WEIRD) societies, but their magnitude and direction can vary across cultural and institutional contexts. Joly et al. (2018) found that the negative association between openness and right-wing ideology was present in both Canada and Flanders, but not in Wallonia, suggesting that local political culture and party systems may moderate these effects [231]. Similarly, Hanania (2017) and other cross-national studies have documented that the openness–liberalism and conscientiousness–conservatism relationships are present but may be attenuated or moderated by local norms and historical legacies.

Systematic reviews of the literature confirm that, while openness and conscientiousness are the most consistent predictors of political ideology, the effect sizes are modest (typically r = 0.10 to 0.20), and much of the variance in political orientation remains unexplained by personality alone [238, 239]. Moreover, the translation of personality traits into political attitudes or behaviors may be constrained by institutional or normative factors, particularly in societies with high power distance or weaker rule of law.

5.4   Evidence from Neuropolitics

Recent advances in neuropolitics have begun to explore the neural correlates of ideological differences in empathy. Zebarjadi et al. (2023) conducted a pioneering study using magnetoencephalography (MEG) to investigate how individuals with different political orientations process vicarious suffering at the neural level [240]

Participants were recruited and categorized along a political spectrum based on self-reported political inclination and validated scales measuring right-wing authoritarianism. During the MEG session, participants were exposed to visual stimuli depicting individuals experiencing pain or distress, designed to elicit vicarious empathic responses. The primary neural measure was alpha-band (8–12 Hz) oscillatory activity in the temporoparietal junction (TPJ), a region implicated in empathy and perspective-taking.

Alpha-band suppression in the TPJ was used as an index of neural empathy response. MEG provides high temporal resolution, allowing the researchers to capture rapid changes in neural activity associated with the perception of others' suffering. The study also collected self-report data on empathy and political attitudes to examine correlations with neural measures.

The results revealed that left-leaning participants exhibited significantly greater alpha-band suppression in the TPJ in response to vicarious suffering compared to right-leaning participants. This neural empathy response was not only categorically stronger in leftists but also showed a parametric association with both self-reported political inclination and right-wing authoritarian values: individuals with higher right-wing/authoritarian scores demonstrated reduced neural empathy responses. These findings suggest that ideological differences in empathy are reflected at the neural level, providing convergent evidence beyond self-report measures that empathy-related processes may underlie some dispositional differences between ideological groups. However, it is important to emphasize that this is a pioneering study, and its findings should be interpreted with appropriate caution. As with any novel research, replication in larger and more diverse samples is necessary to establish the robustness and generalizability of the results. The study demonstrates correlation, not causation, and the operationalization of both "empathy" and "ideology" may influence the observed effects. Furthermore, laboratory-based neuroimaging may not fully capture the complexity of real-world empathy or political behavior. As highlighted in best practices for research interpretation, caution is warranted when drawing broad conclusions from initial findings, and further research is needed to confirm and expand upon these results

5.5   Political Prudence and the Ethics of Leadership

While empirical personality research provides vital insights into the dispositional foundations of political behavior, the cultivation of ethical leadership requires additional considerations of moral reasoning and practical wisdom. Dobel (1998) addresses the concept of political prudence as a central virtue for ethical leadership, defining it as the capacity of leaders to make wise, context-sensitive decisions that balance moral principles with practical realities [241]. Dobel's theoretical framework explores the ethical challenges faced by political leaders, such as conflicts between personal morality and public duty, or between short-term expediency and long-term justice. The article argues that effective leaders must navigate competing values and interests, using prudence to achieve outcomes that are both ethical and effective. This involves judgment, foresight, and the ability to adapt to changing circumstances. While primarily theoretical, Dobel draws on historical examples from political history to illustrate how prudence operates in practice and why it is essential for maintaining public trust and legitimacy. The concept of political prudence complements the personality-based findings from studies like those of Dietrich et al. (2012) and De Neve (2011) by providing a normative framework for understanding how dispositional traits should be channeled toward ethical ends [229, 233].

5.6   Mechanisms and Practical Implications

The mechanisms through which personality traits influence political leadership and orientation are multifaceted. Openness to experience promotes receptivity to change and willingness to challenge established norms, thereby facilitating progressive or reformist leadership. Conscientiousness, by contrast, underpins respect for rules, traditions, and hierarchical authority, aligning with more conservative, stability-oriented leadership. The modest but consistent correlations observed in large-scale studies highlight the probabilistic, rather than deterministic, influence of personality on political orientation and leadership.

For practitioners and scholars, the integration of personality assessment into political leadership development offers a means of identifying and nurturing traits conducive to effective and ethical governance. However, such approaches must be adapted to local cultural and institutional realities, and should not be used to rigidly prescribe or proscribe leadership pathways. The prudence-based framework offered by Dobel (1998) provides guidance on how personality traits should be developed and channeled in service of ethical leadership [241].

5.7   So, Does "Being Good" Make You a Better Politician?

The empirical literature converges on the conclusion that personality traits are significant, albeit modest, predictors of political orientation and leadership style. Openness to experience is the hallmark of left-leaning leadership, while conscientiousness characterizes right-leaning leaders [229, 233]. These associations are strongest in Western societies but are evident, with variation, across diverse cultural contexts. The predictive power of personality traits is further modulated by situational, institutional, and historical factors, underscoring the need for nuanced, context-sensitive approaches to leadership selection and development. The theoretical framework provided by Dobel (1998) suggests that "being good" in politics requires more than favorable personality traits; it demands the cultivation of practical wisdom and ethical judgment that allows leaders to navigate complex moral terrain [241].

It is important to note, however, that the connection between goodness and effectiveness is less straightforward in the realm of politics than in other domains explored in this book. In previous chapters, the evidence consistently indicated that good-heartedness (manifested as empathy, conscientiousness, or integrity) translates relatively directly into better outcomes for drivers, teachers, leaders, or religious individuals. In politics, by contrast, goodness is filtered through a spectrum of ideological, institutional, and cultural priorities. Political systems are inherently pluralistic: what counts as "good" or effective leadership is often contested or interpreted differently depending on the values and priorities of diverse constituencies. Some voters may prefer politicians who champion symbolic or even imaginary issues, sometimes at the expense of policies that serve the broader public interest, while others prioritize pragmatic solutions, moral clarity, or ideological purity. As a result, the virtues that make a "good" politician for one group may be seen as vices by another. This complexity means that, while traits like empathy and prudence can enhance a leader's capacity for just and adaptive governance, they do not guarantee political success or universal approval. Ultimately, the worth of goodness in politics depends not only on individual character but also on the priorities, perceptions, and choices of the public those politicians serve. In this sense, politics stands apart from other arenas: being "good-hearted" may be necessary for ethical leadership, but it is not always sufficient for political victory or influence.

Hence, more specifically, unlike in domains such as driving, teaching, or religious service, where good-heartedness almost universally leads to better outcomes, goodness in politics is not only ambiguous but sometimes even politically disadvantageous. Qualities like empathy, conscientiousness, or integrity, which are celebrated as core virtues in other chapters of this book, are, in the political arena, at times perceived by segments of the electorate as signs of naivety, indecisiveness, or weakness. In polarized or highly competitive contexts, opponents may frame a politician's compassion or ethical restraint as a lack of resolve or the inability to "get tough" on perceived threats. Some voters actively seek leaders who are combative, unyielding, or who focus on divisive or even imaginary issues, valuing symbolic gestures over substantive policy and favoring leaders who represent their grievances, even when such politics may run counter to broader social interests. Thus, in politics, the relationship between goodness and effectiveness is mediated by public opinion, media narratives, and the strategic calculations of both leaders and voters. Whether a politician's good-heartedness is a virtue or a liability depends on where the electorate's priorities stand, the narratives that dominate public discourse, and the institutional incentives at play. This makes the terrain of political life uniquely complex: here, being good-hearted is not always the surest path to influence or success, and sometimes, paradoxically, can even hinder a politician's prospects.

Chapter 6

The Cost–Benefit of Goodness

Up to this point, compelling evidence has been presented that having a fundamentally good character, i.e, being honest, empathetic, and conscientious, translates into better outcomes across a range of roles: from driving and religious observance to education, law enforcement, leadership, and politics. But this raises an important question: does the fact that "being good" leads to such wide-reaching benefits actually make it worthwhile on a personal level? Or, put differently, is there ever a case for being "bad," or does dishonesty and self-interest pay off in the end? This chapter is an exploration of the trade-offs involved in unethical behavior.

6.1 Dishonesty Studies

A systematic investigation of this question starts with an examination of the empirical evidence on how individuals behave when presented with opportunities for dishonesty under controlled conditions. One of the most widely used experimental paradigms for studying dishonesty is the dice-rolling task. In the vast majority of dice-rolling honesty studies, participants are individually instructed to privately roll a standard six-sided die (using a cup to ensure that only they can see the outcome) and then report the number they claim to have rolled to the experimenter [242–244]. The key incentive structure is that participants receive a monetary reward equal to the number they report, except for the number 6, which yields no reward at all; for example, reporting a 1 earns 1 unit of currency, a 2 earns 2 units, up to a 5 earning 5 units, but reporting a 6 results in zero payment. This setup creates a clear temptation to misreport a 6 as a higher-paying number, while the privacy of the roll ensures that dishonesty cannot be detected at the individual level. Instead, researchers statistically analyze the aggregate distribution of reported numbers (expecting a uniform distribution if all participants are honest) to detect deviations such as an overrepresentation of high-paying numbers (especially 5s) and an underrepresentation of 6s, which signal group-level dishonesty. The procedure is conducted in a controlled, private environment, with clear but neutral instructions emphasizing the link between reported outcome and payment, and sometimes includes multiple rounds or group variations to explore additional social or cognitive factors influencing honesty [245, 246].

6.1.1   Partial Lying and Social Image Concerns

A consistent finding across studies is that most people do not lie to the maximum extent possible. Instead, many engage in "partial lying", i.e., reporting a higher number than they actually rolled, but not always the maximum. This behavior is interpreted as an attempt to balance personal gain with the desire to maintain a positive self-image or avoid feeling like a blatant liar. For example, in Fischbacher and Föllmi-Heusi's foundational study, a 6 (which yields no reward) was reported only 6.5% of the time, while 5 was reported 35% of the time to claim the maximum reward. Under conditions of full honesty, each number from 1 to 6 should be reported about 16.7% of the time, since each outcome is equally likely with a fair die. The observed underreporting of 6 (6.5% vs. 16.7%) and overreporting of 5 (35% vs. 16.7%) provide clear evidence of dishonesty at the group level. Moreover, many participants reported intermediate values, suggesting a preference for "plausible" dishonesty over outright maximization [242].

Yet, while partial lying is the norm, studies consistently document the presence of a small but notable subset of participants who engage in extreme dishonesty. In the same foundational experiment, for instance, a few individuals reported the highest possible outcome (such as a 5 in every round) across all their trials. Statistically, the probability of honestly rolling a 5 on every attempt is exceedingly low (for example, 1 in 3,125 for five consecutive rolls), making such behavior virtually impossible by chance alone. These "extreme liars" stand out as statistical outliers, maximizing their payoffs in a way that is unmistakably dishonest and far beyond the more common, subtle forms of cheating observed in the majority of participants [242]. The identification of these extreme cases not only highlights the upper boundary of dishonest behavior in anonymous settings but also underscores the diversity of ethical decision-making strategies among individuals.

Remarkably, while the participants classified as "extreme liars" clearly understood that their pattern of responses would make their dishonesty obvious to the experimenters, they appeared entirely unconcerned about being branded as liars. For them, securing the maximum payment took precedence over any reputational cost, likely reasoning that, since they would never encounter the experimenters again, there was little reason to care about how they were perceived [247, 248]. Given that extreme dishonesty and disregard for reputational consequences are hallmark features of psychopathic personality traits, it would be particularly interesting to test these "extreme liars" for psychopathy, as emerging research suggests a strong link between psychopathic tendencies and a greater propensity for frequent or compulsive lying [249].

Recent research has extended this paradigm to compare individuals and groups. Okano and Goto (2023) found that both individuals and groups lie, but groups (especially pairs of friends) are more likely to engage in partial lying, reporting numbers that yield moderate rather than maximum payoffs [243]. This is attributed to heightened social image concerns within groups: members are more sensitive to being perceived as liars by their peers, leading to more subtle forms of dishonesty.

6.1.2   Cross-Cultural Differences in Dishonesty

A substantial body of research has investigated how rates and patterns of dishonesty in dice-rolling experiments vary across countries and cultures. Large-scale cross-societal studies, including experiments conducted in up to 23 countries, consistently demonstrate that the prevalence of rule violations in a society (such as corruption, tax evasion, and political fraud) correlates with the level of dishonesty observed in experimental tasks. Gächter et al. found that participants from countries with higher rates of societal rule violations are more likely to cheat in the dice-rolling paradigm, suggesting that broader institutional and cultural norms shape individual ethical behavior in incentivized settings [250].

However, the magnitude and nature of these cross-country differences are nuanced. For example, Ariely and colleagues conducted multi-country studies and found that while dishonesty is present everywhere, the average level of dishonesty and the distribution of dishonest behaviors can vary significantly between countries. Some studies found that the baseline tendency to cheat is surprisingly similar across diverse cultures, with only context-specific forms of dishonesty (e.g., bribery) showing substantial variation. Other research, such as Pascual-Ezama et al. (2020), found that the communication channel (e.g., face-to-face vs. anonymous reporting) can amplify or dampen cross-cultural differences, with more distant and anonymous settings leading to more extreme dishonest reporting [245, 251].

Moreover, studies have linked honesty in dice-rolling tasks to broader economic and institutional factors, such as a country's level of economic development and the quality of its institutions. Countries with stronger rule of law and lower corruption tend to exhibit higher levels of honesty in experimental settings [250]. Collectivist cultures may also display different patterns of dishonesty compared to individualist cultures, often showing greater sensitivity to peer behavior and social norms. Recent research demonstrates that dishonest behavior observed in laboratory settings is predictive of dishonest actions in real-world environments. For example, Dai et al. (2018) found that individuals who cheated in lab-based tasks were also more likely to commit fare-dodging on public transportation in the field, providing compelling evidence that experimental measures of dishonesty can reveal meaningful differences in ethical conduct across cultural and societal contexts [183].

6.1.3 Professional and Occupational Differences

While the majority of dice-rolling honesty studies focus on general population samples, there is emerging evidence that professional background and occupational context can influence dishonest behavior. Research examining workplace environments and group dynamics suggests that the moral climate of a profession or organization can affect the likelihood of cheating. For example, studies have found that individuals may behave more dishonestly when acting as part of a group, a dynamic relevant to many professional settings where decisions are made collectively. Communication within groups can drive a "dishonesty shift," indicating that professional environments that encourage group decision-making may see higher rates of dishonest reporting [247, 248].

In the public sector, the dice-rolling paradigm has been used to measure (dis)honesty among individuals and groups in public administration, providing a standardized way to compare dishonesty across different professional backgrounds. Some evidence suggests that environments enabling cheating may attract or select for individuals with lower moral character, potentially leading to higher rates of dishonesty in certain professions over time [252].

Despite these insights, direct, systematic comparisons of dishonesty rates across specific occupations (e.g., lawyers, accountants, teachers, public officials) using the dice-rolling paradigm remain limited.

Most findings to date highlight the influence of group dynamics and workplace culture rather than intrinsic differences between professions.

6.1.4 Demographic and Societal Factors

Meta-analyses and review papers provide robust evidence that demographic factors such as age, gender, and education level also influence dishonest behavior in dice-rolling and related experimental tasks. Across numerous studies and meta-analyses, the following patterns emerge:

– Gender: Males are generally more likely to engage in dishonest behavior than females, both in academic settings and in experimental paradigms like dice-rolling. However, the effect size can vary by context, and some studies find no significant gender differences when controlling for other variables [249, 253].

– Age: Younger individuals tend to be more prone to dishonesty, possibly due to less developed ethical values or greater risk-taking tendencies. Older participants often exhibit lower rates of dishonest behavior, though the effect is not always large [249].

– Education Level: The relationship between education and dishonesty is complex. While higher education may correlate with greater awareness of ethical standards, some evidence suggests that as students progress through their education, they may become more adept at rationalizing dishonest behavior. The specific program or field of study can also play a role [249].

– Personality and Social Context: Traits such as impulsivity and psychopathy are positively associated with dishonesty, while conscientiousness and agreeableness are negatively associated. The perception that peers are cheating increases the likelihood of individual dishonesty, and this peer effect is often stronger in collectivist cultures [254, 255].

– Religiosity and Cultural Values: Higher religiosity is generally associated with lower dishonesty, but the effect size varies by cultural context [256, 257]. Collectivist versus individualist orientations, as well as local social norms, can modulate the extent and form of dishonest behavior [258].

The results of dice-rolling honesty studies reveal that dishonesty is a universal human tendency, but its prevalence and expression are shaped by a complex interplay of cultural, professional, demographic, and societal factors [259]. Cross-country studies show that societal norms and institutional quality matter, while group and professional contexts can amplify or constrain dishonest behavior [260, 261]. Demographic variables such as age and gender, as well as personality traits and social context, further modulate the likelihood and style of dishonesty [262, 263]. These findings underscore the importance of considering both individual and contextual factors when interpreting experimental evidence on ethical behavior.

While experimental studies on honesty highlight the influence of demographic and societal factors on individual behavior, related research in professional contexts (e.g., academic citation practices) demonstrates that these patterns extend beyond the laboratory and shape real-world outcomes as well. Recent large-scale analyses of academic citation practices further illustrate gender-based behavioral differences in professional settings. A notable study by King et al. (2017) examined over 1.5 million research articles and found that male academics are significantly more likely to cite their own work than their female counterparts, with men self-citing up to 70% more frequently in recent decades [264]. This persistent gender gap in self-citation not only highlights systematic behavioral differences but also has important implications for academic recognition and career advancement. Such findings underscore that gender differences in self-promotion and professional conduct are not limited to experimental tasks, but extend to real-world academic practices, reinforcing the broader patterns observed in experimental honesty literature.

6.1.5 Theoretical Models of Lying Behavior

While the empirical evidence from dice-rolling and related honesty experiments reveals clear patterns (such as the prevalence of partial lying, the influence of social image, and the diversity of dishonest strategies) these behavioral regularities prompt a deeper question: what underlying psychological and economic mechanisms drive such nuanced forms of dishonesty? To move beyond mere description and toward explanation, researchers have developed formal theoretical models that capture the cost–benefit calculus individuals perform when deciding whether, and how much, to lie. These models are essential for understanding not only why most people refrain from outright maximization of ill-gotten gains, but also how contextual factors (such as group dynamics and reputational concerns) shape the boundaries of dishonest behavior. In the context of this chapter's broader inquiry into the personal and societal trade-offs of "badness," the following frameworks provide a bridge between observed behavior and the internal and external costs that constrain it.

- Perceived Size of the Lie (Dufwenberg & Dufwenberg Model [265]): This model posits that individuals experience disutility not just from lying, but from the perceived size of the lie. The larger the discrepancy between the reported and actual outcome, the greater the psychological cost. This model fits individual data well but does not fully capture the nuanced behavior of groups, who seem to be influenced by additional social factors.

- Cost of Lying and Social Image (Khalmetski & Sliwka Model [266]): This model incorporates both a fixed cost of lying and a penalty for being perceived as a liar. It predicts that as social image concerns increase (as in group settings), individuals are more likely to engage in partial lying rather than outright maximization. Empirical data show that groups have a lower average cost of lying but are more sensitive to social image, leading to broader distributions of reported numbers and more strategic dishonesty.

Together, these models illuminate the psychological and social trade-offs at the heart of dishonest behavior, extending the classic cost–benefit analysis to include not only material incentives but also the internal discomfort of lying and the external threat to one's social image. The Dufwenberg & Dufwenberg model helps explain why individuals often engage in partial rather than maximal lying, as the psychological cost of a larger lie can outweigh the incremental benefit. However, it is the Khalmetski & Sliwka model that more fully accounts for the strategic adaptation seen in group contexts, where the risk of being perceived as a liar by peers leads to more sophisticated forms of dishonesty; such as randomizing among plausible high numbers to avoid detection. These theoretical perspectives, validated by experimental findings, underscore that the "cost" of badness is not merely a function of external punishment or reward, but is deeply shaped by the interplay of self-concept, social context, and the desire to maintain a positive image in the eyes of oneself and others. In this way, the models provide a conceptual foundation for understanding the limits of dishonesty and the persistent appeal of ethical restraint, even when the immediate material incentives to cheat are strong [243, 265, 266].

6.1.6   Cognitive Load and the Limits of Dishonesty

Another line of research investigates the cognitive demands of lying. Reis et al. (2022) manipulated cognitive load during the dice-rolling task by requiring participants to remember letter strings of varying lengths while reporting their die rolls [244]. The results showed that higher cognitive load (i.e., less available mental capacity) led to less dishonesty, supporting the view that lying is cognitively demanding and that honesty may be the default response when cognitive resources are limited. This effect was robust across different incentive structures, although motivational influences such as gain versus loss framing were less consistent than previously assumed.

Taken together, these studies reveal that dishonesty is widespread but typically bounded by psychological and social constraints. Most people do not maximize their ill-gotten gains, instead opting for partial lies that allow them to benefit while preserving a sense of integrity or social acceptability. Group settings amplify concerns about social image, leading to more nuanced forms of dishonesty. Moreover, lying requires cognitive effort, and honesty tends to prevail when mental resources are taxed. These findings have important implications for understanding ethical decision-making in real-world contexts, from tax compliance to teamwork and organizational behavior.

6.2   The Cognitive and Social Demands of Deception

A growing body of research demonstrates that effective deception is not merely a matter of intent or opportunity, but fundamentally a test of cognitive and social skill. To be a good liar, one must possess a suite of mental abilities that enable the construction, maintenance, and strategic deployment of falsehoods, all while managing the risk of detection and the demands of social interaction.

6.2.1   Cognitive Load and the Mental Effort of Lying

Lying is consistently found to be more cognitively demanding than truth-telling. This increased cognitive load arises because liars must inhibit the automatic, truthful response, construct a plausible alternative, monitor the listener's reactions, and maintain consistency with both known facts and prior statements. Empirical studies using reaction time paradigms reveal that individuals take longer to fabricate lies than to tell the truth, reflecting the additional mental effort required [267]. When cognitive load is experimentally increased (such as by imposing time pressure, requiring dual-task performance, or asking for information in reverse order) liars are more likely to display detectable cues, such as hesitations and inconsistencies, and are more easily identified. These findings underscore that successful deception is a cognitively taxing endeavor [267, 268].

Central to the ability to lie effectively is working memory capacity, i.e., the ability to hold and manipulate information in mind [269, 270]. High working memory capacity allows individuals to juggle the competing demands of suppressing the truth, constructing a coherent falsehood, and tracking what has already been said [269]. Experimental evidence shows that individuals with greater working memory resources are better able to produce plausible and consistent lies, especially under conditions of increased cognitive load [271]. Executive functions, including inhibitory control, cognitive flexibility, and strategic planning, are also critical [270, 272, 273]. Inhibitory control enables the suppression of truthful responses, cognitive flexibility allows for the adaptation of stories in response to new information, and planning supports the construction of lies that can withstand scrutiny [274].

Meta-analyses confirm that executive function is more strongly related to the ability to maintain lies than to the initial act of lying, highlighting the importance of planning and working memory in sustaining deception over time [275].

6.2.2 The Role of Social Intelligence and Theory of Mind

Beyond raw cognitive horsepower, effective deception requires advanced social intelligence and theory of mind (ToM), i.e., the capacity to attribute mental states to others and anticipate their beliefs, intentions, and reactions. Developmental studies show that the emergence of lying in children is closely linked to the development of ToM; children who receive ToM training become more adept at deception [276]. Neuroimaging studies further reveal that deception activates brain regions associated with ToM and social cognition, such as the temporoparietal junction (TPJ) and medial prefrontal cortex (mPFC), particularly in interactive, ecologically valid settings [277, 278]. These regions support the inference of others' beliefs and the strategic manipulation of those beliefs, which are essential for sophisticated forms of deception [279].

Individuals with higher social intelligence and better emotion perception are not only more skilled at producing lies but also at detecting them, suggesting that the same socio-cognitive abilities underpin both sides of the deception equation [280].

Strategic planning is a hallmark of successful liars [281]. The ability to anticipate follow-up questions, construct internally consistent narratives, and adapt to new information is essential, especially in high-stakes or complex situations [282]. Theoretical models such as the Activation–Decision-Construction Model (ADCM) and the Memory and Deception (MAD) Model emphasize that the construction and maintenance of lies draw heavily on planning and working memory resources [272, 283]. Neuroimaging evidence corroborates this, showing increased activation in the prefrontal cortex (i.e., an area associated with executive function and planning) during deception tasks that require complex strategizing [284].

6.2.3 Individual Differences and Neural Correlates of Deception

Not all individuals are equally adept at lying [285, 286]. Individual differences in intelligence, working memory capacity, executive function, and social cognition account for much of the variance in deceptive skill. Experienced or "practiced" liars may show reduced cognitive load and faster response times, indicating that the cognitive cost of lying can decrease with experience [287–289]. Conversely, individuals with lower working memory or executive function are more likely to exhibit detectable cues to deception, particularly under cognitive load [290, 291].

Meta-analyses of neuroimaging studies consistently identify a distributed network of brain regions involved in deception, including the prefrontal cortex (for executive control and planning), anterior cingulate cortex (for conflict monitoring), insula (for emotional processing), and inferior parietal lobule (for attention and working memory) [270, 277, 278]. Socially interactive deception tasks additionally recruit regions associated with theory of mind and moral reasoning, such as the TPJ and mPFC [292, 293].

The ability to lie well is a complex cognitive and social achievement [277, 282]. It requires not only the mental agility to construct and maintain falsehoods under cognitive load, but also the social intelligence to anticipate and manipulate the beliefs of others [279].

Executive functions (working memory, inhibitory control, cognitive flexibility, and planning) form the cognitive backbone of deception, while theory of mind and social intelligence provide the socio-cognitive scaffolding [275, 277, 294]. The neural architecture of deception reflects this complexity, engaging both executive and social brain networks [277, 295]. Thus, to be a good liar, one must indeed be "smart;" not only in terms of general intelligence, but in the specific cognitive and social domains that enable the artful navigation of truth and falsehood [296, 297].

6.3 What Makes People Less Likely to Lie?

Some people would assume that intelligent people are less likely to lie. However, recent meta-analyses and experimental studies do not support the claim that higher intelligence reliably predicts greater honesty. For example, a comprehensive meta-analysis synthesizing results from 565 studies found no strong, consistent link between intelligence and honesty or dishonesty across all contexts [259]. Experimental evidence suggests that higher fluid intelligence is associated with more reliable and sophisticated lying, particularly in oral communication, where cognitive demands are higher. Intelligence does not necessarily reduce the overall likelihood of dishonest behavior. In fact, when opportunities for dishonesty are present, both high- and low-intelligence individuals are similarly likely to lie; intelligence may influence the manner or extent of dishonesty, but not its frequency [297–299].

Instead, the most robust predictors of honest or dishonest behavior are personality traits and cognitive control. Longitudinal and meta-analytic research consistently shows that traits such as conscientiousness, self-control, and low impulsivity are more strongly linked to honesty than intelligence. For instance, individuals with higher self-control and a tendency toward prosocial behavior are less likely to lie, especially when faced with ambiguous moral choices [300–302]. Conscientiousness, in particular, is associated with greater engagement in responsible and honest conduct, and increases in conscientiousness over time are linked to increases in honest behavior [303]. Conversely, higher impulsivity is a stable predictor of dishonest behavior across developmental periods, from childhood through adulthood [301].

Cognitive control, i.e., the capacity to regulate impulses and resolve conflicts between self-interest and moral values, also plays a critical role. Experimental and neuroimaging studies reveal that cognitive control is not inherently "pro-honesty" or "pro-dishonesty," but rather enables individuals to override their default tendencies. For those who are generally honest, cognitive control can facilitate cheating when tempted; for those who are generally dishonest, it can help them act honestly [304, 305]. Reaction time studies further show that honest individuals require more cognitive control (as indicated by longer reaction times) when facing ambiguous moral conflicts, while dishonest responses tend to be more automatic [306]. These findings suggest that the ability to act honestly, especially in morally ambiguous situations, depends on both personality traits and the flexible deployment of cognitive control [304, 305].

Furthermore, recent research highlights the role of creativity in dishonest behavior. Multiple experimental studies have found that individuals with higher creativity are more likely to engage in dishonesty, not because they are less moral, but because their creative thinking enables them to generate more self-serving justifications for unethical actions [307]. This justification mechanism reduces psychological barriers to dishonesty, making it easier for creative individuals to cheat without feeling guilt. Some studies even suggest a bidirectional relationship, where engaging in dishonest behavior can subsequently increase creative thinking [307]. However, the relationship between creativity and dishonesty is nuanced and may depend on contextual and individual factors, such as personality traits and cultural norms [308].

Cross-cultural and age-specific research further enriches our understanding of honesty. For example, honesty tends to increase with age, with older adults being more honest and less tolerant of certain types of lies, a trend partly explained by higher scores on the honesty-humility personality trait [309]. Cross-cultural studies show that while the basic tendency toward minor dishonesty is widespread, the predictors and moralization of honesty and dishonesty are shaped by cultural norms, the strictness of social rules, and the social context in which behavior occurs [261, 310, 311].

Hence, being "clever" does not make one less likely to lie. Rather, honesty is best predicted by traits such as self-control, conscientiousness, and low impulsivity, as well as by a strong capacity for cognitive control. Creativity, on the other hand, may increase the risk of dishonesty by enabling more elaborate justifications for unethical behavior. The most honest individuals may not be those with the highest IQs, but those with personality profiles that favor integrity and the cognitive skills to act in accordance with their moral values.

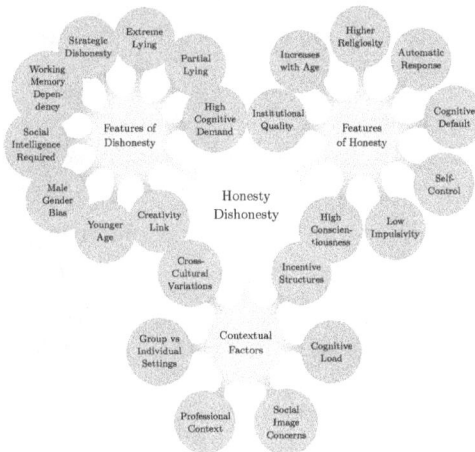

Figure 6.1: Framework illustrating the key features of honesty and dishonesty based on experimental research. The central concept branches into three domains: 'Features of Honesty' encompassing traits like conscientiousness and self-control that predict honest behavior, 'Features of Dishonesty' with patterns ranging from partial to extreme lying, and 'Contextual Factors' that moderate these behaviors across cultural, professional, and social settings, including the influence of group dynamics and institutional quality on ethical decision-making.

Figure 6.1 illustrates the division of factors related to honesty and dishonesty into three main categories: "Features of Honesty," "Features of Dishonesty," and "Contextual Factors,' described in more detail as follows:

1. Features of Honesty
- Personality traits such as high conscientiousness, low impulsivity, and self-control are robust predictors of honest behavior. These are repeatedly highlighted in meta-analyses and experimental studies as the most consistent individual-level correlates of honesty.

- Cognitive default/automatic response: Research shows that honesty is often the default, especially under cognitive load, suggesting that honest responses are less cognitively demanding for most people.

- Sociodemographic factors like higher religiosity, increasing age, and institutional quality are all associated with greater honesty in both experimental and real-world contexts.

- These features are all supported by the literature as primary drivers of honest behavior.

2. Features of Dishonesty
- Cognitive demands: Lying is more cognitively demanding than truth-telling, requiring working memory, planning, and inhibition.

- Behavioral patterns: Partial lying, extreme lying, and strategic dishonesty are all empirically observed in experimental paradigms.

- Demographic and individual factors: Male gender, younger age, and higher creativity are all associated with increased dishonesty, as are certain personality traits (e.g., impulsivity, psychopathy).

- Social intelligence: Effective lying requires theory of mind and social intelligence, as shown in both developmental and neuroimaging studies. These features accurately reflect the complexity and diversity of dishonest behavior.

3. Contextual Factors
- Cultural, professional, and situational influences: Cross-cultural differences, group vs. individual settings, professional context, social image concerns, cognitive load, and incentive structures all moderate the expression of honesty and dishonesty.

- The literature emphasizes that these contextual factors can amplify or constrain both honest and dishonest behavior, and are essential for a complete understanding.

6.4   So, Does "Being Good" Pay?

The evidence reviewed in this chapter paints a nuanced picture of the personal calculus behind honesty and dishonesty. On the one hand, experimental and real-world data consistently show that "being good" (i.e., embodying honesty, conscientiousness, and self-control) yields broad benefits across domains, from professional advancement to social trust and personal well-being. These advantages are not merely theoretical: individuals with high integrity tend to enjoy stronger reputations, more stable relationships, and greater long-term success, both within organizations and in society at large.

Yet, the persistent temptation to be "bad" (e.g., to cheat, lie, or act in pure self-interest) remains a universal human experience. The dice-rolling experiments and related studies reveal that most people, when given the opportunity, do not become extreme liars. Instead, they engage in partial dishonesty, seeking to balance personal gain with the need to maintain a positive self-image and avoid social or psychological costs. Only a small minority, often characterized by specific personality traits such as high impulsivity or psychopathy, are willing to maximize ill-gotten gains regardless of reputational risk.

Crucially, the "cost" of badness is not limited to the risk of external punishment. Theoretical models and empirical findings converge on the idea that internal psychological discomfort, threats to self-concept, and concerns about social image act as powerful brakes on dishonesty. Even when material incentives to cheat are strong, most people refrain from outright maximization because the internal and social costs outweigh the benefits. In group or professional contexts, these social image concerns become even more salient, leading to more subtle and strategic forms of dishonesty rather than blatant cheating.

Moreover, the ability to lie effectively is itself cognitively and socially demanding. Lying requires working memory, executive function, and social intelligence, i.e., resources that are limited and taxed under cognitive load. For most, honesty is the default, especially when mental resources are stretched. This means that, in everyday life, the effort required to sustain dishonesty often makes it an unattractive long-term strategy.

Importantly, intelligence alone does not predict greater honesty or dishonesty. Instead, personality traits such as conscientiousness, self-control, and low impulsivity are the most robust predictors of ethical behavior. Creativity, while valuable in many domains, can sometimes facilitate dishonesty by enabling more elaborate justifications for unethical actions. Contextual factors (e.g., cultural norms, group dynamics, professional environments) further shape the boundaries of honest and dishonest behavior.

So, does "being good" pay? The answer, supported by a wealth of experimental and real-world evidence, is yes; though not always in the most immediate or obvious ways. While minor acts of dishonesty may yield short-term gains, the cumulative psychological, social, and reputational costs tend to make sustained dishonesty a losing proposition for most individuals. The benefits of honesty are often diffuse and long-term, but they are real and substantial, especially in environments where trust, cooperation, and reputation matter.

Conversely, there are rare contexts (characterized by anonymity, lack of accountability, or pathological personality traits) where "badness" may appear to pay off in the short run. But even here, the evidence suggests that such strategies are risky, cognitively taxing, and ultimately isolating.

Thus, the trade-offs explored in this chapter reveal that the personal and societal costs of dishonesty generally outweigh the fleeting rewards. The enduring appeal of ethical restraint is not just a matter of social expectation, but a reflection of deep psychological and social realities. For most people, most of the time, being good is not only the right thing to do, it is also the smart thing to do.

Chapter 7

Barriers to Goodness

The pursuit of goodness is often celebrated as a universal aspiration, yet the path toward ethical and prosocial behavior is frequently obstructed by deep-seated psychological and cultural barriers. Understanding these obstacles is essential for anyone seeking to foster environments where empathy, humility, and openness can flourish. This chapter explores the most significant impediments to goodness, examining how certain personality traits and social dynamics can undermine even the best intentions. By illuminating these barriers, we can better appreciate the challenges inherent in cultivating genuine goodness and identify strategies to overcome them.

7.1 Narcissism and Intellectual Arrogance

Across diverse domains (leadership, teaching, driving, and social engagement) the science of goodness consistently demonstrates that prosocial traits such as empathy, humility, conscientiousness, and openness are foundational for ethical and effective behavior. However, certain personality dispositions act as potent barriers to the cultivation and enactment of goodness. Among these, narcissism and intellectual arrogance stand out for their pervasive and disruptive effects.

Narcissism is typified by grandiosity, entitlement, and a heightened sensitivity to criticism. Individuals with pronounced narcissistic traits often seek validation and admiration, which can manifest as a preoccupation with self-importance and a diminished capacity for genuine concern for others. This self-focus obstructs the development of empathy, which is a core driver of goodness in leadership, teaching, and interpersonal relations. Narcissistic individuals may engage in behaviors that appear superficially prosocial, such as adopting the mantle of a "truth-seeker" or "reformer," but their underlying motivation is frequently self-aggrandizement or control, rather than authentic service or care.

Empirical research has further clarified that both grandiose and vulnerable forms of narcissism are detrimental to goodness [312]. Grandiose narcissists, confident and extraverted, are often resistant to feedback and dismissive of others' perspectives, which impairs collaboration and trust [313]. Vulnerable narcissists, marked by insecurity and neuroticism, are prone to suspicion, defensiveness, and social withdrawal, limiting their capacity for constructive engagement. Both forms erode the psychological foundations of goodness (i.e., empathy, humility, and openness) across professional and personal contexts [314].

Intellectual arrogance compounds these effects. Defined as an exaggerated sense of one's own intellectual capability and an unwillingness to recognize one's limits or errors, intellectual arrogance inhibits the reflective practices essential for growth, ethical reasoning, and learning. Individuals high in intellectual arrogance are less likely to seek feedback, admit mistakes, or revise their judgments. In fields where the science of goodness shows that trust, adaptability, and humility are vital (such as leadership, teaching, and even safe driving) arrogance obstructs the very processes that enable ethical and effective action.

Rather than fostering environments of trust and cooperation, narcissism and intellectual arrogance can create climates of fear, mistrust, and conflict, undermining the social bonds and psychological safety that are central to goodness. The result is not only decreased effectiveness but also increased risk of unethical conduct, group polarization, and social harm. The psychological pathways by which narcissism and intellectual arrogance erode the foundations of goodness (such as empathy, humility, and openness) are illustrated in Figure 7.1.

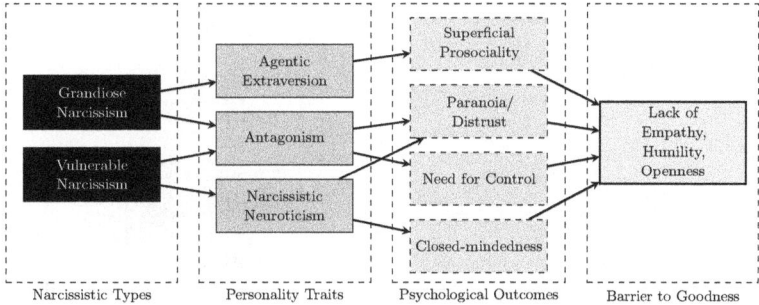

Narcissistic Types   Personality Traits   Psychological Outcomes   Barrier to Goodness

Figure 7.1: This conceptual model illustrates how different forms of narcissism (grandiose and vulnerable) undermine the development and expression of goodness in domains such as leadership, teaching, and social engagement. Personality traits like agentic extraversion and antagonism (often linked to grandiose narcissism), as well as narcissistic neuroticism (linked to vulnerable narcissism), give rise to psychological outcomes such as superficial prosociality, paranoia, excessive need for control, and closed-mindedness [312, 315]. These pathways ultimately erode core ingredients of goodness (including empathy, humility, and openness) thereby impeding ethical behavior, collaboration, and trust in relevant disciplines. Arrows indicate empirically supported causal pathways.

7.2   The Paradox of Expertise

While education and expertise are frequently assumed to promote ethical and prosocial behavior, recent research identifies a paradox: under certain conditions, greater education or specialized knowledge may actually impede goodness, especially when coupled with narcissism or intellectual arrogance (as illustrated in Figure 7.2).

This "paradox of expertise" emerges when formal credentials or advanced training foster a sense of superiority or infallibility, rather than humility and responsibility. Individuals with impressive academic or professional backgrounds may begin to conflate their domain-specific expertise with universal competence. Such "credentialed arrogance" can lead to overconfidence in unfamiliar areas, diminished receptiveness to dissenting views, and the misuse of technical language to obscure, rather than clarify, complex issues.

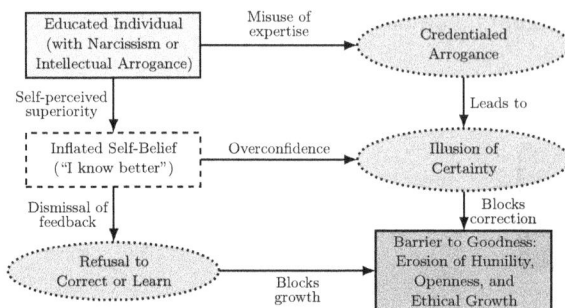

Figure 7.2: This conceptual model illustrates how education, when combined with narcissism or intellectual arrogance, can paradoxically create barriers to goodness. Educated individuals with inflated self-belief may develop "credentialed arrogance" and an "illusion of certainty," leading them to overestimate their competence and dismiss feedback. This refusal to correct or learn undermines humility, openness, and ethical growth, i.e., core ingredients of goodness in any discipline. Arrows indicate the psychological and behavioral pathways that block the cultivation of goodness.

The consequences are evident in settings where technical expertise is invoked to override collective wisdom or ethical norms. For instance, professionals leveraging unrelated credentials to promote unsound practices (whether in public health, education, or policy) may inadvertently amplify misinformation and erode public trust. This dynamic is particularly dangerous when audiences defer to credentials rather than evaluate the substance of claims, undermining the epistemic humility and critical reflection that are essential for goodness in any discipline.

The paradox is further exacerbated by systems that reward confidence over caution, and assertion over inquiry. In such environments, individuals who project certainty (regardless of the accuracy or benevolence of their views) are often elevated to positions of influence. This "confidence illusion" can enable the proliferation of charismatic but misguided voices, sidelining those who practice the humility and self-scrutiny fundamental to moral and effective action.

For example, the educational paradox manifests vividly in anti-vaccine communities. Influencers with unrelated expertise frequently weaponize their educational background to lend credibility to pseudoscientific claims, framing opposition to immunization protocols as "skeptical inquiry" while ignoring population-level evidence. Their followers, often educated professionals scoring high in narcissistic traits, proudly assert "I know better" while rejecting peer-reviewed literature. As a result, credentialed individuals and their followers, motivated by narcissism or intellectual arrogance, reject humility and critical reflection in favor of overconfidence and misplaced authority [316].

7.2.1 Resilience Limited by Personality Traits

It is tempting to assume that resilience, intelligence, or higher education will, by themselves, equip individuals to act ethically and prosocially. However, the science of goodness reveals that these attributes are not sufficient when personality traits such as narcissism or intellectual arrogance are present.

Intellectual humility (i.e., the recognition of one's cognitive limitations and the willingness to revise beliefs in light of new evidence) is more predictive of goodness-oriented behaviors than intelligence or advanced training alone. Without humility, intelligence can serve to rationalize self-serving or harmful actions, and education can become a tool for justifying unethical conduct. High-achieving individuals lacking in humility are often less receptive to correction, more resistant to feedback, and more likely to persist in error, thereby undermining the collective good.

These limitations are not restricted to the individual; they can become institutionalized. Organizations or communities that valorize confidence, status, or credentials above character and humility risk normalizing behaviors that are antithetical to goodness, such as exclusion, dogmatism, and the rationalization of harm.

7.3 Deflection as Self-Preservation

A less discussed but critical barrier to goodness arises not only from the internal traits of toxic individuals, but also from the strategies they employ to maintain their self-image and avoid self-correction. For many with entrenched narcissism or deep-seated insecurity, genuine self-reflection and personal growth are experienced as intolerable threats. Rather than confront their own shortcomings, such individuals often seek out those who embody goodness (traits like empathy, humility, and openness) as targets.

The presence of genuinely good-hearted people poses a unique problem for these individuals: it creates the risk of comparison, both internally and externally. Internally, the mere presence of someone who demonstrates authentic goodness serves as a constant reminder of their own deficiencies, threatening their already fragile self-concept. Externally, others may begin to notice the contrast, comparing the toxic individual unfavorably to those who model integrity and kindness. For those deeply invested in protecting their self-image, either form of comparison is intolerable.

To resolve this threat, toxic individuals often attempt to eliminate the good-hearted person from their environment (whether through ostracism, undermining, or character attacks) so that no such comparison is possible. In this way, the virtues of good people become not just a silent rebuke but a direct threat to those who are unwilling or unable to engage in self-improvement. Rather than being inspired to change, toxic individuals may instead be driven to isolate or discredit those who represent what they most lack.

If you find yourself targeted by individuals who seem threatened by your positive traits, it is important to recognize that their hostility is not a reflection of your shortcomings, but of their own inability to self-reflect and grow. Here are some steps to consider:

- Maintain Perspective: Remind yourself that being targeted is often a sign that your goodness is making a difference. Do not internalize the toxic person's projections or criticisms.

- Set Boundaries: Protect your emotional and psychological well-being by establishing clear boundaries. Limit unnecessary interactions and avoid being drawn into their manipulative dynamics.

- Seek Support: Connect with others who value and reinforce your positive traits. Trusted friends, mentors, or support groups can provide perspective and encouragement.

– Avoid Retaliation: Resist the urge to respond in kind. Retaliation often reinforces the toxic dynamic and can undermine your own values.

– Prioritize Self-Care: Engage in practices that restore your sense of self-worth and resilience, such as mindfulness, reflection, or creative pursuits.

– Document Interactions: If the targeting occurs in a professional or organizational context, keep careful records of any problematic interactions. This documentation can be vital if escalation or intervention becomes necessary, such as reporting to HR or seeking external support. A simple and effective method is to send yourself a summary email after each incident, describing what occurred, when and where it happened, and who was present. These timestamped messages create a reliable, chronological record that can be invaluable if you need to establish a pattern of behavior or defend yourself against misrepresentation.

– Consider Professional Guidance: In cases of severe or persistent targeting, consulting with a counselor, coach, or HR professional may be warranted.

By understanding the psychological dynamics at play and responding with clarity and self-compassion, you can preserve your integrity and continue to embody the goodness that provokes such reactions in others. Ultimately, the challenge is not only to withstand such targeting, but to remain steadfast in your commitment to ethical and prosocial behavior, regardless of the obstacles placed in your path.

7.4   Implications for Cultivating Goodness

Recognizing the barriers posed by narcissism, intellectual arrogance, and the paradox of expertise is essential for the deliberate cultivation of goodness in any discipline. Interventions that promote self-awareness, empathy, and intellectual humility (such as reflective practice, feedback mechanisms, and collaborative learning) are vital. Environments that reward curiosity, openness, and the ethical use of knowledge foster the development of good-hearted professionals and citizens.

Conversely, systems that reward only technical achievement, status, or visibility risk empowering individuals whose traits may undermine the very qualities that define goodness. The science of goodness thus calls for a holistic approach to development and selection; one that integrates character, humility, and prosocial motivation with knowledge and skill.

Thus, while education, expertise, and intelligence are valuable assets, their contribution to goodness is contingent upon the presence of humility, empathy, and a commitment to the collective well-being. Narcissism, intellectual arrogance, and the paradox of expertise represent persistent threats to the realization of goodness across disciplines. Effective strategies to promote goodness must therefore address not only cognitive and technical capacities, but also the personality traits and cultural values that shape our ability to act ethically and for the good of others.

7.4.1   Personality Testing in Role Selection

Given the robust evidence linking personality traits such as empathy, humility, and conscientiousness to ethical and effective behavior across domains, it is tempting to propose that individuals be systematically screened for these traits prior to selection for roles of responsibility. In principle, personality assessments (particularly those based on well-validated models such as the Big Five) could be used to identify candidates most likely to embody the qualities associated with goodness in leadership, teaching, healthcare, or other professions. Indeed, research has demonstrated that certain traits are predictive of positive outcomes in these roles, while others, such as narcissism or intellectual arrogance, are associated with an increased risk of cultivating dysfunctional group dynamics, poor collaboration, and diminished trust.

However, the practical implementation of personality testing as a gatekeeping tool faces significant challenges, both ethical and methodological. First, personality is a complex and multifaceted construct, influenced by situational factors, cultural context, and developmental history. While trait measures can provide valuable insights, they are not deterministic; individuals may compensate for certain dispositional weaknesses through training, reflection, or supportive environments. Moreover, the predictive validity of personality assessments, though statistically significant at the group level, is often insufficient for making high-stakes decisions about individuals. False positives and negatives are inevitable, and the risk of unjust exclusion or misclassification is nontrivial.

Second, the use of personality testing in selection processes raises concerns about privacy, fairness, and potential discrimination. There is a longstanding debate about the ethical implications of using psychological assessments to limit access to employment or advancement, particularly when such tools may inadvertently disadvantage certain groups or reinforce existing biases. Legal frameworks in many jurisdictions restrict the use of personality testing for employment decisions, especially when the relevance of specific traits to job performance is not clearly established.

Third, the dynamic and context-dependent nature of goodness further complicates the use of static trait measures. Goodness is not merely a function of inherent disposition, but is shaped by organizational culture, leadership, training, and ongoing feedback. Individuals may grow, adapt, and develop prosocial qualities over time, especially when supported by environments that value and reinforce such behaviors. Overreliance on pre-selection testing risks neglecting the importance of developmental processes and the potential for positive change.

Finally, there are practical limitations related to the reliability and validity of available assessment tools. Self-report measures are susceptible to social desirability bias and faking, particularly when individuals are motivated to present themselves in a favorable light. While observer ratings and multi-source feedback can mitigate some of these issues, they are resource-intensive and not always feasible at scale.

For these reasons, while personality assessment can play a valuable role in professional development, coaching, and team composition, its use as a primary selection mechanism for roles requiring goodness is fraught with limitations. A more effective approach is to integrate personality insights with holistic evaluation methods, ongoing training, and the cultivation of organizational cultures that support ethical and prosocial behavior. By recognizing both the promise and the limits of personality testing, institutions can better balance the goals of fairness, effectiveness, and the promotion of goodness across disciplines.

Bibliography

[1] Timothy A. Judge, Joyce E. Bono, Remus Ilies, and Megan W. Gerhardt. Personality and leadership: A qualitative and quantitative review. *Journal of Applied Psychology*, 87(4):765–780, 2002. doi:10.1037/0021-9010.87.4.765.

[2] D. Scott Drue, Jennifer D. Nahrgang, Ned Wellman, and Stephen E. Humphrey. Trait and behavioral theories of leadership: An integration and meta-analytic test of their relative validity. *Personnel Psychology*, 64(1):7–52, February 2011. doi:10.1111/j.1744-6570.2010.01201.x.

[3] Anoop A. Javalagi, Daniel A. Newman, and Mengtong Li. Personality and leadership: Meta-analytic review of cross-cultural moderation, behavioral mediation, and honesty-humility. *Journal of Applied Psychology*, 109(9):1489–1511, September 2024. doi:10.1037/apl0001182.

[4] Colin Silverthorne. Leadership effectiveness and personality: a cross cultural evaluation. *Personality and Individual Differences*, 30(2):303–309, January 2001. doi:10.1016/s0191-8869(00)00047-7.

[5] Erna Suwardi, Muhamad Suhaimi Taat, Roslee Talip, and Mohd Sobrye Paimin. Big five personality traits as a catalyst for instructional competency: A scoping review in educational leadership. *International Journal of Research and Innovation in Social Science*, IX(XIX):80–94, 2025. doi:10.47772/ijriss.2025.901900008.

[6] Anshika Grover and Dr Amit. The big five personality traits and leadership: A comprehensive analysis. *International Journal For Multidisciplinary Research*, 6(1), January 2024. doi:10.36948/ijfmr.2024.v06i01.11820.

[7] John D. Mayer, Peter Salovey, and David R. Caruso. Emotional intelligence: Theory, findings, and implications. *Psychological Inquiry*, 15(3):197–215, July 2004. doi:10.1207/s15327965pli1503_02.

[8] Muhammad Habib, Syed Muhammad Ali Naqi, and Mohsan Ali. Emotional intelligence: Understanding, assessing, and cultivating the key to personal and professional success. *sjesr*, 6(2):50–55, June 2023. doi:10.36902/sjesr-vol6-iss2-2023(50-55).

[9] Peter Salovey and John D. Mayer. Emotional intelligence. *Imagination, Cognition and Personality*, 9(3):185–211, March 1990. `doi:10.2190/dugg-p24e-52wk-6cdg`.

[10] Peter Salovey and John D. Mayer. What is emotional intelligence? In Peter Salovey and David J. Sluyter, editors, *Emotional Development and Emotional Intelligence: Educational Implications*, pages 3–31. Basic Books, New York, 1997.

[11] John D. Mayer, Peter Salovey, and David R. Caruso. Emotional intelligence as zeitgeist, as personality, and as a mental ability. In Reuven Bar-On and James D. A. Parker, editors, *Handbook of Emotional Intelligence: Theory, Development, Assessment, and Application at Home, School, and in the Workplace*, pages 92–117. Jossey-Bass, San Francisco, 2000.

[12] K. V. Petrides and Adrian Furnham. Trait emotional intelligence: Psychometric investigation with reference to established trait taxonomies. *European Journal of Personality*, 15(6):425–448, 2001. `doi:10.1002/per.416`.

[13] K. V. Petrides. Psychometric properties of the trait emotional intelligence questionnaire (teique). In Con Stough, Donald H. Saklofske, and James D. A. Parker, editors, *Assessing Emotional Intelligence: Theory, Research, and Applications*, pages 85–101. Springer, New York, 2009.

[14] Reuven Bar-On. *Bar-On Emotional Quotient Inventory (EQ-i): Technical manual*. Multi-Health Systems, 1997.

[15] Daniel Goleman. *Emotional Intelligence: Why It Can Matter More Than IQ*. Bantam Books, 1995.

[16] Jim McCleskey. Emotional intelligence and leadership: A review of the progress, controversy, and criticism. *International Journal of Organizational Analysis*, 22(1):76–93, March 2014. `doi:10.1108/ijoa-03-2012-0568`.

[17] Ning Hsu, Daniel A. Newman, and Katie L. Badura. Emotional intelligence and transformational leadership: Meta-analysis and explanatory model of female leadership advantage. *Journal of Intelligence*, 10(4):104, November 2022. `doi:10.3390/jintelligence10040104`.

[18] Jorge López González, Jesús Manuel Martínez, Maven Lomboy, and Luis Expósito. Study of emotional intelligence and leadership competencies in university students. *Cogent Education*, 11(1), October 2024. `doi:10.1080/2331186x.2024.2411826`.

[19] Lane Mills. A meta-analysis of the relationship between emotional intelligence and effective leadership. *Journal of Curriculum and Instruction*, page 22, 2009. `doi:10.3776/joci.2009.v3n2p22`.

[20] Raquel Gómez-Leal, Allison A. Holzer, Christina Bradley, Pablo Fernández-Berrocal, and Janet Patti. The relationship between emotional intelligence and leadership in school leaders: a systematic review. *Cambridge Journal of Education*, 52(1):1–21, June 2021. `doi:10.1080/0305764x.2021.1927987`.

[21] Augusty Pa and Jain Mathew. A meta analytic review of the relationship between emotional intelligence and leadership effectiveness. *Restaurant Business*, 118(9):118–126, September 2019. doi:10.26643/rb.v118i9.7972.

[22] Peter Edelman and Daan van Knippenberg. Emotional intelligence, management of subordinate's emotions, and leadership effectiveness. *Leadership & Organization Development Journal*, 39(5):592–607, June 2018. doi:10.1108/lodj-04-2018-0154.

[23] David Rosete and Joseph Ciarrochi. Emotional intelligence and its relationship to workplace performance outcomes of leadership effectiveness. *Leadership & Organization Development Journal*, 26(5):388–399, July 2005. doi:10.1108/01437730510607871.

[24] Robert Kerr, John Garvin, Norma Heaton, and Emily Boyle. Emotional intelligence and leadership effectiveness. *Leadership & Organization Development Journal*, 27(4):265–279, June 2006. doi:10.1108/01437730610666028.

[25] Stéphane Côté, Paulo N. Lopes, Peter Salovey, and Christopher T.H. Miners. Emotional intelligence and leadership emergence in small groups. *The Leadership Quarterly*, 21(3):496–508, June 2010. doi:10.1016/j.leaqua.2010.03.012.

[26] Jonathan Westover. Leading with empathy: How understanding others creates connection and drives success. *Human Capital Leadership Review*, 14(2), November 2024. doi:10.70175/hclreview.2020.14.2.12.

[27] Jonathan Westover. Building the compassionate culture: How empathetic leadership breeds engagement and performance. *Human Capital Leadership Review*, 12(3), September 2024. doi:10.70175/hclreview.2020.12.3.10.

[28] Vivek Mehra and Dr Sanjay Srivastava. The role of empathy in leadership on employee satisfaction and organizational performance: A qualitative analysis. *Economic Sciences*, 20(2):107–115, September 2024. doi:10.69889/zvvekm14.

[29] Vatsalya Sharma, Mohit Suyal, and Tara Datt Tiwari. Exploring empathy in management: Compassionate leadership - the ratan tata way. *International Journal of Advanced Research in Science, Communication and Technology*, page 508–512, July 2024. doi:10.48175/ijarsct-19162.

[30] Lauren S. Simon, Christopher C. Rosen, Ravi S. Gajendran, Sibel Ozgen, and Emily S. Corwin. Pain or gain? understanding how trait empathy impacts leader effectiveness following the provision of negative feedback. *Journal of Applied Psychology*, 107(2):279–297, February 2022. doi:10.1037/apl0000882.

[31] Golnaz Sadri, Todd J. Weber, and William A. Gentry. Empathic emotion and leadership performance: An empirical analysis across 38 countries. *The Leadership Quarterly*, 22(5):818–830, October 2011. doi:10.1016/j.leaqua.2011.07.005.

[32] Jinyoung Hwang. The role of emotional intelligence in team dynamics. *International Journal of Science and Research Archive*, 13(2):1396–1406, November 2024. `doi:10.30574/ijsra.2024.13.2.1875`.

[33] Xiao Wu, Quanliang Liu, Huanli Yao, and Banerjee Srikrishna. The role of emotional intelligence in leadership and team dynamics. *International Journal For Multidisciplinary Research*, 5(6), November 2023. `doi:10.36948/ijfmr.2023.v05i06.8140`.

[34] Brigette Ann Rapisarda. The impact of emotional intelligence on work team cohesiveness and performance. *The International Journal of Organizational Analysis*, 10(4):363–379, April 2002. `doi:10.1108/eb028958`.

[35] Valentyn Bannikov, Kostiantyn Horchakov, and Vita Baidyk. The role of emotional intelligence in the formation of team efficiency. *Economics. Finances. Law*, 10/2024:11–15, October 2024. `doi:10.37634/efp.2024.10.2`.

[36] John Ugoani. Emotional intelligence: Leading, managing, conflict management and result in organizations. *SSRN Electronic Journal*, 2024. `doi:10.2139/ssrn.4735252`.

[37] Peter Johnathon Reilly. Developing emotionally intelligent work teams improves performance and organizational wellbeing: A literature review. *New Review of Academic Librarianship*, 29(2):203–217, August 2022. `doi:10.1080/13614533.2022.2112716`.

[38] Joann Farrell Quinn and David Wilemon. Emotional intelligence as a facilitator of project leader effectiveness. In *PICMET '09 – 2009 Portland International Conference on Management of Engineering & Technology*, page 1267–1275. IEEE, August 2009. `doi:10.1109/picmet.2009.5262022`.

[39] Isabel Coronado-Maldonado and María-Dolores Benítez-Márquez. Emotional intelligence, leadership, and work teams: A hybrid literature review. *Heliyon*, 9(10):e20356, October 2023. `doi:10.1016/j.heliyon.2023.e20356`.

[40] Vishal Arghode, Ann Lathan, Meera Alagaraja, Kumaran Rajaram, and Gary N. McLean. Empathic organizational culture and leadership: conceptualizing the framework. *European Journal of Training and Development*, 46(1/2):239–256, August 2021. `doi:10.1108/ejtd-09-2020-0139`.

[41] Olga M. Klimecki. The role of empathy and compassion in conflict resolution. *Emotion Review*, 11(4):310–325, July 2019. `doi:10.1177/1754073919838609`.

[42] Shivani and Prakash Karuna. The critical role of emotional intelligence in navigating workplace conflict: An introduction. *International Journal of Management and Development Studies*, 14(8):16–24, August 2025. `doi:10.53983/ijmds.v14n8.003`.

[43] Vandana, Neeta, Anil, Swapnil, Shaina Gaur, Gupta, Bhatt, Gaur, and Parveez. Conflict management in organizations: Psychological strategies

and sociological dynamics. *Lex localis – Journal of Local Self-Government*, 23(S4), 2025. doi:10.52152/800850.

[44] Ilmira Gerasimova and Natalia Khasanova. Personality self-regulation management in conflict situations. In *2019 XXI International Conference Complex Systems: Control and Modeling Problems (CSCMP)*, page 742–745. IEEE, September 2019. doi:10.1109/cscmp45713.2019.8976636.

[45] Jean Costa, Malte F. Jung, Mary Czerwinski, François Guimbretière, Trinh Le, and Tanzeem Choudhury. Regulating feelings during interpersonal conflicts by changing voice self-perception. In *Proceedings of the 2018 CHI Conference on Human Factors in Computing Systems*, CHI '18, page 1–13. ACM, April 2018. doi:10.1145/3173574.3174205.

[46] Song Xu. Uncovering the cognitive mechanism of emotional validity in conflict management. *International Journal of Public Health and Awareness*, 05(02):15–21, July 2022. doi:10.55640/ijpha-523.

[47] R.S Mekhala and K Sandhya. An empirical study on the impact of emotional intelligence on occupational performance. *Indian Journal of Public Health Research & Development*, 10(4):342, 2019. doi:10.5958/0976-5506.2019.00715.0.

[48] Abd Ullah, Sarfaraz Khan, and Faheem Uddin. Building emotionally intelligent teams: A survey on the impact of emotional intelligence on organizational success. *Journal of Asian Development Studies*, 13(3):749–763, September 2024. doi:10.62345/jads.2024.13.3.62.

[49] Amanda Moore and Ketevan Mamiseishvili. Examining the relationship between emotional intelligence and group cohesion. *Journal of Education for Business*, 87(5):296–302, January 2012. doi:10.1080/08832323.2011.623197.

[50] Grace Yulianti, Mohammad Chaidir, and Dadang Irawan. Exploring the role of emotional intelligence in leadership effectiveness: A qualitative study. *International Journal of Management, Accounting & Finance (KBIJMAF)*, 1(2):38–49, May 2024. doi:10.70142/kbijmaf.v1i2.192.

[51] Xiangyi Zhou. A study on the impact of inclusive leadership on employee loyalty: The mediating role of psychological safety. *The EUrASEANs: journal on global socio-economic dynamics*, 5(48):270–284, September 2024. doi:10.35678/2539-5645.5(48).2024.270-284.

[52] Anjali Vaishal. The impact of psychological safety on leader decision-making: An empirical analysis of the relationship. *INTERANTIONAL JOURNAL OF SCIENTIFIC RESEARCH IN ENGINEERING AND MANAGEMENT*, 07(07), July 2023. doi:10.55041/ijsrem24958.

[53] Emma Clarke, Katharina Näswall, Annick Masselot, and Sanna Malinen. Feeling safe to speak up: Leaders improving employee wellbeing through psychological safety. *Economic and Industrial Democracy*, 46(1):152–176, February 2024. doi:10.1177/0143831x231226303.

[54] Caroline Muss, Dana Tüxen, and Bärbel Fürstenau. Empathy in leadership: a systematic literature review on the effects of empathetic leaders in organizations. *Management Review Quarterly*, January 2025. doi:10.1007/s11301-024-00472-7.

[55] Natalie H. Longmire and David A. Harrison. Seeing their side versus feeling their pain: Differential consequences of perspective-taking and empathy at work. *Journal of Applied Psychology*, 103(8):894–915, August 2018. doi:10.1037/apl0000307.

[56] Waseem Bahadur, Ali Nawaz Khan, Ahsan Ali, and Muhammad Usman. Investigating the effect of employee empathy on service loyalty: The mediating role of trust in and satisfaction with a service employee. *Journal of Relationship Marketing*, 19(3):229–252, November 2019. doi:10.1080/15332667.2019.1688598.

[57] Julie A. Ruestow. *The effect of a leader's emotional intelligence on follower job satisfaction and organizational commitment: An exploratory mixed methodology study of emotional intelligence in public human services.* Ph.d. dissertation, Capella University, Minneapolis, MN, October 2008.

[58] Jahanvash Karim. The relationship between emotional intelligence, leader-member exchange and organizational commitment. *Euro Asia Journal of Management*, 18(36):153–171, December 2008. URL: https://ssrn.com/abstract=1819299.

[59] Yolonda T. Sanders. Empirical connections between followers' emotional intelligence and followership styles. *Journal of Behavioral and Applied Management*, 24(3), December 2024. doi:10.21818/001c.126833.

[60] J. Irudhaya Rajesh, Verma Prikshat, Paul Shum, and L. Suganthi. Follower emotional intelligence: A mediator between transformational leadership and follower outcomes. *Personnel Review*, 48(5):1239–1260, August 2019. doi:10.1108/pr-09-2017-0285.

[61] Peter J. Jordan and Ashlea Troth. Emotional intelligence and leader member exchange: The relationship with employee turnover intentions and job satisfaction. *Leadership & Organization Development Journal*, 32(3):260–280, May 2011. doi:10.1108/01437731111123915.

[62] Kujtim Hameli, Lekë Ukaj, and Lum undefinedollaku. The role of self-efficacy and psychological empowerment in explaining the relationship between emotional intelligence and work engagement. *EuroMed Journal of Business*, 20(2):378–398, November 2023. doi:10.1108/emjb-08-2023-0210.

[63] Saad M. Alotaibi, Muslim Amin, and Jonathan Winterton. Does emotional intelligence and empowering leadership affect psychological empowerment and work engagement? *Leadership & Organization Development Journal*, 41(8):971–991, September 2020. doi:10.1108/lodj-07-2020-0313.

[64] Sonia A. Udod, Karon Hammond-Collins, and Megan Jenkins. Dynamics of emotional intelligence and empowerment: The perspectives of middle managers. *Sage Open*, 10(2), April 2020. doi:10.1177/2158244020919508.

[65] Guangya Ma, Weilin Wu, Chenlin Liu, Junhan Ji, and Xiaoxiao Gao. Empathetic leadership and employees' innovative behavior: examining the roles of career adaptability and uncertainty avoidance. *Frontiers in Psychology*, 15, May 2024. doi:10.3389/fpsyg.2024.1371936.

[66] Nor Hanan Abd Nasir and Nomahaza Mahadi. Emotional intelligent organizations: Integrating moods and emotions into organizational development strategies. *International Journal of Academic Research in Business and Social Sciences*, 15(8), August 2025. doi:10.6007/ijarbss/v15-i8/26168.

[67] Ali Ridho. Beyond iq: Why emotional intelligence is the key to exceptional leadership. *Riwayat: Educational Journal of History and Humanities*, 7(4):2855–2862, December 2024. doi:10.24815/jr.v7i4.41942.

[68] Sanjay Kumar. Establishing linkages between emotional intelligence and transformational leadership. *Industrial Psychiatry Journal*, 23(1):1, 2014. doi:10.4103/0972-6748.144934.

[69] S. Venkat Raghav and Padmavathi SM. Emotional intelligence in leadership: A cross-cultural analysis of employee engagement and retention. *ShodhKosh: Journal of Visual and Performing Arts*, 5(7), July 2024. doi:10.29121/shodhkosh.v5.i7.2024.2772.

[70] Paul B. Pedersen and Mark Pope. Inclusive cultural empathy for successful global leadership. *American Psychologist*, 65(8):841–854, November 2010. doi:10.1037/0003-066x.65.8.841.

[71] Ilan Alon and James M. Higgins. Global leadership success through emotional and cultural intelligences. *Business Horizons*, 48(6):501–512, November 2005. doi:10.1016/j.bushor.2005.04.003.

[72] Chao Miao, Ronald H. Humphrey, and Shanshan Qian. A cross-cultural meta-analysis of how leader emotional intelligence influences subordinate task performance and organizational citizenship behavior. *Journal of World Business*, 53(4):463–474, June 2018. doi:10.1016/j.jwb.2018.01.003.

[73] Kristina Mullamaa. Empathetic leadership and cultural consciousness in leading: Lessons from iceland, sweden, estonia, latvia, lithuania, and finland. *European Journal of Business and Management Research*, 9(6):7–14, November 2024. doi:10.24018/ejbmr.2024.9.6.2460.

[74] Talat Islam, Saleha Sharif, Hafiz Fawad Ali, and Saqib Jamil. Zooming into paternalistic leadership: evidence from high power distance culture. *European Journal of Management and Business Economics*, 33(4):505–525, May 2022. doi:10.1108/ejmbe-05-2021-0149.

[75] Judy van Zyl and Dr. Claudia Sigamoney. Cultural intelligence as a leadership competence. *The International Journal of Business & Management*, August 2025. doi:10.24940/theijbm/2025/v13/i5/bm2503-015.

[76] K. Y. Ng, L. Van Dyne, and S. Ang. From experience to experiential learning: Cultural intelligence as a learning capability for global leader development. *Academy of Management Learning & Education*, 8(4):511–526, December 2009. doi:10.5465/amle.8.4.zqr511.

[77] Hackjin Kim. A neuroscientific exploration of empathy. *Transversal Humanities*, 20:1–46, June 2025. doi:10.37123/th.2025.20.1.

[78] Zahra Kanch, Hebron Bekele, Ava Kashfi, and Mulugeta Semework. Empathy unmasked: Exploring the neural mechanisms of empathy and cognitive functions in understanding others. *Journal of Student Research*, 12(4), November 2023. doi:10.47611/jsr.v12i4.2281.

[79] Lydia Kogler, Veronika I. Müller, Elena Werminghausen, Simon B. Eickhoff, and Birgit Derntl. Do i feel or do i know? neuroimaging meta-analyses on the multiple facets of empathy. *Cortex*, 129:341–355, August 2020. doi:10.1016/j.cortex.2020.04.031.

[80] Carme Uribe, Arnau Puig-Davi, Alexandra Abos, Hugo C. Baggio, Carme Junque, and Barbara Segura. Neuroanatomical and functional correlates of cognitive and affective empathy in young healthy adults. *Frontiers in Behavioral Neuroscience*, 13, May 2019. doi:10.3389/fnbeh.2019.00085.

[81] Robert Eres, Jean Decety, Winnifred R. Louis, and Pascal Molenberghs. Individual differences in local gray matter density are associated with differences in affective and cognitive empathy. *NeuroImage*, 117:305–310, August 2015. doi:10.1016/j.neuroimage.2015.05.038.

[82] Raeanne C. Moore, Sheena I. Dev, Dilip V. Jeste, Isabel Dziobek, and Lisa T. Eyler. Distinct neural correlates of emotional and cognitive empathy in older adults. *Psychiatry Research: Neuroimaging*, 232(1):42–50, April 2015. doi:10.1016/j.pscychresns.2014.10.016.

[83] Eres Robert, Decety Jean, Louis Winnifred, and Molenberghs Pascal. Anatomical differences in empathy related brain areas: A voxel-based morphometry study. *Frontiers in Human Neuroscience*, 9, 2015. doi: 10.3389/conf.fnhum.2015.217.00187.

[84] Henrik Walter. Social cognitive neuroscience of empathy: Concepts, circuits, and genes. *Emotion Review*, 4(1):9–17, January 2012. doi: 10.1177/1754073911421379.

[85] Christine L. Cox, Lucina Q. Uddin, Adriana Di Martino, F. Xavier Castellanos, Michael P. Milham, and Clare Kelly. The balance between feeling and knowing: affective and cognitive empathy are reflected in the brain's intrinsic functional dynamics. *Social Cognitive and Affective Neuroscience*, 7(6):727–737, September 2011. doi:10.1093/scan/nsr051.

[86] Simone G. Shamay-Tsoory. The neural bases for empathy. *The Neuroscientist*, 17(1):18–24, November 2010. doi:10.1177/1073858410379268.

[87] Amee D. Baird, Ingrid E. Scheffer, and Sarah J. Wilson. Mirror neuron system involvement in empathy: A critical look at the evidence. *Social Neuroscience*, 6(4):327–335, August 2011. doi:10.1080/17470919.2010. 547085.

[88] V Rajmohan and E Mohandas. Mirror neuron system. *Indian Journal of Psychiatry*, 49(1):66, 2007. doi:10.4103/0019-5545.31522.

[89] Jennifer H. Pfeifer, Marco Iacoboni, John C. Mazziotta, and Mirella Dapretto. Mirroring others' emotions relates to empathy and interpersonal competence in children. *NeuroImage*, 39(4):2076–2085, February 2008. doi:10.1016/j. neuroimage.2007.10.032.

[90] Hillary Anger Elfenbein, Zhike Lei, Naomi Beth Rothman, Gerben Alexander Van Kleef, Arik Cheshin, and Nale Lehmann-Willenbrock. When affect collides: The influence of emotional contagion on interpersonal and group outcomes. *Academy of Management Proceedings*, 2017(1):14560, August 2017. doi:10.5465/ambpp.2017.14560symposium.

[91] Arkadiy Aleksandrovich Kudryashov and Luiza Gagikovna Simonyan. The phenomenon of emotional contagion in psychology and psychophysiology. *Psychology & Psychophysiology*, 12(4):12–23, January 2020. URL: http: //dx.doi.org/10.14529/jpps190402, doi:10.14529/jpps190402.

[92] Seung-Yoon Rhee, Hyewon Park, and Jonghoon Bae. Network structure of affective communication and shared emotion in teams. *Behavioral Sciences*, 10(10):159, October 2020. URL: http://dx.doi.org/10.3390/bs10100159, doi:10.3390/bs10100159.

[93] Joy Hirsch. Two-person multimodal imaging using functional near infrared spectroscopy reveals neural mechanisms for emotional contagion. In *2022 IEEE Photonics Conference (IPC)*, page 1–2. IEEE, November 2022. doi: 10.1109/ipc53466.2022.9975753.

[94] Omer Eldadi, Hila Sharon-David, and Gershon Tenenbaum. Interpersonal emotions in team sports: Effects of emotional contagion on emotional, social and performance outcomes of a team. *Scientific Journal of Sport and Performance*, 2(4):473–491, August 2023. doi:10.55860/kcdx3917.

[95] Joy Hirsch, Xian Zhang, J. Adam Noah, and Aishwarya Bhattacharya. Neural mechanisms for emotional contagion and spontaneous mimicry of live facial expressions. *Philosophical Transactions of the Royal Society B: Biological Sciences*, 378(1875), March 2023. doi:10.1098/rstb.2021.0472.

[96] Sarah Boukarras, Donato Ferri, Laura Borgogni, and Salvatore Maria Aglioti. Neurophysiological markers of asymmetric emotional contagion: implications for organizational contexts. *Frontiers in Integrative Neuroscience*, 18, January 2024. doi:10.3389/fnint.2024.1321130.

[97] Cameron Anderson and Dacher Keltner. The role of empathy in the formation and maintenance of social bonds. *Behavioral and Brain Sciences*, 25(1):21–22, February 2002. doi:10.1017/s0140525x02230010.

[98] Helen Riess. The science of empathy. *Journal of Patient Experience*, 4(2):74–77, May 2017. doi:10.1177/2374373517699267.

[99] Kengo Miyazono and Kiichi Inarimori. Empathy, altruism, and group identification. *Frontiers in Psychology*, 12, December 2021. doi:10.3389/fpsyg.2021.749315.

[100] Irene G. Wilkinson. In praise of empathy: The glue that holds caring communities together in a fractured world. *Canadian Journal of Family and Youth*, 11(1):234–291, January 2019. doi:10.29173/cjfy29415.

[101] Lian T. Rameson, Sylvia A. Morelli, and Matthew D. Lieberman. The neural correlates of empathy: Experience, automaticity, and prosocial behavior. *Journal of Cognitive Neuroscience*, 24(1):235–245, January 2012. doi:10.1162/jocn_a_00130.

[102] Birgit Derntl, Andreas Finkelmeyer, Simon Eickhoff, Thilo Kellermann, Dania I. Falkenberg, Frank Schneider, and Ute Habel. Multidimensional assessment of empathic abilities: Neural correlates and gender differences. *Psychoneuroendocrinology*, 35(1):67–82, January 2010. doi:10.1016/j.psyneuen.2009.10.006.

[103] Tania Singer and Claus Lamm. The social neuroscience of empathy. *Annals of the New York Academy of Sciences*, 1156(1):81–96, March 2009. doi:10.1111/j.1749-6632.2009.04418.x.

[104] Sylvia A. Morelli, Lian T. Rameson, and Matthew D. Lieberman. The neural components of empathy: Predicting daily prosocial behavior. *Social Cognitive and Affective Neuroscience*, 9(1):39–47, September 2012. doi:10.1093/scan/nss088.

[105] Jonathan Levy, Karen Yirmiya, Abraham Goldstein, and Ruth Feldman. The neural basis of empathy and empathic behavior in the context of chronic trauma. *Frontiers in Psychiatry*, 10, August 2019. doi:10.3389/fpsyt.2019.00562.

[106] Jonathan Levy, Karen Yirmiya, Abraham Goldstein, and Ruth Feldman. Chronic trauma impairs the neural basis of empathy in mothers: Relations to parenting and children's empathic abilities. *Developmental Cognitive Neuroscience*, 38:100658, August 2019. doi:10.1016/j.dcn.2019.100658.

[107] Jonas P. Nitschke and Jennifer A. Bartz. The association between acute stress & empathy: A systematic literature review. *Neuroscience & Biobehavioral Reviews*, 144:105003, January 2023. doi:10.1016/j.neubiorev.2022.105003.

[108] Jeroen Stouten, Marius Dijke, and David De Cremer. Ethical leadership. *Journal of Personnel Psychology*, 11(1):1–6, 2011. doi:10.1027/1866-5888/a000059.

[109] Anna Kazanskaia. Ethical leadership: Traits, practices, and impact on organizational culture, 2025. doi:10.64357/neya-gjnps-eth-ds-mk-06.

[110] John Ughulu. Ethical leadership in modern organizations: Navigating complexity and promoting integrity. *International Journal of Economics Business and Management Research*, 08(05):52–62, 2024. doi:10.51505/ijebmr.2024.8505.

[111] Jonathan H. Westover. Authentic leadership: Building an ethical culture for long-term success. *Human Capital Leadership Review*, 24(1), August 2025. doi:10.70175/hclreview.2020.24.1.1.

[112] Fajr Noor ain. Ethical leadership in the age of technological advancements navigating moral dilemmas and building trust. *Cognizance journal*, 3(12):346–366, 2023. doi:10.47760/cognizance.2023.v03i12.025.

[113] Kamalesh Kishore Shrivastava. Ethical leadership's influence on workplace behavior and culture: A qualitative study. *Integrated Journal for Research in Arts and Humanities*, 3(5):335–337, 2023. doi:10.55544/ijrah.3.5.37.

[114] Anna Kazanskaia. Ethical decision-making in organizations: Foundations, frameworks, and emerging challenges, 2025. doi:10.64357/neya-gjnps-eth-ds-mk-01.

[115] Anna Kazanskaia. Ethical decision-making models: Frameworks for organizational integrity and practice, 2025. doi:10.64357/neya-gjnps-eth-ds-mk-04.

[116] Qutaib Hussein, Sharif Mustawfyah, and Fazıl Efstath Haneh. Corporate governance and ethical leadership: Key factors in preventing financial statement fraud and money laundering. *Journal Economic Business Innovation*, 1(2):195–216, 2024. doi:10.69725/jebi.v1i2.175.

[117] Marlond Antunez, Nélson Ramalho, and Tania Marques. Context matters less than leadership in preventing unethical behaviour in international business. *Journal of Business Ethics*, 2023. doi:10.1007/s10551-023-05520-y.

[118] Asan Vernyuy Wirba. Ethical leadership in organisation. a literature review, 2023. doi:10.31124/advance.23537070.v1.

[119] Connie Deng, Duygu Biricik Gulseren, Carlo Isola, Kyra Grocutt, and Nick Turner. Transformational leadership effectiveness: an evidence-based primer. *Human Resource Development International*, 26(5):627–641, 2022. doi:10.1080/13678868.2022.2135938.

[120] Irfan Ullah Khan, Rooh Ul Amin, and Naveed Saif. Individualized consideration and idealized influence of transformational leadership: Mediating role of inspirational motivation and intellectual stimulation. *International Journal of Leadership in Education*, pages 1–11, 2022. doi:10.1080/13603124.2022.2076286.

[121] Weichun Zhu, Xiaoming Zheng, Ronald E. Riggio, and Xi Zhang. A critical review of theories and measures of ethics-related leadership. *New Directions for Student Leadership*, 2015(146):81–96, 2015. doi:10.1002/yd.20137.

[122] Robert K. Greenleaf. *Servant Leadership: A Journey into the Nature of Legitimate Power and Greatness*. Paulist Press, 25th anniversary edition, November 2002.

[123] Digvijaysinh Thakore. Servant leadership. *International Letters of Social and Humanistic Sciences*, 7:23–32, 2013. doi:10.18052/www.scipress.com/ilshs.7.23.

[124] Rose O. Sherman. The case for servant leadership. *Nurse Leader*, 17(2):86–87, 2019. doi:10.1016/j.mnl.2018.12.001.

[125] Tina Mertel and Carol Brill. What every leader ought to know about becoming a servant leader. *Industrial and Commercial Training*, 47(5):228–235, 2015. doi:10.1108/ict-02-2015-0013.

[126] Christoph Lumer. Introduction: The relevance of rational decision theory for ethics. *Ethical Theory and Moral Practice*, 13(5):485–496, May 2010. doi:10.1007/s10677-010-9228-9.

[127] Joann Franklin Klinker and Donald G. Hackmann. An analysis of principals' ethical decision making using rest's four component model of moral behavior. *Journal of School Leadership*, 14(4):434–456, July 2004. doi:10.1177/105268460401400404.

[128] Gavin Enck. Six-step framework for ethical decision making. *Journal of Health Services Research & Policy*, 19(1):62–64, December 2013. doi:10.1177/1355819613511599.

[129] Simone De Colle. A stakeholder management model for ethical decision making. *International Journal of Management and Decision Making*, 6(3/4):299, 2005. doi:10.1504/ijmdm.2005.006555.

[130] Robert House, Mansour Javidan, Paul Hanges, and Peter Dorfman. Understanding cultures and implicit leadership theories across the globe: an introduction to project globe. *Journal of World Business*, 37(1):3–10, March 2002. doi:10.1016/s1090-9516(01)00069-4.

[131] Robert J. House, Paul J Hanges, Mansour Javidan, Peter W Dorfman, and Vipin Gupta, editors. *Culture, leadership, and organizations*. SAGE Publications, Thousand Oaks, CA, July 2004.

[132] Peter B. Smith. Book review: Culture, leadership, and organizations: The globe study of 62 societies. *Journal of Cross-Cultural Psychology*, 36(5):628–630, September 2005. doi:10.1177/0022022105278546.

[133] Nebojsa Janicijevic. The impact of national culture on leadership. *Economic Themes*, 57(2):127–144, June 2019. doi:10.2478/ethemes-2019-0008.

[134] Geert Hofstede. Dimensions of national cultures in fifty countries and three regions. In J. B. Deregowski, S. Dziurawiec, and R. C. Annis, editors, *Expiscations in Cross-Cultural Psychology*, pages 335–355. Swets & Zeitlinger, Lisse, 1983.

[135] C. Muhammad Siddique, Hinna Fatima Siddique, and Shama Urooj Siddique. Linking authoritarian leadership to employee organizational embeddedness, lmx and performance in a high-power distance culture: a mediation-moderated analysis. *Journal of Strategy and Management*, 13(3):393–411, April 2020. doi:10.1108/jsma-10-2019-0185.

[136] Naresh Khatri. Consequences of power distance orientation in organisations. *Vision: The Journal of Business Perspective*, 13(1):1–9, January 2009. doi:10.1177/097226290901300101.

[137] Nebojsa Janicijevic and Ivana Marinkovic. Empirical testing of hofstede's measures of national culture and their impact on leadership in four countries. *Ekonomika preduzeca*, 63(5–6):264–278, 2015. doi:10.5937/ekopre1506264j.

[138] Mladen Adamovic. The cultural influence on employees' preferences for reward allocation rules: A two-wave survey study in 28 countries. *Human Resource Management Journal*, 33(4):889–921, January 2023. doi:10.1111/1748-8583.12486.

[139] Terri Scandura and Peter Dorfman. Leadership research in an international and cross-cultural context. *The Leadership Quarterly*, 15(2):277–307, April 2004. doi:10.1016/j.leaqua.2004.02.004.

[140] Hein Wendt, Martin C. Euwema, and I.J. Hetty van Emmerik. Leadership and team cohesiveness across cultures. *The Leadership Quarterly*, 20(3):358–370, June 2009. doi:10.1016/j.leaqua.2009.03.005.

[141] Danna Booyens Strydom. Ethical leadership and performance: The effect of follower individualism-collectivism. *International Journal of Cross Cultural Management*, 21(2):261–283, May 2021. doi:10.1177/14705958211013395.

[142] Andrian Gaju. Uncertainty avoidance and crisis management: Theoretical insights into cultural dynamics in navigating crises. *Proceedings of the International Conference on Applied Research in Business, Management and Economics*, 2(1):1–16, July 2025. doi:10.33422/bmeconf.v2i1.994.

[143] Dana L. Ott and Snejina Michailova. Cultural intelligence: A review and new research avenues. *International Journal of Management Reviews*, 20(1):99–119, August 2016. doi:10.1111/ijmr.12118.

[144] Kevin S. Groves, Ann Feyerherm, and Minhua Gu. Examining cultural intelligence and cross-cultural negotiation effectiveness. *Journal of Management Education*, 39(2):209–243, July 2014. doi:10.1177/1052562914543273.

[145] Kavita Sharma and Tarun Kumar Makhija. Bridging the cultural divides: The transformative power of cultural intelligence in global business leadership and negotiation. *Journal of Global Research in Education and Social Science*, 18(2):15–24, April 2024. doi:10.56557/jogress/2024/v18i28647.

[146] Carole Ann Creque and Doreen J. Gooden. Cultural intelligence and global business competencies: A framework for organizational effectiveness in the

global marketplace. *International Journal of Management & Information Systems (IJMIS)*, 15(4):141, September 2011. doi:10.19030/ijmis.v15i4.5812.

[147] Jonathan Freking. How cultural intelligence shapes communication and decision-making in multicultural teams. *The Scholarship Without Borders Journal*, 3(2), August 2025. doi:10.57229/2834-2267.1069.

[148] Emma Kilduff and Kathryn Cormican. Do you really understand me? an analysis of cultural intelligence in global projects. *Procedia Computer Science*, 196:824–831, 2022. doi:10.1016/j.procs.2021.12.081.

[149] Emerson K. Keung and Amanda J. Rockinson-Szapkiw. The relationship between transformational leadership and cultural intelligence: A study of international school leaders. *Journal of Educational Administration*, 51(6):836–854, September 2013. doi:10.1108/jea-04-2012-0049.

[150] Kunning Zhang. Leadership in early childhood education from a cultural adaptation perspective: An effective integration of distributed and pedagogical leadership. *Education Reform and Development*, 7(6):20–26, July 2025. doi:10.26689/erd.v7i6.11018.

[151] Florin Lucian Isac and Eugen Florin Remes. Culture and business ethics – a comparative perspective. *Studia Universitatis "Vasile Goldis" Arad – Economics Series*, 27(3):54–65, September 2017. doi:10.1515/sues-2017-0012.

[152] Osita Ejikeme and Uzoma Ebubechukwu. Ethical challenges in international business. *ANUSANDHAN – NDIM's Journal of Business and Management Research*, 2(2):27–39, August 2020. doi:10.56411/anusandhan.2020.v2i2.27-39.

[153] Turgut Guvenli and Rajib Sanyal. Perception and understanding of bribery in international business. *Ethics & Behavior*, 22(5):333–348, September 2012. URL: http://dx.doi.org/10.1080/10508422.2012.706140, doi:10.1080/10508422.2012.706140.

[154] Achinto Roy. Bribes vs. gifts. *The International Journal of Knowledge, Culture, and Change Management: Annual Review*, 8(9):143–152, 2008. doi:10.18848/1447-9524/cgp/v08i09/50665.

[155] Lauren Rogers-Sirin and Selcuk R. Sirin. Cultural competence as an ethical requirement: Introducing a new educational model. *Journal of Diversity in Higher Education*, 2(1):19–29, March 2009. doi:10.1037/a0013762.

[156] Shiyu Yang, Jackson Lu, Jennifer Chatman, Mansour Javidan, Carolyn Egri, Peter W. Dorfman, Richard Cotton, Ya-Ru Chen, Jean SK Lee, Joel Brockner, Xiao-Ping Chen, Misha Mariam, Xiaoran Hu, Qiongjing Hu, Jihyeon Kim, and Jackson Lu. Leadership in a multicultural world: Developing and identifying effective leaders on a global stage. *Academy of Management Proceedings*, 2023(1), August 2023. doi:10.5465/amproc.2023.16919symposium.

[157] Andrew I. Ellestad and Bradley Gene Winton. The push and pull between culture and integrity in the workplace: an ethical decision-making context. *International Journal of Ethics and Systems*, July 2024. doi:10.1108/ijoes-02-2024-0042.

[158] Ekene Ezinwa Nwankwo, Damilola Emmanuel Ogedengbe, James Olakumle Oladapo, Oluwatobi Timothy Soyombo, and Chinwe Chinazo Okoye. Cross-cultural leadership styles in multinational corporations: A comparative literature review. *International Journal of Science and Research Archive*, 11(1):2041–2047, February 2024. doi:10.30574/ijsra.2024.11.1.0273.

[159] Constantin Bratianu, Dan Paiuc, and Ruxandra Bejinaru. The impact of knowledge dynamics on multicultural leadership and the mediating role of cultural intelligence. *European Conference on Knowledge Management*, 25(1):103–108, September 2024. doi:10.34190/eckm.25.1.2465.

[160] Barry L. Boyd, Christina Armstrong-Smith, Amy Forbes, and Aja C. Holmes. Understanding the leadership learner: Priority 3 of the national leadership education research agenda 2020–2025. *Journal of Leadership Studies*, 14(3):50–55, November 2020. doi:10.1002/jls.21718.

[161] Lisa E. Kim, Verena Jörg, and Robert M. Klassen. A meta-analysis of the effects of teacher personality on teacher effectiveness and burnout. *Educational Psychology Review*, 31(1):163–195, January 2019. doi:10.1007/s10648-018-9458-2.

[162] Gordana Digic. The relationship between personal and professional characteristics of teachers. *Facta Universitatis, Series: Philosophy, Sociology, Psychology and History*, page 001, August 2018. doi:10.22190/fupsph1801001d.

[163] Renon P. Tobias, Dr. Ryan Romnick B. Sanchez, Dr. Tony G. Zamora, and Dr. Emil B. Ferdinez. Exploring emotional intelligence and teaching performance of new generation educators. *International Journal of Research and Innovation in Social Science*, IX(VI):4902–4913, 2025. doi:10.47772/ijriss.2025.906000373.

[164] Sal Meyers, Katherine Rowell, Mary Wells, and Brian C. Smith. Teacher empathy: A model of empathy for teaching for student success. *College Teaching*, 67(3):160–168, April 2019. doi:10.1080/87567555.2019.1579699.

[165] Bridget Cooper. Empathy, interaction and caring: Teachers' roles in a constrained environment. *Pastoral Care in Education*, 22(3):12–21, August 2004. doi:10.1111/j.0264-3944.2004.00299.x.

[166] Debora L. Roorda, Helma M. Y. Koomen, Jantine L. Spilt, and Frans J. Oort. The influence of affective teacher–student relationships on students' school engagement and achievement: A meta-analytic approach. *Review of Educational Research*, 81(4):493–529, December 2011. doi:10.3102/0034654311421793.

[167] Tulay Bozkurt and Melis Seray Ozden. The relationship between empathetic classroom climate and students' success. *Procedia - Social and Behavioral Sciences*, 5:231–234, 2010. doi:10.1016/j.sbspro.2010.07.078.

[168] Bijender, Kuldeep Nara, and Parveen Kumar. Aging, personality, and teaching aptitude in school grade physical education teachers. *Pedagogy of Physical Culture and Sports*, 27(4):297–304, August 2023. doi:10.15561/ 26649837.2023.0405.

[169] Sherub x Sherub Gyeltshen and Nima Gyeltshen. The impact of supportive teacher-student relationships on academic performance. *Asian Journal of Advanced Research and Reports*, page 15–34, November 2022. doi: 10.9734/ajarr/2022/v16i12446.

[170] Violeta Lozano Botellero, Stine M. Ekornes, Siv M. Gamlem, Wenche Torrissen, and Helga Synnevåg Løvoll. Perceived teacher support in secondary education from 1980 to 2019: An integrative review. *Cogent Education*, 10(1), February 2023. doi:10.1080/2331186x.2022.2164648.

[171] Shila Devi, Zaira Wahab, and Afaq Ahmed Siddiqui. Exploratory assessment of the factors of personality trait of mathematics teacher's that effects on the academic achievements: A statistical surveyed approach. *Journal of Basic & Applied Sciences*, 13:674–680, December 2017. doi:10.6000/1927-5129.2017.13.107.

[172] Lisa E. Kim, Ilan Dar-Nimrod, and Carolyn MacCann. Teacher personality and teacher effectiveness in secondary school: Personality predicts teacher support and student self-efficacy but not academic achievement. *Journal of Educational Psychology*, 110(3):309–323, April 2018. doi:10.1037/edu0000217.

[173] Olivia E. Atherton, Angelina R. Sutin, Antonio Terracciano, and Richard W. Robins. Stability and change in the big five personality traits: Findings from a longitudinal study of mexican-origin adults. *Journal of Personality and Social Psychology*, 122(2):337–350, February 2022. doi:10.1037/pspp0000385.

[174] Oliver P. John and Sanjay Srivastava. The big five trait taxonomy: History, measurement, and theoretical perspectives. In Lawrence A. Pervin and Oliver P. John, editors, *Handbook of Personality: Theory and Research*, chapter 4, pages 102–138. The Guilford Press, New York, 2nd edition, 1999.

[175] Lewis R. Goldberg. An alternative "description of personality": The big-five factor structure. *Journal of Personality and Social Psychology*, 59(6):1216–1229, 1990. doi:10.1037/0022-3514.59.6.1216.

[176] William J. Chopik and Shinobu Kitayama. Personality change across the life span: Insights from a cross-cultural, longitudinal study. *Journal of Personality*, 86(3):508–521, July 2017. doi:10.1111/jopy.12332.

[177] Ruggero Andrisano Ruggieri, Pietro Crescenzo, Anna Iervolino, Pier Giorgio Mossi, and Giovanni Boccia. Predictability of big five traits in high school

teacher burnout. detailed study through the disillusionment dimension. *Epidemiology, Biostatistics, and Public Health*, 15(3), February 2022. doi: 10.2427/12923.

[178] Ziyan Liu, Yingnan Li, Wenying Zhu, Yuanping He, and Dongbin Li. A meta-analysis of teachers' job burnout and big five personality traits. *Frontiers in Education*, 7, March 2022. doi:10.3389/feduc.2022.822659.

[179] Robert S. Bledsoe and Deborah S. Richardson. The role of personality traits in responses to active learning. *Active Learning in Higher Education*, September 2025. doi:10.1177/14697874251372404.

[180] Atif Bilal, Syed Harris Laeeque, Muhammad Ali Saeed, and Mohsin Mumtaz. Teacher-perpetrated sexual harassment and student performance: roles of emotional exhaustion and neuroticism. *Equality, Diversity and Inclusion: An International Journal*, 41(5):793–812, February 2022. doi:10.1108/edi-06-2021-0155.

[181] Reza Pishghadam and Samaneh Sahebjam. Personality and emotional intelligence in teacher burnout. *The Spanish journal of psychology*, 15(1):227–236, March 2012. doi:10.5209/rev_sjop.2012.v15.n1.37314.

[182] Jessica L. Grayson and Heather K. Alvarez. School climate factors relating to teacher burnout: A mediator model. *Teaching and Teacher Education*, 24(5):1349–1363, July 2008. doi:10.1016/j.tate.2007.06.005.

[183] Zhixin Dai, Fabio Galeotti, and Marie Claire Villeval. Cheating in the lab predicts fraud in the field: An experiment in public transportation. *Management Science*, 64(3):1081–1100, March 2018. doi:10.1287/mnsc.2016.2616.

[184] Ying Wang and Brian H. Kleiner. Defining employee dishonesty. *Management Research News*, 28(2/3):11–22, February 2005. doi:10.1108/01409170510785057.

[185] Richard A. Bernardi, Caitlin A. Banzhoff, Abigail M. Martino, and Katelyn J. Savasta. Challenges to academic integrity: Identifying the factors associated with the cheating chain. *Accounting Education*, 21(3):247–263, June 2012. doi:10.1080/09639284.2011.598719.

[186] David T. Welsh, Lisa D. Ordóñez, Deirdre G. Snyder, and Michael S. Christian. The slippery slope: How small ethical transgressions pave the way for larger future transgressions. *Journal of Applied Psychology*, 100(1):114–127, 2015. doi:10.1037/a0036950.

[187] Crystal Reeck and Dan Ariely. Dishonest behavior can transition to continuous ethical transgressions. *Scientific Reports*, 15(1), July 2025. doi:10.1038/s41598-025-10097-9.

[188] Irene Blanken, Niels van de Ven, and Marcel Zeelenberg. A meta-analytic review of moral licensing. *Personality and Social Psychology Bulletin*, 41(4):540–558, February 2015. doi:10.1177/0146167215572134.

[189] Anna C. Merritt, Daniel A. Effron, and Benoît Monin. Moral self-licensing: When being good frees us to be bad: Moral self-licensing. *Social and Personality Psychology Compass*, 4(5):344–357, May 2010. doi:10.1111/j. 1751-9004.2010.00263.x.

[190] Anton Aluja, Ferran Balada, Oscar García, and Luis F. García. Psychological predictors of risky driving: the role of age, gender, personality traits (zuckerman's and gray's models), and decision-making styles. *Frontiers in Psychology*, 14, May 2023. doi:10.3389/fpsyg.2023.1058927.

[191] Xiaohui Luo, Yan Ge, and Weina Qu. The association between the big five personality traits and driving behaviors: A systematic review and meta-analysis. *Accident Analysis & Prevention*, 183:106968, April 2023. doi:10.1016/j.aap.2023.106968.

[192] Pauline Gulliver and Dorothy Begg. Personality factors as predictors of persistent risky driving behavior and crash involvement among young adults. *Injury Prevention*, 13(6):376–381, December 2007. doi:10.1136/ip.2007. 015925.

[193] Dragan Jovanović, Krsto Lipovac, Predrag Stanojević, and Dragana Stanojević. The effects of personality traits on driving-related anger and aggressive behaviour in traffic among serbian drivers. *Transportation Research Part F: Traffic Psychology and Behaviour*, 14(1):43–53, January 2011. doi:10.1016/j.trf.2010.09.005.

[194] Zhenhao Yu, Weina Qu, and Yan Ge. Trait anger causes risky driving behavior by influencing executive function and hazard cognition. *Accident Analysis & Prevention*, 177:106824, November 2022. doi:10.1016/j.aap. 2022.106824.

[195] Charles Atombo, Chaozhong Wu, Emmanuel O. Tettehfio, and Aaron A. Agbo. Personality, socioeconomic status, attitude, intention and risky driving behavior. *Cogent Psychology*, 4(1):1376424, September 2017. doi: 10.1080/23311908.2017.1376424.

[196] Paul T. Costa and Robert R. McCrae. *The Revised NEO Personality Inventory (NEO-PI-R)*, page 179–198. SAGE Publications Ltd, 2008. doi: 10.4135/9781849200479.n9.

[197] Paul Costa and R. Mccrae. Neo PI-R professional manual. *Psychological Assessment Resources*, 396:223–256, 1992.

[198] Robert R. McCrae and Oliver P. John. An introduction to the five-factor model and its applications. *Journal of Personality*, 60(2):175–215, June 1992. doi:10.1111/j.1467-6494.1992.tb00970.x.

[199] Christopher J. Soto and Oliver P. John. The next big five inventory (BFI-2): Developing and assessing a hierarchical model with 15 facets to enhance bandwidth, fidelity, and predictive power. *Journal of Personality and Social Psychology*, 113(1):117–143, July 2017. doi:10.1037/pspp0000096.

[200] Xiaohui Luo, Yan Ge, and Weina Qu. The association between the big five personality traits and driving behaviors: A systematic review and meta-analysis. *Accident Analysis & Prevention*, 183:106968, April 2023. doi:10.1016/j.aap.2023.106968.

[201] Maryam Akbari, B Lankarani Kamran, Seyed Taghi Heydari, Seyed Abbas Motevalian, Reza Tabrizi, Zohreh Asadi-Shekari, and Mark JMSullman. Meta-analysis of the correlation between personality characteristics and risky driving behaviors. *Journal of Injury and Violence Research*, 11(2):107–122, 2019. doi:10.5249/jivr.v11i2.1172.

[202] Mahsa Bayat, Kayvan Aghabayk, and Nirajan Shiwakoti. Investigating the driving skills-attitudes nexus for safer roads. *IATSS Research*, 48(4):496–505, December 2024. doi:10.1016/j.iatssr.2024.10.001.

[203] Adnan Yousaf and Jianping Wu. Cross-cultural behaviors: A comparative analysis of driving behaviors in pakistan and china. *Sustainability*, 16(12):5225, June 2024. doi:10.3390/su16125225.

[204] Burcu Arslan and Türker Özkan. Role of culture, income level and governance quality on driver behaviours. *Journal of Road Safety*, 35(3):10–23, August 2024. doi:10.33492/jrs-d-24-3-2319349.

[205] Yesim Üzümcüoğlu, Türker Özkan, and Timo Lajunen. The relationships between cultural variables, law enforcements and driver behaviours across 37 nations. *Transportation Research Part F: Traffic Psychology and Behaviour*, 58:743–753, October 2018. doi:10.1016/j.trf.2018.07.009.

[206] Ariadna Claudia Moreno, Mailyn Moreno, Cynthia Porras, and Juan Pavón. Human and environmental factors analysis in traffic using agent-based simulation. *Applied Sciences*, 13(6):3499, March 2023. doi:10.3390/app13063499.

[207] Xiaoxiao Wang and Liangjie Xu. Factors influencing drivers' queue-jumping behavior at urban intersections: A covariance-based structural equation modeling analysis. *Electronic Research Archive*, 32(3):1439–1470, 2024. doi:10.3934/era.2024067.

[208] Yaoshan Xu, Yongjuan Li, and Li Jiang. The effects of situational factors and impulsiveness on drivers' intentions to violate traffic rules: Difference of driving experience. *Accident Analysis & Prevention*, 62:54–62, January 2014. doi:10.1016/j.aap.2013.09.014.

[209] Liping Yang, Mengmeng Zhang, Lidong Zhang, and Qinghai Lin. Evolutionary game analysis of queue-jumping and yielding behaviours of drivers with type A and type B personality traits. *Journal of Advanced Transportation*, 2024(1), January 2024. doi:10.1155/2024/5567329.

[210] Kazufumi Suzuki, Keshuang Tang, Wael Alhajyaseen, Koji Suzuki, and Hideki Nakamura. An international comparative study on driving attitudes and behaviors based on questionnaire surveys. *IATSS Research*, 46(1):26–35, April 2022. doi:10.1016/j.iatssr.2021.10.002.

[211] Trond Nordfjærn, Stig Jørgensen, and Torbjorn Rundmo. A cross-cultural comparison of road traffic risk perceptions, attitudes towards traffic safety and driver behaviour. *Journal of Risk Research*, 14(6):657–684, June 2011. doi:10.1080/13669877.2010.547259.

[212] Türker Özkan, Timo Lajunen, Joannes El. Chliaoutakis, Dianne Parker, and Heikki Summala. Cross-cultural differences in driving behaviours: A comparison of six countries. *Transportation Research Part F: Traffic Psychology and Behaviour*, 9(3):227–242, May 2006. doi:10.1016/j.trf.2006.01.002.

[213] Dakota McCarty and Hyun Woo Kim. Risky behaviors and road safety: An exploration of age and gender influences on road accident rates. *PLOS ONE*, 19(1):e0296663, January 2024. doi:10.1371/journal.pone.0296663.

[214] World Health Organization. *Global Status Report on Road Safety 2018*. World Health Organization, Geneva, Switzerland, 2018. URL: https://www.who.int/publications/i/item/9789241565684.

[215] Pierluigi Cordellieri, Francesca Baralla, Fabio Ferlazzo, Roberto Sgalla, Laura Piccardi, and Anna Maria Giannini. Gender effects in young road users on road safety attitudes, behaviors and risk perception. *Frontiers in Psychology*, 7, September 2016. doi:10.3389/fpsyg.2016.01412.

[216] Shraddha Sagar, Nikiforos Stamatiadis, Rachel Codden, Marco Benedetti, Larry Cook, and Motao Zhu. Socioeconomic and demographic factors effect in association with driver's medical services after crashes. *International Journal of Environmental Research and Public Health*, 19(15):9087, July 2022. doi:10.3390/ijerph19159087.

[217] Diana Mitsova, Eric Dumbaugh, and Dibakar Saha. Crash risk for low-income and minority populations: An examination of at-risk population segments and underlying risk factors. Final Report CSCRS-R31, Collaborative Sciences Center for Road Safety, University of North Carolina at Chapel Hill, Chapel Hill, NC, 2021. Supported by the U.S. Department of Transportation's University Transportation Centers Program. URL: https://www.roadsafety.unc.edu/publications/.

[218] National Highway Traffic Safety Administration. Fatality analysis reporting system (fars) 2020. Technical report, U.S. Department of Transportation, Washington, DC, 2021. URL: https://www.nhtsa.gov/crash-data-systems/fatality-analysis-reporting-system.

[219] Paweł Łowicki and Marcin Zajenkowski. No empathy for people nor for god: The relationship between the dark triad, religiosity and empathy. *Personality and Individual Differences*, 115:169–173, September 2017. doi:10.1016/j.paid.2016.02.012.

[220] Paweł Łowicki and Marcin Zajenkowski. Religiousness is associated with higher empathic concern—evidence from self- and other-ratings. *Psy-

chology of Religion and Spirituality, 13(2):127–135, May 2021. doi: 10.1037/rel0000299.

[221] Irene Cristofori, Wanting Zhong, Shira Cohen-Zimerman, Joseph Bulbulia, Barry Gordon, Frank Krueger, and Jordan Grafman. Brain networks involved in the influence of religion on empathy in male vietnam war veterans. *Scientific Reports*, 11(1), May 2021. doi:10.1038/s41598-021-90481-3.

[222] Tatsunori Ishii and Katsumi Watanabe. Do empathetic people have strong religious beliefs? survey studies with large japanese samples. *The International Journal for the Psychology of Religion*, 33(1):1–18, April 2022. doi:10.1080/10508619.2022.2057059.

[223] Abdullah M. Abu Al Ghanam. Religiosity, empathy, and its relationship with prosocial behaviour, the mediating role of peer's relationship. *International Journal of Religion*, 5(2):256–266, February 2024. doi:10.61707/z3xbh904.

[224] Laila van Ments, Peter Roelofsma, and Jan Treur. Modelling the effect of religion on human empathy based on an adaptive temporal–causal network model. *Computational Social Networks*, 5(1), January 2018. doi:10.1186/s40649-017-0049-z.

[225] Bart Duriez. Are religious people nicer people? taking a closer look at the religion–empathy relationship. *Mental Health, Religion & Culture*, 7(3):249–254, September 2004. doi:10.1080/13674670310001606450.

[226] Laura R. Saslow, Robb Willer, Matthew Feinberg, Paul K. Piff, Katharine Clark, Dacher Keltner, and Sarina R. Saturn. My brother's keeper?: Compassion predicts generosity more among less religious individuals. *Social Psychological and Personality Science*, 4(1):31–38, April 2012. doi:10.1177/1948550612444137.

[227] Amy Wilson and Andrea D. Clements. A correlation study between religiosity and empathy toward victims of crime. Master's thesis, East Tennessee State University, 2017. Undergraduate Honors Thesis. URL: https://hdl.handle.net/10419/245404.

[228] Richard Hanania. The personalities of politicians: A big five survey of american legislators. *Personality and Individual Differences*, 108:164–167, 2017. doi:10.1016/j.paid.2016.12.020.

[229] Bryce J. Dietrich, Scott Lasley, Jeffery J. Mondak, Megan L. Remmel, and Joel Turner. Personality and legislative politics: The big five trait dimensions among u.s. state legislators. *Political Psychology*, 33(2):195–210, March 2012. doi:10.1111/j.1467-9221.2012.00870.x.

[230] Devin K. Joshi. A new conceptualization of the political left and right: One dimension, multiple domains. *Canadian Journal of Political Science*, 54(3):534–554, June 2021. doi:10.1017/s0008423921000408.

[231] Jeroen K. Joly, Joeri Hofmans, and Peter Loewen. Personality and party ideology among politicians. a closer look at political elites from canada and

belgium. *Frontiers in Psychology*, 9:552, 2018. doi:10.3389/fpsyg.2018.00552.

[232] Chris G. Sibley, Danny Osborne, and John Duckitt. Personality and political orientation: Meta-analysis and test of a threat-constraint model. *Journal of Research in Personality*, 46(6):664–677, December 2012. doi:10.1016/j.jrp.2012.08.002.

[233] Jan-Emmanuel De Neve. Personality, childhood experience, and political ideology. *SSRN Electronic Journal*, 2011. doi:10.2139/ssrn.1857533.

[234] ALAN S. GERBER, GREGORY A. HUBER, DAVID DOHERTY, CONOR M. DOWLING, and SHANG E. HA. Personality and political attitudes: Relationships across issue domains and political contexts. *American Political Science Review*, 104(1):111–133, February 2010. doi:10.1017/s0003055410000031.

[235] Rolfe Daus Peterson and Carl L. Palmer. The dark triad and nascent political ambition. *Journal of Elections, Public Opinion and Parties*, 32(2):275–296, 2019. doi:10.1080/17457289.2019.1660354.

[236] Marta Rogoza, Marta Marchlewska, and Dagmara Szczepańska. Why dark personalities participate in politics? *Personality and Individual Differences*, 186:111319, 2022. doi:10.1016/j.paid.2021.111319.

[237] Matejas Mackin and Neal J. Roese. The dark triad predicts public display of offensive political products. *Journal of Research in Personality*, 112:104516, 2024. doi:10.1016/j.jrp.2024.104516.

[238] Adrian Furnham and George Horne. Personality and demographic correlates of political ideology. *Personality and Individual Differences*, 186:111320, 2022. doi:10.1016/j.paid.2021.111320.

[239] Filipe Falcão, Bárbara Sousa, Daniela S. M. Pereira, Renato Andrade, Pedro Moreira, Anna Quialheiro, Carlos Jalali, and Patrício Costa. We vote for the person, not the policies: a systematic review on how personality traits influence voting behaviour. *Discover Psychology*, 3:1, 2023. doi:10.1007/s44202-022-00057-z.

[240] Niloufar Zebarjadi, Eliyahu Adler, Annika Kluge, Mikko Sams, and Jonathan Levy. Ideological values are parametrically associated with empathy neural response to vicarious suffering. *Social Cognitive and Affective Neuroscience*, 18(1):1–10, 2023. doi:10.1093/scan/nsad001.

[241] J. Patrick Dobel. Political prudence and the ethics of leadership. *Public Administration Review*, 58(1):74, January 1998. doi:10.2307/976892.

[242] Urs Fischbacher and Franziska Föllmi-Heusi. Lies in disguise-an experimental study on cheating: Lies in disguise. *Journal of the European Economic Association*, 11(3):525–547, June 2013. doi:10.1111/jeea.12014.

[243] Yoshitaka Okano and Eiji Goto. Groups versus individuals, partial lying, and social image concern in a dice-rolling experiment. *The Japanese Economic Review*, 75(2):301–331, September 2023. doi:10.1007/s42973-023-00139-0.

[244] Moritz Reis, Roland Pfister, and Anna Foerster. Cognitive load promotes honesty. *Psychological Research*, 87(3):826–844, June 2022. doi:10.1007/s00426-022-01686-8.

[245] David Pascual-Ezama, Drazen Prelec, Adrián Muñoz, and Beatriz Gil-Gómez de Liaño. Cheaters, liars, or both? a new classification of dishonesty profiles. *Psychological Science*, 31(9):1097–1106, August 2020. doi:10.1177/0956797620929634.

[246] Erez Siniver, Yossef Tobol, and Gideon Yaniv. Collective punishment and cheating in the die-under-the-cut task. *Experimental Psychology*, 69(1):40–45, January 2022. doi:10.1027/1618-3169/a000543.

[247] Ori Weisel and Shaul Shalvi. The collaborative roots of corruption. *Proceedings of the National Academy of Sciences*, 112(34):10651–10656, August 2015. doi:10.1073/pnas.1423035112.

[248] Martin G. Kocher, Simeon Schudy, and Lisa Spantig. I lie? we lie! why? experimental evidence on a dishonesty shift in groups. *SSRN Electronic Journal*, 2016. doi:10.2139/ssrn.2828600.

[249] Johannes Abeler, Anke Becker, and Armin Falk. Representative evidence on lying costs. *Journal of Public Economics*, 113:96–104, May 2014. doi:10.1016/j.jpubeco.2014.01.005.

[250] Simon Gächter and Jonathan F. Schulz. Intrinsic honesty and the prevalence of rule violations across societies. *Nature*, 531(7595):496–499, March 2016. doi:10.1038/nature17160.

[251] Dan Ariely, Ximena Garcia-Rada, Lars Hornuf, and Heather Mann. The (true) legacy of two really existing economic systems. *SSRN Electronic Journal*, 2014. doi:10.2139/ssrn.2457000.

[252] Alain Cohn, Ernst Fehr, Benedikt Herrmann, and Frédéric Schneider. Social comparison and effort provision: Evidence from a field experiment: Social comparison and effort provision. *Journal of the European Economic Association*, 12(4):877–898, March 2014. doi:10.1111/jeea.12079.

[253] Valerio Capraro. Gender differences in lying in sender-receiver games: A meta-analysis. *Judgment and Decision Making*, 13(4):345–355, July 2018. doi:10.1017/s1930297500009220.

[254] Samuel D. Lee, Nathan R. Kuncel, and Jacob Gau. Personality, attitude, and demographic correlates of academic dishonesty: A meta-analysis. *Psychological Bulletin*, 146(11):1042–1058, November 2020. doi:10.1037/bul0000300.

[255] Constantin Yves Plessen, Marton Laszlo Gyimesi, Bettina Manuela Johanna Kern, Tanja Marie Fritz, Marcela Victoria Catalán Lorca, Martin Voracek,

and Ulrich S. Tran. Associations between academic dishonesty and personality: A pre-registered multilevel meta-analysis. *PsyArXiv*, January 2020. doi:10.31234/osf.io/pav2f.

[256] Olga Stavrova and Pascal Siegers. Religious prosociality and morality across cultures: How social enforcement of religion shapes the effects of personal religiosity on prosocial and moral attitudes and behaviors. *Personality and Social Psychology Bulletin*, 40(3):315–333, November 2013. doi:10.1177/0146167213510951.

[257] Aaron D. Nichols, Martin Lang, Christopher Kavanagh, Radek Kundt, Junko Yamada, Dan Ariely, and Panagiotis Mitkidis. Replicating and extending the effects of auditory religious cues on dishonest behavior. *PLOS ONE*, 15(8):e0237007, August 2020. doi:10.1371/journal.pone.0237007.

[258] Li Zhao, Haiying Mao, Brian J. Compton, Junjie Peng, Genyue Fu, Fang Fang, Gail D. Heyman, and Kang Lee. Academic dishonesty and its relations to peer cheating and culture: A meta-analysis of the perceived peer cheating effect. *Educational Research Review*, 36:100455, June 2022. doi:10.1016/j.edurev.2022.100455.

[259] Philipp Gerlach, Kinneret Teodorescu, and Ralph Hertwig. The truth about lies: A meta-analysis on dishonest behavior. *Psychological Bulletin*, 145(1):1–44, January 2019. doi:10.1037/bul0000174.

[260] Alessandra Cassar, Giovanna d'Adda, and Pauline Grosjean. Institutional quality, culture, and norms of cooperation: Evidence from behavioral field experiments. *The Journal of Law and Economics*, 57(3):821–863, August 2014. doi:10.1086/678331.

[261] Diego Aycinena, Lucas Rentschler, Benjamin Beranek, and Jonathan F. Schulz. Social norms and dishonesty across societies. *Proceedings of the National Academy of Sciences*, 119(31), July 2022. doi:10.1073/pnas.2120138119.

[262] Benjamin E. Hilbig, Isabel Thielmann, and Daniel W. Heck. Filling in the missing pieces: Personality traits (un)related to dishonest behavior. *European Journal of Personality*, 39(5):732–746, October 2024. doi:10.1177/08902070241293621.

[263] David Martincik and Olga Martincikova-Sojkova. Effect of personality traits and social value orientation on the tendency to dishonesty: An empirical study. *Communications of International Proceedings*, 2023. doi:10.5171/2023.4247623.

[264] Molly M. King, Carl T. Bergstrom, Shelley J. Correll, Jennifer Jacquet, and Jevin D. West. Men set their own cites high: Gender and self-citation across fields and over time. *Socius: Sociological Research for a Dynamic World*, 3, January 2017. doi:10.1177/2378023117738903.

[265] Martin Dufwenberg and Martin A. Dufwenberg. Lies in disguise – a theoretical analysis of cheating. *Journal of Economic Theory*, 175:248–264, May 2018. doi:10.1016/j.jet.2018.01.013.

[266] Kiryl Khalmetski and Dirk Sliwka. Disguising lies—image concerns and partial lying in cheating games. *American Economic Journal: Microeconomics*, 11(4):79–110, November 2019. doi:10.1257/mic.20170193.

[267] David A. Neequaye. A metatheoretical review of cognitive load lie detection. *Collabra: Psychology*, 9(1), 2023. doi:10.1525/collabra.87497.

[268] Jeffrey J. Walczyk, Frank P. Igou, Alexa P. Dixon, and Talar Tcholakian. Advancing lie detection by inducing cognitive load on liars: A review of relevant theories and techniques guided by lessons from polygraph-based approaches. *Frontiers in Psychology*, 4, 2013. doi:10.3389/fpsyg.2013.00014.

[269] Yu-Hui Lo and Philip Tseng. Electrophysiological markers of working memory usage as an index for truth-based lies. *Cognitive, Affective, & Behavioral Neuroscience*, 18(6):1089–1104, July 2018. doi:10.3758/s13415-018-0624-2.

[270] S. E. Christ, D. C. Van Essen, J. M. Watson, L. E. Brubaker, and K. B. McDermott. The contributions of prefrontal cortex and executive control to deception: Evidence from activation likelihood estimate meta-analyses. *Cerebral Cortex*, 19(7):1557–1566, November 2008. doi:10.1093/cercor/bhn189.

[271] Anna Van 't Veer, Mariille Stel, and Ilja van Beest. Limited capacity to lie: Cognitive load interferes with being dishonest. *SSRN Electronic Journal*, 2013. doi:10.2139/ssrn.2351377.

[272] Fabiana Battista, Henry Otgaar, Ivan Mangiulli, and Antonietta Curci. The role of executive functions in the effects of lying on memory. *Acta Psychologica*, 215:103295, April 2021. doi:10.1016/j.actpsy.2021.103295.

[273] Wang Yue, Ng Wu Chun, Ng Khoon Siong, Wu Tiecheng, and Li Xiaoping. An eeg source localization and connectivity study on deception of autobiography memories. In *2013 6th International IEEE/EMBS Conference on Neural Engineering (NER)*, page 468–471. IEEE, November 2013. doi:10.1109/ner.2013.6695973.

[274] Victor A. Gombos. The cognition of deception: The role of executive processes in producing lies. *Genetic, Social, and General Psychology Monographs*, 132(3):197–214, August 2006. doi:10.3200/mono.132.3.197-214.

[275] Liyang Sai, Siyuan Shang, Cleo Tay, Xingchen Liu, Tingwen Sheng, Genyue Fu, Xiao Pan Ding, and Kang Lee. Theory of mind, executive function, and lying in children: a meta-analysis. *Developmental Science*, 24(5), March 2021. doi:10.1111/desc.13096.

[276] Xiao Pan Ding, Henry M. Wellman, Yu Wang, Genyue Fu, and Kang Lee. Theory-of-mind training causes honest young children to lie. *Psychological Science*, 26(11):1812–1821, October 2015. doi:10.1177/0956797615604628.

[277] Nina Lisofsky, Philipp Kazzer, Hauke R. Heekeren, and Kristin Prehn. Investigating socio-cognitive processes in deception: A quantitative meta-analysis of neuroimaging studies. *Neuropsychologia*, 61:113–122, August 2014. doi:10.1016/j.neuropsychologia.2014.06.001.

[278] Maribel Delgado-Herrera, Azalea Reyes-Aguilar, and Magda Giordano. What deception tasks used in the lab really do: Systematic review and meta-analysis of ecological validity of fmri deception tasks. *Neuroscience*, 468:88–109, August 2021. doi:10.1016/j.neuroscience.2021.06.005.

[279] Maya Zheltyakova, Maxim Kireev, Alexander Korotkov, and Svyatoslav Medvedev. Neural mechanisms of deception in a social context: an fMRI replication study. *Scientific Reports*, 10(1), July 2020. doi:10.1038/s41598-020-67721-z.

[280] Suzanne L. K. Stewart, Clea Wright, and Catherine Atherton. Deception detection and truth detection are dependent on different cognitive and emotional traits: An investigation of emotional intelligence, theory of mind, and attention. *Personality and Social Psychology Bulletin*, 45(5):794–807, September 2018. doi:10.1177/0146167218796795.

[281] Kayo Sakamoto, Tei Laine, and Ilya Farber. Deciding whether to deceive: Determinants of the choice between deceptive and honest communication. *Journal of Economic Behavior & Organization*, 93:392–399, September 2013. doi:10.1016/j.jebo.2013.05.003.

[282] Jeffrey J. Walczyk, Laura L. Harris, Terri K. Duck, and Devyani Mulay. A social-cognitive framework for understanding serious lies: Activation-decision-construction-action theory. *New Ideas in Psychology*, 34:22–36, August 2014. doi:10.1016/j.newideapsych.2014.03.001.

[283] Alison M. O'Connor, Victoria W. Dykstra, and Angela D. Evans. Executive functions and young children's lie-telling and lie maintenance. *Developmental Psychology*, 56(7):1278–1289, July 2020. doi:10.1037/dev0000955.

[284] Nobuhito Abe. The neurobiology of deception: evidence from neuroimaging and loss-of-function studies. *Current Opinion in Neurology*, 22(6):594–600, December 2009. doi:10.1097/wco.0b013e328332c3cf.

[285] Chih-Chen Lee, Tingting (Rachel) Chung, and Robert B. Welker. Behavioral genetics of deception detection performance. *Journal of Managerial Psychology*, 33(1):106–120, January 2018. doi:10.1108/jmp-07-2017-0228.

[286] Charles F. Bond and Bella M. DePaulo. Individual differences in judging deception: Accuracy and bias. *Psychological Bulletin*, 134(4):477–492, July 2008. doi:10.1037/0033-2909.134.4.477.

[287] B. Van Bockstaele, B. Verschuere, T. Moens, Kristina Suchotzki, Evelyne Debey, and Adriaan Spruyt. Learning to lie: Effects of practice on the cognitive cost of lying. *Frontiers in Psychology*, 3, 2012. doi:10.3389/fpsyg.2012.00526.

[288] Julie Gawrylowicz, Samuel Fairlamb, Emily Tantot, Zehra Qureshi, Amadeus Redha, and Anne M. Ridley. Does practice make the perfect liar? the effect of rehearsal and increased cognitive load on cues to deception. *Applied Cognitive Psychology*, 30(2):250–259, December 2015. doi:10.1002/acp.3199.

[289] Jennifer M. C. Vendemia, Robert F. Buzan, and Eric P. Green. Practice effects, workload, and reaction time in deception. *The American Journal of Psychology*, 118(3):413–429, October 2005. doi:10.2307/30039073.

[290] Ted Maldonado, Frank M. Marchak, Danielle M. Anderson, and Keith A. Hutchison. The role of working memory capacity and cognitive load in producing lies for autobiographical information. *Journal of Applied Research in Memory and Cognition*, 7(4):574–586, December 2018. doi:10.1016/j.jarmac.2018.05.007.

[291] George Visu-Petra, Mircea Miclea, and Laura Visu-Petra. Reaction time-based detection of concealed information in relation to individual differences in executive functioning. *Applied Cognitive Psychology*, 26(3):342–351, September 2011. doi:10.1002/acp.1827.

[292] Mei Chen, Tingyu Zhang, Ruqian Zhang, Ning Wang, Qing Yin, Yangzhuo Li, Jieqiong Liu, Tao Liu, and Xianchun Li. Neural alignment during face-to-face spontaneous deception: Does gender make a difference? *Human Brain Mapping*, 41(17):4964–4981, August 2020. doi:10.1002/hbm.25173.

[293] S Lissek, M Brüne, S Peters, N Fuchs, H Witthaus, V Nicolas, G Juckel, and M Tegenthoff. Reasoning about cooperation and deception leads to differential brain activation in theory of mind tasks. *Klinische Neurophysiologie*, 39(01), March 2008. doi:10.1055/s-2008-1072872.

[294] Shanna Williams, Kelsey Moore, Angela M. Crossman, and Victoria Talwar. The role of executive functions and theory of mind in children's prosocial lie-telling. *Journal of Experimental Child Psychology*, 141:256–266, January 2016. doi:10.1016/j.jecp.2015.08.001.

[295] Nobuhito Abe, Maki Suzuki, Etsuro Mori, Masatoshi Itoh, and Toshikatsu Fujii. Deceiving others: Distinct neural responses of the prefrontal cortex and amygdala in simple fabrication and deception with social interactions. *Journal of Cognitive Neuroscience*, 19(2):287–295, February 2007. doi:10.1162/jocn.2007.19.2.287.

[296] Justyna Sarzynska, Marcel Falkiewicz, Monika Riegel, Justyna Babula, Daniel S. Margulies, Edward Necka, Anna Grabowska, and Iwona Szatkowska. More intelligent extraverts are more likely to deceive. *PLOS ONE*, 12(4):e0176591, April 2017. doi:10.1371/journal.pone.0176591.

[297] Justyna Sarzynska-Wawer, Krzysztof Hanusz, Aleksandra Pawlak, Julia Szymanowska, and Aleksander Wawer. Are intelligent people better liars? relationships between cognitive abilities and credible lying. *Journal of Intelligence*, 11(4):69, April 2023. doi:10.3390/jintelligence11040069.

[298] Michalis Drouvelis and Graeme Pearce. Understanding the link between intelligence and lying. CESifo Working Paper 9223, Center for Economic Studies and ifo Institute (CESifo), Munich, July 2021. URL: https://hdl.handle.net/10419/245404.

[299] Michalis Drouvelis and Graeme Pearce. Is there a link between intelligence and lying? *Journal of Economic Behavior & Organization*, 206:182–203, February 2023. doi:10.1016/j.jebo.2022.12.008.

[300] Tianxin Mao, Weigang Pan, Yingying Zhu, Jian Yang, Qiaoling Dong, and Guofu Zhou. Self-control mediates the relationship between personality trait and impulsivity. *Personality and Individual Differences*, 129:70–75, July 2018. doi:10.1016/j.paid.2018.03.013.

[301] Elliott T. MacDonell and Teena Willoughby. Investigating honesty-humility and impulsivity as predictors of aggression in children and youth. *Aggressive Behavior*, 46(1):97–106, November 2019. doi:10.1002/ab.21874.

[302] Yusuke Takahashi, Grant W. Edmonds, Joshua J. Jackson, and Brent W. Roberts. Longitudinal correlated changes in conscientiousness, preventative health-related behaviors, and self-perceived physical health. *Journal of Personality*, 81(4):417–427, January 2013. doi:10.1111/jopy.12007.

[303] Wiebke Bleidorn, Ted Schwaba, Anqing Zheng, Christopher J. Hopwood, Susana S. Sosa, Brent W. Roberts, and D. A. Briley. Personality stability and change: A meta-analysis of longitudinal studies. *Psychological Bulletin*, July 2022. doi:10.1037/bul0000365.

[304] Sebastian P. Speer, Ale Smidts, and Maarten A. S. Boksem. Cognitive control promotes either honesty or dishonesty, depending on one's moral default. *The Journal of Neuroscience*, 41(42):8815–8825, September 2021. doi:10.1523/jneurosci.0666-21.2021.

[305] Sebastian P.H. Speer, Ale Smidts, and Maarten A.S. Boksem. Cognitive control and dishonesty. *Trends in Cognitive Sciences*, 26(9):796–808, September 2022. doi:10.1016/j.tics.2022.06.005.

[306] Hao-Ming Li, Wen-Jing Yan, Yu-Wei Wu, and Zi-Ye Huang. Cognitive control in honesty and dishonesty under different conflict scenarios: insights from reaction time. *Frontiers in Psychology*, 15, March 2024. doi:10.3389/fpsyg.2024.1271916.

[307] Francesca Gino and Dan Ariely. The dark side of creativity: Original thinkers can be more dishonest. *Journal of Personality and Social Psychology*, 102(3):445–459, March 2012. doi:10.1037/a0026406.

[308] Karolina A Scigala, Christoph Schild, and Ingo Zettler. Dark, gray, or bright creativity? (re)investigating the link between creativity and dishonesty. *European Journal of Personality*, 36(1):108–129, May 2021. doi:10.1177/08902070211010993.

[309] Alison M. O'Connor, Deston Chung Eng Kea, Qinggong Li, Xiao Pan Ding, and Angela D. Evans. Older adults are more approving of blunt honesty than younger adults: a cross-cultural study. *Current Psychology*, 42(30):26758–26771, September 2022. doi:10.1007/s12144-022-03785-6.

[310] Heather Mann, Ximena Garcia-Rada, Lars Hornuf, Juan Tafurt, and Dan Ariely. Cut from the same cloth: Similarly dishonest individuals across countries. *Journal of Cross-Cultural Psychology*, 47(6):858–874, May 2016. doi:10.1177/0022022116648211.

[311] Alejandro Erut. Cross-cultural studies on concepts of lying: Methodological approaches and their findings. *Advances in Experimental Philosophy of Lying*, page 137–168, 2025. doi:10.5040/9781350377837.ch-6.

[312] Daniel G. Lannin, Max Guyll, Zlatan Krizan, Stephanie Madon, and Marilyn Cornish. When are grandiose and vulnerable narcissists least helpful? *Personality and Individual Differences*, 56:127–132, January 2014. doi:10.1016/j.paid.2013.08.035.

[313] Maria Leniarska, Marcin Zajenkowski, Virgil Zeigler-Hill, Jeremiasz Górniak, and Anna Turek. You better not tell me i'm not intelligent! grandiose narcissism and reaction to negative intelligence feedback. *Personality and Individual Differences*, 221:112548, April 2024. doi:10.1016/j.paid.2024.112548.

[314] Pascal Simard, Valérie Simard, Olivier Laverdière, and Jean Descôteaux. The relationship between narcissism and empathy: A meta-analytic review. *Journal of Research in Personality*, 102:104329, February 2023. doi:10.1016/j.jrp.2022.104329.

[315] Aleksandra Cichocka, Marta Marchlewska, and Mikey Biddlestone. Why do narcissists find conspiracy theories so appealing? *Current Opinion in Psychology*, 47:101386, October 2022. doi:10.1016/j.copsyc.2022.101386.

[316] Tylor J. Cosgrove and Christopher P. Murphy. Narcissistic susceptibility to conspiracy beliefs exaggerated by education, reduced by cognitive reflection. *Frontiers in Psychology*, 14, July 2023. doi:10.3389/fpsyg.2023.1164725.

Dawning Research Press

Founded in 2019, Dawning Research Press is dedicated to publishing scholarly works that bridge academic rigor with public understanding. Our mission is to illuminate complex issues at the intersection of science, society, and human experience.

Contact Information

Email: admin@dawningresearch.org
Website: www.dawningresearch.org

For information about permissions, bulk purchases, educational discounts, or media inquiries, please contact us at the email address above.

Committed to evidence-based scholarship and accessible science communication.